Science

ESL Support

Grade 6

Harcourt
SCHOOL PUBLISHERS

Orlando   Austin   New York   San Diego   Toronto   London

Visit *The Learning Site!*
www.harcourtschool.com

Contents

Strategies for Success

Throughout the United States, students with limited English proficiency and their teachers face daily challenges in the classroom. One of the greatest challenges for students is learning subjects taught in a language they have not yet mastered. The challenge for teachers is providing instruction that these students clearly understand. Academic instruction designed especially for the English language learner (ELL) meets these challenges. These strategies do not lower standards or change academic expectations for ELLs. Instead, they modify instruction to meet students' diverse linguistic and cultural needs. Through these strategies, students gain equal access to the curriculum and they experience academic success.

Rationale and Research

Research has shown that five to seven years of appropriate instruction are needed to acquire academic proficiency in a second language (Krashen, 1982). Postponing content instruction until students gain full mastery of English would be unreasonable and a disservice to these students. Educators realize that with carefully planned lessons and the use of a variety of research-based practices designed to meet the needs of ELLs, these students can meet content standards while demonstrating growth in English language proficiency.

Stages of English Language Acquisition

Proficiency Level: BEGINNER	
Pre-Production	**Early Production**
Listening/Speaking • associate utterances with meanings • use unanalyzed phrases sporadically • may need to use native language to demonstrate comprehension • respond nonverbally or with one or two words and short phrases • participate in songs, chants, and rhymes	**Listening/Speaking** • begin to model verb tenses, such as present participles • ask and answer simple questions about familiar concepts • participate in face-to-face conversations with peers • begin to self-check and self-correct
Reading • decode but have difficulty with English phonological awareness • comprehend simple content • begin to read single words and short phrases	**Reading** • comprehend and recall main ideas of a simple story or other content • improve pronunciation and phonological awareness • read student-generated text
Writing • copy, label, and list • write familiar words and phrases	**Writing** • use graphic organizers and writing frames • write simple questions and answers

Proficiency Level: INTERMEDIATE

Speech Emergence

Listening/Speaking
- express thoughts and use original language
- use complete simple sentences
- produce sustained conversation

Reading
- interact with a variety of print
- use writing for a variety of purposes

Writing
- transfer reading and oral language to writing
- write for a variety of purposes
- participate fully in editing

Intermediate Fluency

Listening/Speaking
- use the listening process to improve comprehension and oral skills
- clarify, distinguish, and evaluate ideas and responses
- demonstrate adequate pronunciation and grammar usage

Reading
- use a variety of reading strategies
- use various study skills

Writing
- use extended written production in all content areas
- use adjectives, adverbs, and figurative language in writing

Proficiency Level: ADVANCED

Advanced Fluency

Listening/Speaking
- Create, clarify, critique, and evaluate ideas and responses
- Comprehend concrete and abstract topics and concepts
- Use effortless, fluent speech

Reading
- Use graphophonic cues, syntax, context, and prior knowledge to make meaning
- Read grade-level materials with limited difficulty

Writing
- Use graphophonic cues, syntax, context, and prior knowledge to make meaning
- Write to meet social needs and academic demands

Teaching Strategies

Language is learned in a variety of ways, but experience and time are important factors that foster proficiency. To acquire a second language, students must receive large amounts of *comprehensible input* (Krashen, 1982). Comprehensible input describes the understandable and meaningful language directed toward learners acquiring a second language. Language and the delivery of concepts are either decontextualized (with few clues) or contextualized (rich with clues). Traditional instruction has been very decontextualized, but English language learners rely on contextualized instruction and materials for comprehensible input (Cummins, 1994). Characteristics of comprehensible input include the following:

- Focus on communicating a meaningful message rather than on language forms
- Frequent use of concrete contextual referents, such as visuals, manipulatives, and graphics
- Acceptance of primary language use by the learner
- Minimal overt correction by the instructor
- Establishment of positive and motivating learning environments.

Language learning is developmental. When students receive comprehensible input, they progress through predictable levels of language proficiency. Students at various proficiency levels have specific characteristics and need different instructional strategies.

Teaching Strategies: BEGINNER	
• Provide opportunities for purposeful listening and speaking • Surround students with environmental print • Use rhymes, chants, songs, and games • Group students by mixed language ability and provide for paired learning • Use students' prior knowledge • Address all learning modalities • Provide a low-anxiety environment • Ask questions that can be answered with one- or two-word responses	• Incorporate both cooperative and collaborative group opportunities • Use non-verbal role-playing • Incorporate visual aids, realia, or manipulatives when possible • Use multisensory lessons when introducing new information • Provide opportunities to apply vocabulary • Write key points and directions on board or chart

Teaching Strategies: INTERMEDIATE

- Provide opportunities for listening comprehension with contextual support

- Ask questions requiring yes/no, either/or, and listing responses

- Ask questions that require group discussion responses

- Have students label and/or categorize visuals or manipulatives

- Use patterned or predictable text

- Provide structure for writing and reading

- Incorporate shared reading and writing lessons

- Have students use numerical symbols

- Have students use a variety of graphic organizers

- Review frequently to reinforce learning

- Provide notes or outlines and use journal writing for new information

- Ask open-ended questions, and encourage students to describe, restate, and expand language

- Model mathematical concepts and conduct guided lessons using concrete models

- Use visuals, role-playing, and skits to promote conceptual learning

- Focus on vocabulary/concept development

- Provide a variety of texts (genres and levels) for independent reading and concept attainment

- Encourage students to compare and contrast mathematical concepts

Teaching Strategies: ADVANCED

- Provide structure for discussions and assignments

- Guide use of reference material for research and independent work

- Provide opportunities for students to create oral and written narratives

- Provide a variety of realistic writing and speaking experiences

- Encourage creative expression

- Focus on sustained vocabulary/concept development

- Continue direct, explicit skill instruction

- Provide opportunities for students to support and defend positions or opinions

- Model and guide students in predicting outcomes

- Provide age-appropriate reading and writing materials

- Continue ongoing language development through integrated language arts and content-area activities

Scaffolding Principles and Strategies

To encourage students to develop cognition, handle complex language tasks, and take risks, use scaffolding strategies to organize instruction. The lesson format and strategies in this book incorporate the following scaffolding principles and strategies.

Comprehensible Input

Use rich context to introduce vocabulary and concepts. Restate the content in different ways, such as simplifying the language, to help students understand the content. Speak slowly and enunciate words exactly. Avoid the use of idioms and colloquialisms. Use gestures, facial expressions, and dramatization. Use visuals such as realia, pictures, and graphic organizers. Use hands-on experience and manipulatives.

Language and Vocabulary

Explore language, clarifying how the lesson vocabulary and other words in the English language work. Explore words with multiple meanings and examine how prefixes and suffixes affect the meaning of words. Teach about the meaning of abstract terms and look at unique spellings. Teach word origins and examine compound words. Divide words into syllables or phonemes, and teach correct pronunciation and intonation by blending words.

Background/Experience

Activate and build on students' prior knowledge by accessing experience the students may already have with the content or some aspect of it. While students progress from the known to the unknown, help them make connections to previous learning. Have students describe verbally, graphically, or dramatically what they know about a topic, such as family life or concepts involving social interaction. Encourage them to brainstorm and to relate personal stories.

How to Use *ESL Support* Strategies and Lessons

The goal of this book is to teach grade-level content and to develop English language proficiency. You can modify the strategies to meet the needs of students at various levels of language acquisition. Scaffolding structures are built into each lesson and a variety of language experiences are offered. Chapter Openers and Lessons are organized in the following way.

Chapter Opener — Develop Scientific Concepts and Vocabulary

This section presents a summary of the scientific concepts, skills, and vocabulary that make up the content of each lesson in the chapter. The number of lessons in each chapter may vary.

Preview Scientific Principles

This section includes suggestions to help students become familiar with and understand the scientific principles of each lesson. A variety of motivational strategies address the different modalities of learning, such as visual, contextual, and metacognitive that are important for students learning English. The strategies set the tone for each lesson, preparing students for the activities they will encounter as they learn the concepts presented in each lesson.

Practice

An activity that focuses on the chapter topic, vocabulary words, and/or scientific principles forms the essential point for this section. Strategies are typically interactive, including the use of graphic organizers, and they accommodate different learning styles.

Apply

Through the use of poems, songs, or sentences, this section helps students apply what they learned in the Practice section. It also reinforces content while introducing and practicing language structures with students.

Lesson

1 Build Background

The clock icon that begins each of the three main sections of the lesson is followed by the approximate duration in minutes of the activities in the section. The activities are suitable for at least two of the three proficiency levels (Beginning, Intermediate, Advanced) as indicated by the check marks next to each proficiency level.

Access Prior Knowledge

This section previews the concept or concepts of the lesson by encouraging discussion of the main ideas and vocabulary. The activity in this section is appropriate for at least two of the three student proficiency levels (Beginning, Intermediate, and Advanced) and serves as motivation to gain students' attention.

Preteach Lesson Vocabulary

Successful lessons for ELLs include direct instruction of vocabulary. The lesson lists the same vocabulary as the *Science* Student Edition along with several activities to reinforce the words and concepts. The activities may include suggestions to help students relate vocabulary and ideas to their experiences and backgrounds. The words should be used throughout the day and made part of students' working vocabulary. Repetition and reinforcement are essential.

Build Fluency

These strategies build and extend the activities presented in **Access Prior Knowledge** and **Preteach Lesson Vocabulary** activities. Students engage in repetition of chants, choral responses, and clapping of rhythm of words and sentences in order to develop language, practice language skills, and learn language patterns. Additional fluency-building strategies include role play or dramatization of back and forth conversations of familiar social situations.

2 Scaffold the Content

Scaffolding structures are used throughout the activities in this main section in order to ensure students' success as they become exposed to and acquire the main concepts of the lesson.

Preview the Lesson

Students walk through the pages of their science text, looking at the illustrations and the main headings in order to become exposed to the focus of the lesson. You may use the headings and art to introduce and elicit predictions about the concepts of the lesson in order to present the learning goal of the lesson.

Investigate

This section provides an alternative instructional activity for the **Investigate** feature in the science text. It may include an instructional strategy that clarifies the directions or an explanation of language structures, such as idioms, that may be confusing to students as they develop their cognitive skills and learn to handle complex language tasks.

Modify Instruction—Multilevel Strategies

This section employs alternative instruction in the areas of Comprehensible Input, Language and Vocabulary, and Background/Experience, which were previously described. Interactive exercises designed to reinforce the lesson focus are provided at the Beginning, Intermediate, and Advanced levels. **For All Students** provides a way to have students apply the alternative activities under **Modify Instruction** as they continue with the lesson in their textbooks.

Extend

This section provides an extension of the **Investigate** or **Modify Instruction** activity. Students are encouraged to think about how they learn, and why what they learn is important and useful in their lives. Students will complete the **Show What You Know** page at home to demonstrate understanding of the lesson.

③ Apply and Assess

The first section under **Apply and Assess** includes a short title describing an interactive exercise which illustrates the instructional area goal of the **Modify Instruction** section. It incorporates language and concept understandings and encourages independent comprehension of ideas with peer-to-peer features.

Informal Assessment

Activities in this section check students' understanding of the alternative instructional strategies for Beginning, Intermediate, and Advanced proficiency levels under **Modify Instruction**.

Show What You Know

The blackline master in this section is intended to be reproduced as a take home sheet. It is a graphic organizer designed to have students practice and apply the concepts and vocabulary presented in the lesson. It also allows students an opportunity to summarize, review, and share with family members what they have learned in the lesson.

Bibliography

Archibald, J. (ed.) (2000). *Second Language Acquisition and Linguistic Theory*. Oxford: Blackwell.

Bilingual Education Handbook: Designing Instruction for LEP Students. (1990). Sacramento, CA: California Department of Education.

Campbell, L., Campbell, B., and Dickinson, D. (1999). *Teaching and Learning Through Multiple Intelligences*. Needham, MA: Allyn & Bacon.

Cantoni-Harvey, G. (1987). *Content-Area Language Instruction: Approaches and Strategies*. Reading, MA: Addison-Wesley.

Cummins, J. (1994). "The Acquisition of English as a Second Language" in *Kids Come in All Languages: Reading Instruction for ESL Students*. Newark, DE: International Reading Association.

Dobb, Fred (2004). *Essential Elements of Effective Science Instruction for English Learners,* 2nd Edition. California Science Project: Los Angeles, CA.

Holt, Daniel (Ed.). (1993). *Cooperative Learning: Response to Linguistic and Cultural Diversity*. Washington, D.C.: Center for Applied Linguistics.

Krashen, S. (1982). *Principles and Practice in Second Language Acquisition*. New York: Pergamon Press.

Krashen, S., and Terrell, T. (1983). *The Natural Approach*. San Francisco: Pergamon/ Alemany Press.

Mohan, B. (1986). *Language and Content*. Reading, MA: Addison-Wesley.

Randall, J.A. (Ed.). (1987). *ESL Through Content-Area Instruction*. Englewood Cliffs, NJ: Prentice Hall Regents/ERIC Clearinghouse on Languages and Linguistics. (ERIC Document Reproduction Service No. ED 283387)

Reyhner, J., Davison, D.M. (1992). "Improving Mathematics and Science Instruction for LEP Middle and High School Students Through Language Activities" in *Third National Research Symposium on Limited English Proficient Student Issues*.

Schifini, Alfredo. (1991). "Language, Literacy, and Content Instruction: Strategies for Teachers" in *Kids Come in All Languages: Reading Instruction for ESL Students*. Newark, DE: International Reading Association.

Willetts, K. (Ed.). (1986). *Integrating Language and Content Instruction*. Los Angeles: Center for Language Education and Research, UCLA. (ERIC Document Reproduction Service No. ED 278262)

Willetts, K., and Crandall, J.A. (1986). *Content-Based Language Instruction*. ERIC/ CLL News Bulletin, 9 (2). Washington, D.C.: ERIC Clearinghouse on Languages and Linguistics.

1 Cells, Reproduction, and Heredity

Develop Scientific Concepts and Vocabulary

In this chapter, students will explore how plant and animal cells are alike and different and how cells work together as tissues and organs. They will also learn how cells reproduce and how traits are passed from one generation to another.

Preview Scientific Principles

Walk through the chapter with students, pausing to read aloud or to have volunteers read aloud the four questions that are lesson titles. Encourage students to look at the illustrations on the pages. Have them share what they already know that might help them answer the questions in the titles.

When to Use With Chapter Opener	Proficiency Levels
⏱ 20 minutes	✔ Beginning ✔ Intermediate ✔ Advanced

Lesson 1: How Do Plant and Animal Cells Differ?

- Ask students to explain how animals and plants are alike and different.
- Explain that both plants and animals are made of cells. A cell is very tiny and cannot be seen with the naked eye.
- Ask if students think plant and animal cells are different, like plants and animals are different. Tell them they will find the answer to this question in this lesson.

Lesson 2: How Do Cells Work Together?

- Have students name as many body organs as possible, such as the heart, the stomach, the liver, and so on.
- Explain that these organs are made of tissues, and tissues are made of cells working together. Cells in different tissues and organs look different and have different jobs.

Lesson 3: How Do Cells Reproduce?

- Ask students how they think their bodies grow. Guide them to realize that their bodies use the food they eat to produce new cells. These cells make them taller and help them change into adults.

© Harcourt

- Explain that cells reproduce, or make copies of themselves, in different ways. Lesson 3 will help students learn how their bodies grow—and how other living things, from robins to pine trees, grow. They will also learn how living things produce offspring.

Lesson 4: How Are Traits Inherited?

- Explain that a *trait* is a feature or characteristic that is inherited, or passed, from parent to child. Traits include hair, eye, and skin color, along with height and other characteristics.

- Ask students if they have ever seen a cat or a dog with a litter of babies. In what ways were the kittens or puppies like their parents? Explain that the offspring inherited these traits from their parents. Lesson 4 will help students understand how this happens.

Practice

Involve students in writing this chapter's vocabulary words on cards, one term per card. Invite them to share what they know and what they would like to learn about cells, reproduction, and heredity. You might summarize this information in a chart and refer to it as students progress through the lesson.

Apply

Write the following chart on the board and have students take turns echoing or reading the lines aloud. You might use gestures or draw pictures to help explain some of the sentences.

Tiny Cells

Cells are so tiny that you can only see them through a microscope.

Muscle tissue makes me strong.

Tissues work together to form organs, like my brain.

Growth begins when one cell divides into two cells.

The two cells then divide into four cells.

The four cells then divide into eight cells, and so on.

I inherited my hair color and skin color from my parents.

Some traits are stronger than others.

Strong traits are inherited more often than weak traits.

How Do Plant and Animal Cells Differ?

① Build Background

Access Prior Knowledge

When to Use	Proficiency Levels
Before introducing the lesson	✔ Beginning
🕐 15 minutes	✔ Intermediate
	Advanced

Give students an opportunity to share what they know about cells, which are very small parts of living things. Have students ever seen a cell under a microscope? What did it look like? Was it from a plant or an animal? If no students have seen a cell, what do they think one might look like? Explain that this lesson will help students learn more about cells.

Preteach Lesson Vocabulary

> **chloroplasts, cell wall, nucleus, chromosomes, DNA**

List the vocabulary words on the board.

Have students look at pages 34–36 and find the words on the board. Then:

- Ask which words on the board have the /k/ sound. *(chloroplasts, nucleus, chromosomes)*

- Ask students what spelling pattern they see for the /k/ sound in these words. *(ch, c)* Have students repeat all three words with you, clapping out three syllables for each word.

- Explain that *chloroplasts* help plants make their food and are found only in plant cells. The *nucleus* is the control center of a cell. *Chromosomes* contain information about the main characteristics of a plant or animal cell.

- Have students say *cell wall* with you. Explain that only plants have cell walls, which protect the cells and give them their shape.

- Explain that chromosomes are made of *DNA*. Students will find out what DNA stands for in this lesson.

Build Fluency

Have students work in pairs to practice dialogues such as the following:

Where do you find chloroplasts? You find them only in _____ cells. *(plant)*

What controls the cell? It is the _____. *(nucleus)*

Do you know what deoxyribonucleic acid is? I think that's what _____ stands for. *(DNA)*

② Scaffold the Content

Preview the Lesson

When to Use With pp. 30–36	Proficiency Levels
🕐 20 minutes	✔ Beginning ✔ Intermediate ✔ Advanced

- Read the title on page 30 aloud. Explain that students will find the answer to this question in the lesson.
- Have students look at the pictures on pages 32 through 36. Ask them to use the captions to identify which pictures show plant cells and which show animal cells.
- Ask students how we can see cells. *(with a microscope)* How is a microscope different from a magnifying glass? *(A microscope can magnify things much more than a magnifying glass can.)*

Investigate, p. 31

Before students begin the Investigate:

- Review the steps in the Procedure and have a volunteer demonstrate them.
- Explain that *gelatin* is the correct name for a familiar dessert. Have volunteers tell about times when they helped make this dessert. Did they follow the steps in the Procedure?
- Make sure students understand the terms *section*, *twist tie*, and *set*.
- After students complete the activity, discuss their conclusions.

Modify Instruction—Multilevel Strategies

Language and Vocabulary Write the words *cell* and *sell* on the board and have students define them. Point out that there is no difference in the way the two words sound, but they are spelled differently and have different meanings. *Cell* and *sell* are homophones: they sound the same. Have volunteers construct sentences that use *cell* and *sell*. Ask the class to point to the correct spelling of the word in each sentence.

Beginning On the board, write other pairs of homophones that appear in this chapter, such as *know/no*, *knew/new*, *there/their/they're*, *piece/peace*, and *eye/I*. Explain the meanings of each pair of words, using gestures and words. Use one word in each pair in a sentence and have students point to the word you used.

Intermediate Add other homophones to the list on the board, such as *to/too/two*, *one/won*, *here/hear*, *ate/eight*, and *aloud/allowed*. After reviewing the meanings, assign a pair of words to a pair of students and have them use their words in two sentences.

Advanced Have students identify other homophones, if possible. Ask them to use pairs of homophones in pairs of sentences that indicate the different meanings of the words.

For All Students Invite students to add more homophones to the list as they progress through the chapter. Review the meanings of all the suggested additions.

Extend

Have students complete the **Show What You Know** activity on page 7 to demonstrate their understanding of the differences between plant and animal cells.

③ Apply and Assess

Make a Model

When to Use With Reading Review p. 37 ⏱ 20 minutes	Proficiency Levels ✔ Beginning ✔ Intermediate ✔ Advanced

Materials: colored paper, scissors, paste, or other art materials

- Have small groups use colored paper or other media to make models of plant and animal cells.
- Ask the groups to label each cell and its parts. Write the parts (cell wall, cell membrane, nucleus, cytoplasm, chloroplasts, chromosomes, vacuoles, mitochondria, nuclear membrane) on the board to help with spelling.
- Have groups display and compare their models. Discuss how plant and animal cells differ.

Informal Assessment

Beginning	Intermediate	Advanced
Ask individual students to point to the kind of cell and the cell parts that you name. (*Answers will vary.*)	Have each student name the cell part you indicate on an unlabeled model. You might allow him or her to refer to the parts written on the board.	Have each student describe similarities and differences between plant and animal cells. (*Answers will vary. Example: Both plant and animal cells have a nucleus and chromosomes, but only plant cells have cell walls and chloroplasts.*)

Comparing Plant and Animal Cells

Show how plant and animal cells are the same and different. Name the parts found only in plant cells in the left circle. Name the parts found only in animal cells in the right circle. Name the parts found in both kinds of cells in the center section.

Plant Cells   Both   Animal Cells

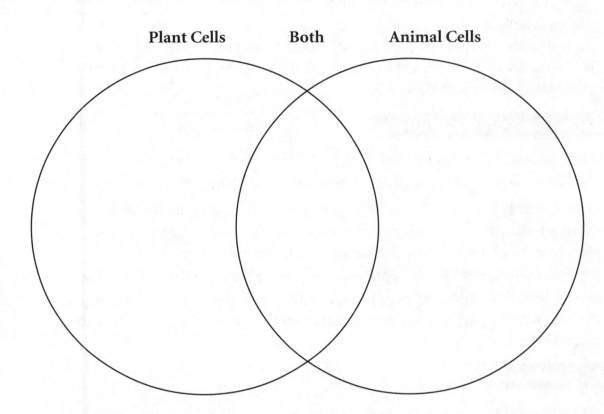

School-Home Connection: Have students take this page home to share with family members. They can use this page to tell about plant and animal cells.

How Do Cells Work Together?

① Build Background

Access Prior Knowledge

When to Use	Proficiency Levels
Before introducing the lesson 15 minutes	✔ Beginning ✔ Intermediate Advanced

Ask students where they think they could find cells in their bodies. For example, is their skin made of cells? How about their blood? Guide them to recall from Lesson 1 that their entire bodies are made of cells. See if students can name kinds of cells, such as muscle, bone, and blood cells.

Preteach Lesson Vocabulary

> tissue, organ

List the vocabulary words on the board.

Have students find the words on the board on pages 40 and 42. Then:

- Have students say the word *tissue* with you. Explain that *tissue* has several meanings. It can mean the soft paper we use to blow our noses, and it can also mean "a group of cells," such as muscle tissue and nerve tissue.

- Have students say the word *organ* with you. Explain that this word also has several meanings. It can mean a musical instrument much like a piano, and it can also mean a part of a living organism that does a certain job, such as the heart or brain.

Build Fluency

Have pairs practice dialogues with questions and answers such as the following: What is an organ? It's a structure in living things, but it's also a _____. *(musical instrument)*

What do you call a group of cells that has a special job? You call it a _____, just like the paper you use when you sneeze. *(tissue)*

② Scaffold the Content

Preview the Lesson

When to Use With pp. 38–46 20 minutes	Proficiency Levels
	✔ Beginning
	✔ Intermediate
	✔ Advanced

Read the title on page 38 aloud. Explain that students will find the answer to this question in the lesson.

- Ask students to look at the pictures on pages 40–46 and name the parts of the body shown there. What kinds of cells, tissues, and organs are shown? What do their jobs seem to be?
- Write *organ* and *organism* on the board and have a volunteer underline the *-ism* suffix. Ask students what these two words mean. Guide them to understand that an *organ* is part of a living thing, such as a heart, lungs, roots, and stems. An *organism* is the whole living thing, such as a person, dog, or tree.

Investigate, p. 39

Before students begin the Investigate:

- Write the word *lungs* on the board and have students say it with you. Ask them where their lungs are and what they do. Ask what represents the lungs in this activity. *(the balloon)* Discuss how a balloon is like the lungs. *(The balloon becomes larger and smaller, just like lungs when we breathe.)*
- Review the steps in the Procedure and have students explain them in their own words. Use words and gestures to make sure they understand the meanings of *stretch*, *mouth*, *secure*, and *slack*.

Modify Instruction—Multilevel Strategies

Language and Vocabulary Write the words *organ* and *organism* on the board and have students say them with you and define them (see Lesson Preview). Explain that these and several other words are based on a Greek word that means "work." Ask students to explain how an organ and an organism work. *(Organs help a living thing stay alive; organisms find food and so on.)*

Beginning Add the word *organize* to the board and have students repeat it after you. Explain that *organize* means "to put things in order," which is one kind of work. Use each of the three words in sentences and have students point to the word you used.

Intermediate Add *organize* and *organization* to the board and have students repeat these words, clapping the syllables. Construct sentences that can be completed by one of the four words and encourage students to point to or say the missing word.

Advanced Add *organize*, *organization*, *organizer*, and *organic* to the board and have students repeat them, clapping the syllables. Discuss how these words each relate to work. Have students use them each in sentences.

For All Students Encourage students to look for words based on *organ* and think about how they relate to work.

Extend

Have students complete the **Show What You Know** activity on page 11 to demonstrate their understanding of cells and tissues.

③ Apply and Assess

Make a Poster

When to Use With Reading Review p. 47 ⏱ 20 minutes	Proficiency Levels ✔ Beginning ✔ Intermediate ✔ Advanced

Materials: drawing supplies, poster board

- Have students work in small groups to make an outline of the organization of cells, starting with a single cell, moving to groups of specialized cells (tissues), and ending with organs. They might draw examples at each level.
- Have students suggest the words they need as labels so you can write them on the board.
- Provide time for the groups to share their posters with the class and name the parts and examples that they included.

Informal Assessment

Beginning	Intermediate	Advanced
Ask individual students to point to pictures of cells, tissue, and organs, or point to these items and ask students to name them.	Have students each complete a sentence related to their group's poster. *(Answers will vary. Example: A cell is the smallest unit of a _____. [living thing, organism])*	Have each student describe the functions of specific cells, types of tissue, and organs. *(Answers will vary. Example: Connective tissue adds support and structure to the body.)*

Name _____

Date _____

Cells and Tissues at Work

Draw each kind of cell or tissue named below.

Cheek cell

Muscle cell

Tissue lining the small intestine

School-Home Connection: Have students take this page home to share with family members. They can use this page to tell about different cells and tissues.

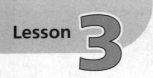

How Do Cells Reproduce?

1 Build Background

Access Prior Knowledge

When to Use	Proficiency Levels
Before introducing the lesson	✔ Beginning
⏱ 15 minutes	✔ Intermediate
	Advanced

Ask students to explain how people and animals reproduce. How do students think tiny cells reproduce? Do cells have male sex cells (sperm) and female sex cells (eggs)? If not, how do cells make more cells—how do living things grow? (Note students' responses so you can correct any misconceptions during the lesson.)

Preteach Lesson Vocabulary

sexual reproduction, genes

List the vocabulary words on the board.

Have students find the terms on the board on pages 50 and 51. Then:

- Have students say *sexual reproduction* with you, clapping out the syllables.

- Write the base word *produce* under *reproduction*. Ask students what they do when they produce something. *(They make it.)* Discuss how the prefix *re-* affects the meaning of the word. *(Then it means "make something again.")* Explain that the suffix *-tion* means "the act of." So *reproduction* means "the act of making something again."

- Have students say the word *genes* with you. Write the word *jeans* below it and have them say this word. Discuss the different meanings of these homophones: "information in cells" and "a kind of pants." Invite volunteers to use each homophone in a sentence.

Build Fluency

Have students work in pairs. Model dialogues with questions and answers such as the following:

People say I look like my father. What do you think? *(You do. You must have his genes.)*

What is reproduction? *(It's how animals make babies.)*

© Harcourt

② Scaffold the Content

Preview the Lesson

When to Use	Proficiency Levels
With pp. 48–56	✔ Beginning
	✔ Intermediate
⏱ 20 minutes	✔ Advanced

- Read the title on page 48 aloud. Explain that this lesson will answer the question.

- Have students follow the steps in sexual reproduction shown on page 50 as you explain the process in simple terms. Point out that one cell divides into two; then these two cells divide into four and so on. Explain that cells can divide in two ways: mitosis and meiosis.

- Review the steps in mitosis, shown on pages 52–53. Explain that this process produces body cells. As a cell divides, the new cell gets a copy of all the chromosomes that were in the old cell.

- Finally, review the steps in meiosis, shown on page 55. Explain that this process produces reproductive cells. As a cell divides in two, each new cell gets half of the chromosomes in the old cell.

Investigate, p. 49

Use before students begin the Investigate:

- Review the steps in the Procedure. Have a volunteer demonstrate what to do or ask students to read the steps and explain them in their own words.

- Use gestures and words to make sure that students understand the meanings of these words: *slide, focus, observe, adjust, stage, division.*

- Tell or remind students that *sequence* means "order." You might write the numbers 1–4 on separate cards and ask a volunteer to put them in sequence or order.

- After students complete the activity, discuss their conclusions as a class.

Modify Instruction—Multilevel Strategies

Language and Vocabulary Point out that several words in this lesson have more than one meaning. As an example, write *rest* on the board and have students say it with you. Invite a volunteer to define this word and use it in a sentence. Make sure students are aware that *rest* can mean "to sit quietly" (*He will rest after the race.*) or "what is left" (*I will eat the rest of the cake.*).

Beginning Add the words *slide* and *tip* to the board. Have students say them with you. Then help them recognize at least two meanings for each word—*Slide*: "a slide in the park, a slide for a microscope, to slide on the ice"; *tip*: "the end, a suggestion, to push over."

© Harcourt

Intermediate In addition to *slide* and *tip*, help students recognize two meanings for *way* ("a path, a process") and *kind* ("a type, caring"). Use each meaning in a sentence and have students explain what the word means in that context.

Advanced In addition to the words above, help students recognize different meanings for *stage* ("a platform, a period of development") and *draw* ("to make a picture, to select"). Encourage students to use both meanings of the words in sentences.

For All Students Have students contribute to a running list of words with multiple meanings as they study this chapter and others.

Extend

Have students complete the Show What You Know activity on page 15 to demonstrate their understanding of how cells reproduce. *(Answers: Both, meiosis, mitosis)*

③ Apply and Assess

Make a Diagram

When to Use	Proficiency Levels
With Reading Review p. 57  20 minutes	✔ Beginning ✔ Intermediate ✔ Advanced

Materials: drawing supplies, butcher paper

- Have small groups make diagrams to show the stages of mitosis or meiosis. (You might assign the types of reproduction to make sure both will be represented.)

- Ask the groups to label the stages, copying words you have written on the board. Some groups might be able to add a sentence or two explaining what happens at each stage.

- Provide time for each group to present its diagram to the class.

Informal Assessment

Beginning	Intermediate	Advanced
Ask individual students to point to the stage that you describe on their group's diagram. Encourage them to use words and gestures to explain what is happening at that stage.	Have each student complete a sentence or answer a question about his or her group's diagram. *(Example question: In mitosis, what happens after the chromosomes separate? Answer: They move to opposite sides of the cell.)*	Have each student describe the stages of mitosis or meiosis in complete sentences. *(Answers will vary. Example for mitosis: In the first stage, each chromosome makes a copy of itself.)*

Comparing Mitosis and Meiosis

Read the sentences below. Decide what they tell about. Then choose the correct
sentence to copy under *Mitosis*, *Meiosis*, and *Both*.

> The cell splits in two.
>
> Each new cell has half of the chromosomes of the old cell.
>
> Each new cell has the same number of chromosomes as the old cell.

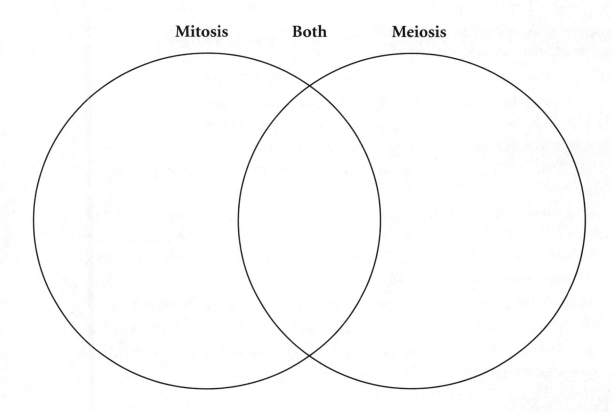

Mitosis   **Both**   **Meiosis**

School-Home Connection: Have students take this page home to share with
family members. They can use this page to tell how cells reproduce.

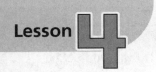
How Are Traits Inherited?

① Build Background

Access Prior Knowledge

When to Use	Proficiency Levels
Before introducing the lesson	✔ Beginning
⏱ 15 minutes	✔ Intermediate
	Advanced

Ask students if they know someone who looks like his or her parents. In what ways do these people look alike? *(examples: hair color, eye color, skin color, tallness)* Ask students how they think parents pass some of these traits on to their children.

Preteach Lesson Vocabulary

> **dominant, recessive**

List the vocabulary words on the board.

Have students find the words on the board on page 62. Then:

- Have them say the word *dominant* with you, clapping out the syllables. Ask a volunteer to read the definition that precedes the word. *(stronger)* Explain that *dominant* is from a Latin word that means "master." When you *dominate*, you rule.

- Have students say and clap out the word *recessive*. Have a volunteer find its definition in the text. *(weaker)* Explain that *recessive* is from a Latin word that means "to recede or pull back." At school, *recess* is a time to "pull back" from working and just have fun.

- Explain that *dominant* and *recessive* are adjectives, or describing words.

- Use *dominant* and *recessive* in sentences, such as these: *Carla is the dominant player on her basketball team. Jake becomes shy around strangers because he has a recessive personality.*

Build Fluency

Have students work in pairs. Model dialogues by completing questions and answers such as the following:

What is your dominant language? It's English, but I also understand Spanish.

What does *recessive* mean? It means "weaker," which is the opposite of stronger.

© Harcourt

② Scaffold the Content

Preview the Lesson

When to Use
With pp. 58–64

🕐 20 minutes

Proficiency Levels
✔ Beginning
✔ Intermediate
✔ Advanced

Read the title on page 58 aloud. Tell students the lesson will answer this question.

- Write *inherited* on the board. Explain that it means "received from a parent." Traits are received from a parent.
- Challenge students to restate the lesson title in their own words. For example: "How are characteristics received from a parent?"
- Explain that each characteristic we have, such as eye color, can be dominant (strong) or recessive (weak). For example, brown eye color is dominant, while blue eye color is recessive. If even one of your parents has brown eyes, you will probably have brown eyes because brown eyes are a dominant trait.

Investigate, p. 59

Before students begin the Investigate:

- Write the word *ear* on the board and have students define it. Then have them use context clues to figure out what the word *ear* means on page 59. Guide them to understand that an *ear of corn* is the part of the corn that contains the seeds or kernels.
- Review the steps in the Procedure. Ask a volunteer to demonstrate how to complete each step, or invite students to explain what they are to do in their own words.
- Make sure students understand that to *predict* is to guess what will happen. To *estimate* is to guess a number instead of counting. A *ratio* is a comparison between two numbers. For example, if there are 10 white kernels and 20 purple kernels, the ratio is 1:2.

Modify Instruction—Multilevel Strategies

Comprehensible Input Show students pictures of pet families, such as a mother cat and her kittens. Ask which traits students think the kittens inherited from their mother. Which inherited traits probably came from their father?

Beginning Have students cut out magazine pictures or draw pictures of a human or animal family. Ask them to point to characteristics that the offspring inherited from their parents.

Intermediate Help students name inherited traits and construct simple sentences that compare these traits. For instance: *My dog has brown spots, just like his mother.* Write their sentences on the board and encourage them to read them aloud.

Advanced Have students write a paragraph explaining how traits are inherited by offspring.

For All Students Ask students to notice human and animal families around them and watch for inherited traits.

Extend

Have students complete the **Show What You Know** activity on page 19 to demonstrate their understanding of how traits are inherited.

③ Apply and Assess

Make a Diagram

When to Use With Reading Review p. 65 ⏱ 20 minutes	Proficiency Levels ✔ Beginning ✔ Intermediate ✔ Advanced

Materials: drawing supplies, poster board

- Have groups diagram what would happen if dominant and recessive traits were combined. First, have each group choose a plant or animal (not a human) that is real or make-believe. Then each group will choose a dominant trait and a recessive trait for its living thing, such as curly and straight fur or red and white petals.

- Next, the group will draw a simple diagram showing both parent plants or both parent animals. They will mark each parent with a capital letter for a dominant trait or a lowercase letter for a recessive trait.

- Finally, the group will discuss and then draw what happens when the parent plants or animals produce four offspring. They will show the traits inherited by each offspring and how each offspring looks as a result. Provide time for groups to share their diagrams.

Informal Assessment

Beginning	Intermediate	Advanced
Ask individual students to point out examples of dominant and recessive traits, or you might point to examples and have students identify them as dominant or recessive. *(Answers will vary.)*	Have each student construct or complete simple sentences about his or her group's diagram. *(Answers will vary. Example: The mother dog has _____. [long ears] This trait is _____. [dominant])*	Have each student describe the dominant and recessive traits in his or her group's diagram in complete sentences. *(Answers will vary. Example: The father's long ears are a dominant trait, so all his puppies have long ears, too.)*

Name _____

Date _____

Traits Word Web

Complete the word web by adding words that tell about inherited traits. Use the words from the box.

chromosomes	plastic	genes	dominant
paper	electricity	recessive	

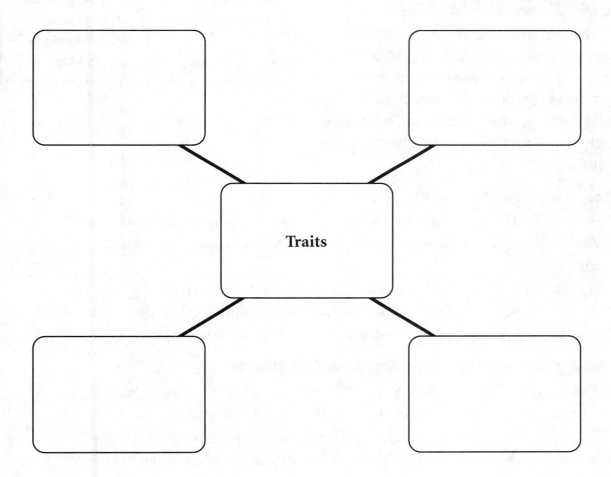

Traits

 School-Home Connection: Have students take this page home to share with family members. They can use this page to tell how traits are inherited.

© Harcourt

2 Classifying Living Things ●

Develop Scientific Concepts and Vocabulary

In this chapter, students will learn how to classify and name living things. All living things, or organisms, are classified according to their characteristics in order to better identify and study them. Organisms are divided into main groups, called kingdoms, then subdivided into smaller and smaller groups.

Preview Scientific Principles

Walk through the chapter with students, pausing to read aloud or to have volunteers read aloud the three questions that are lesson titles. Encourage students to briefly discuss each question and to tell what they already know that might help them answer the questions.

When to Use With Chapter Opener ⏱ 25 minutes	Proficiency Levels ✔ Beginning ✔ Intermediate ✔ Advanced

Lesson 1: How Are Organisms Classified?

- Have students work in groups to sort white and yellow index cards or chalk into two groups. Ask them to explain their reason for sorting the objects they way they did.

- Explain that students have *classified* the objects into two groups. Discuss that classification means putting similar objects into groups. Explain that living things—also called *organisms*—can also be classified into groups.

Lesson 2: What Are the Major Groups of Organisms?

- Write *dog, cat, horse* on the board. Ask students how these organisms are alike. Guide them to the understanding that they are all animals.

- Explain that organisms are divided into broad groups that have similar features. Preview that the groups are animals, plants, fungi, protists, and bacteria.

- Help students organize this information into a word web with ORGANISMS in the center and the five group names around it.

Lesson 3: How Do Scientists Name Organisms?

- Explain that scientists have given organisms a special name to identify them.
- Write *Homo sapiens* on the board. Say that this is the scientific name for humans.
- Explain that the name comes from two of the scientific groups to which humans belong. The first word is the *genus* name and the second word is the *species* name.

Practice

Materials: seven large sheets of tag board, marking pens

- Point out that the classification system used today divides organisms into seven levels from *Kingdom* to *Species*. Each level down contains fewer organisms that have more in common.
- Write the names of the seven levels on the board, in proper order: *Kingdom, Phylum, Class, Order, Family, Genus,* and *Species*. Have students copy the terms onto seven sheets of tag board as you read them and students repeat them.
- Then have students take turns holding the cards and putting themselves in order.

Apply

- Write the first two lines of *It's Easy to Remember!* on the board. Have students practice saying it as a chant to help learn the seven classification groups.
- Write the last three lines and underline the first letter of each word. Show students how each line works as a mnemonic to remember the seven levels. Have students read the lines, then choose and memorize one of them. They can also write their own.

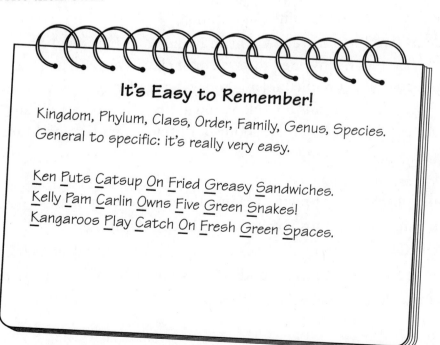

It's Easy to Remember!

Kingdom, Phylum, Class, Order, Family, Genus, Species.
General to specific: it's really very easy.

Ken Puts Catsup On Fried Greasy Sandwiches.
Kelly Pam Carlin Owns Five Green Snakes!
Kangaroos Play Catch On Fresh Green Spaces.

How Are Organisms Classified?

① Build Background

Access Prior Knowledge

When to Use	Proficiency Levels
Before introducing the lesson 15 minutes	✔ Beginning ✔ Intermediate Advanced

Ask students to describe some differences between plants and animals. Explain to students that scientists have been classifying living things into groups, such as plants and animals, for thousands of years. Ask them why they think it is important to classify organisms and discuss how classification helps identify, sort, name, and better study living things. Have students help list about 15 organisms on the board. Allow time for them to suggest ways they might separate the living things into groups.

Preteach Lesson Vocabulary

classification

Write the vocabulary word on the board.

- Write *classify* on the board and ask students to discuss what it means to classify. Ask them for synonyms of this term, such as sort, group, or organize. Explain that *classification* is the noun form of the verb classify. Have students point to the vocabulary word on page 76.

- Tell students that they will be learning how living things, or organisms, are classified in science. Explain that similar things, or things that are alike in many ways, are put into the same classification.

- Have students find the picture of Carl von Linné (Carl Linnaeus) on page 77. Explain that he invented the system of classifying and naming organisms used—in a modified form—today. It is called the *Linnaean System.* Von Linné divided organisms into plant and animal *kingdoms.* Explain that scientists have since added new kingdoms for bacteria, protists, and fungi.

Build Fluency

Have students complete and practice reading these sentence frames:

Sorting similar things into groups is called _____. *(classification)*

_____ invented the system of classification for living things. *(Von Linné)*

It originally had groups for _____ and animals. *(plants)*

Today, the system also includes fungi, protists, and _____. *(bacteria)*

② Scaffold the Content

Preview the Lesson

When to Use	Proficiency Levels
With pp. 74–78	✔ Beginning
🕐 15 minutes	✔ Intermediate
	✔ Advanced

- Have students read the section head on page 76 and discuss why it might be useful to classify organisms. Ask them to suggest ways they would divide organisms into broad groups and identify which traits they would use for classification.

- Preview page 77 and discuss why it is important for scientists to agree on one system of classification. Ask what would happen if different people used different systems.

- Have students turn to page 78. Remind them that, today, scientists use a version of the Linnaean system. This system divides organisms into large groups. Ask students to scan the page and identify the name for these large groups. *(kingdoms)*

Investigate, p. 75

Materials: variety of beans

- Before students begin the Investigate, explain that they will observe a variety of beans. Display the mixed beans to preview these objects for students.

- Tell students that they will need to observe how the beans are alike and different. Ask them to identify properties or characteristics they might use to classify the beans and write the answers on the board. *(Possible answers: shape, size, color, texture)*

- Explain that students will then use their observations to classify the beans in a way that they choose. Review what it means to classify.

Modify Instruction—Multilevel Strategies

Language and Vocabulary This lesson introduces new vocabulary that serves as the basis for the rest of the chapter. These activities will reinforce the meaning of the new terms.

Beginning Have partners choose one term from this list and present an oral definition to the group: *organism, classification, kingdom, Linnaean system.*

Intermediate Have students make vocabulary cards for these terms in the lesson: *organism, classification, kingdom, Linnaean system.* Have them write each term on one side of an index card and a definition on the other side.

Advanced Have students use these four scientific words from the lesson and use each one in a complete sentence: *organism, classification, kingdom, Linnaean system.*

For All Students Encourage students to make vocabulary cards or update a lesson dictionary to track the new terms they learn throughout the lesson.

Extend

Have the students complete the **Show What You Know** activity on page 25 to demonstrate their understanding of classification systems.

③ Apply and Assess

Plants and Animals Poster

When to Use With Reading Review p. 79 🕐 25 minutes	Proficiency Levels ✔ Beginning ✔ Intermediate Advanced

Materials: markers or paints, poster board

- Divide the students into two groups. Assign one group the category of *plants* and the other the category of *animals*.
- Give each group a large sheet of poster board and ask them to paint or draw 10 examples in that category.
- Have students write one sentence about each picture, including its classification. If necessary, present sentence frames for students to complete: This hippopotamus is an _____. *(animal)* This redwood tree is a _____. *(plant)*
- Have volunteers from each group share the names of all the items on the poster and read the sentences aloud to the group.

Informal Assessment

Beginning	Intermediate	Advanced
Ask students to define a term from the list. *(Answers: organism: a living thing; classification: sorting similar objects into groups; kingdom: the largest groups in the Linnaean system; Linnaean system: a system of classification for organisms)*	Ask students to define two of the terms using their cards as a reference. *(Answers: organism: a living thing; classification: sorting similar objects into groups; kingdom: the largest groups in the Linnaean system; Linnaean system: a system of classification for organisms)*	Select two of the vocabulary words and ask students to define them in their own words. Ask them *yes/no* questions about the words. Then reverse roles and have students ask you *yes/no* questions about the word. *(Answers: organism: a living thing; classification: sorting similar objects into groups; kingdom: the largest groups in the Linnaean system; Linnaean system: a system of classification for organisms)*

Classification Chart

Cut out 12 pictures of living things. Classify each one as a plant, animal, or other. Tape or glue each picture into the correct column of the chart. Then explain how you classified the pictures.

Plants	Animals	Others

_____

_____

_____

_____

School-Home Connection: Have students take this page home to share with family members. They can use this page to tell about the classification of organisms.

Lesson 2 What Are the Major Groups of Organisms?

① Build Background

Access Prior Knowledge

When to Use	Proficiency Levels
Before introducing the lesson 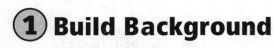 20 minutes	✔ Beginning ✔ Intermediate ✔ Advanced

Remind students that they already know about two kingdoms—plant and animal. Write *plants* and *animals* on the board. Ask students to identify any other kingdoms they know and write the names on the board. Fill out the list with bacteria, fungi, and protists. Allow time for students to identify members of each kingdom and tell about the characteristics of each one.

Preteach Lesson Vocabulary

> **adaptation, fungus, protist**

List the vocabulary words on the board.

- Have students find the vocabulary words on pages 82 to 85 and help them with the spelling and pronunciation of each term, including the plural of *fungus (fungi)*.

- Have students point to *adaptation* on page 82 and preview the definition. Summarize that an adaptation is a trait or characteristic that helps an organism survive. Ask students to name adaptations that help them survive. Point out that adaptations are one way that scientists classify organisms.

- Explain that fungi and protists are kingdoms, like plants and animals. Have students preview page 84 to identify types of fungi and their features. Repeat for protists on page 85.

- Have students go back through the lesson to find the words *chloroplasts*, *vertebrates*, and *invertebrates* (pages 82–83). Explain that these important features help scientists classify organisms into kingdoms or into smaller groups within the kingdoms.

Build Fluency

Ask students to sing the following lines to the tune of *Frère Jacques (Are You Sleeping?)*:

What's a *mushroom*? What's a *mushroom*? Do you know? Do you know?

It's a *fungus*. It's a *fungus*. This I know. This I know.

Repeat the tune substituting the following words in additional verses: pine tree/ a plant; a lizard/an animal; an amoeba/a protist; a spider, an animal.

② Scaffold the Content

Preview the Lesson

When to Use With pp. 80–86	Proficiency Levels
🕐 15 minutes	✔ Beginning ✔ Intermediate ✔ Advanced

- Have students preview the section heads to identify the five kingdoms and have them write the names on separate index cards.
- Have them preview the pictures and write names or draw pictures on the back of each card to identify two or three members of each kingdom.
- Tell students that within kingdoms, organisms are put into smaller subgroups. For example, plants are classified as *vascular* or *nonvascular*. Explain that *vascular* comes from the Latin word for "little vessel." Explain that plants are sorted by whether or not they have tubes inside them.

Investigate, p. 81

- Before students begin the Investigate, explain that they will categorize foods into groups and subgroups in this Investigate. Remind them that kingdoms are also divided into subgroups.
- Ask a volunteer to define the prefix *sub-* and use that definition to define *subgroup*. Point out that subgroups make up levels of classification.
- Review the different food groups by asking students to identify examples of: fruit, vegetables, meat, bread or grains, and dairy products.

Modify Instruction—Multilevel Strategies

Language and Vocabulary In this lesson, students will learn the names and characteristics of the five kingdoms as well as some of the subgroups within those kingdoms. The key to mastering this skill is to say and write the five terms and begin to understand the characteristics that distinguish each one from the others.

Beginning Have students say the five kingdom names.

Intermediate Have students write the five kingdom names on a sheet of paper and illustrate or write an example of each one.

Advanced Have students write the names of the five kingdoms on separate index cards and write a sentence or phrase of the back of each one telling a distinctive feature of that kingdom.

For All Students Have students begin a word web for each of the kingdoms. Have them add to the word webs as they learn more about each one during the lesson.

Have the students complete the **Show What You Know** activity on page 29 to demonstrate their understanding of the five kingdoms.

③ Apply and Assess

Interactive Kingdom Chart

When to Use With Reading Review p. 87 🕐 15 minutes	Proficiency Levels ✔ Beginning ✔ Intermediate ✔ Advanced

Materials: magazines, butcher paper, glue, scissors, markers or colored pencils

- Have each student find and cut out a picture of one example of each of the five kingdoms. If a picture is not available, ask them to draw one.
- Let students arrange their pictures on the butcher paper as follows:
  1. Glue only the top edge of the picture to the butcher paper.
  2. Write the name of the appropriate kingdom underneath the picture so that it will only show if the picture is lifted up.
- Have partners trade posters and try to identify the kingdom for each picture, telling each other why they think their answer is correct. They can lift the pictures to check their answers.

Informal Assessment

Beginning	Intermediate	Advanced
Have students say the five names to you and write down as many as they can. *(Answers: plant, animal, protist, fungus, bacterium)*	Ask students to read their list of names. Ask them *true/false* questions about each kingdom. *(Answers: plant, animal, protist, fungus, bacterium)*	Ask students to name the five kingdoms and tell as much as they know about one of the kingdoms. *(Answers: plant, animal, protist, fungus, bacterium)*

Kingdom Chart

Write the name of one of the five kingdoms in each box. Write one example of an organism and two features or facts about that kingdom.

Kingdom: _____

example: _____

fact 1: _____

fact 2: _____

Kingdom: _____

example: _____

fact 1: _____

fact 2: _____

Kingdom: _____

example: _____

fact 1: _____

fact 2: _____

Kingdom: _____

example: _____

fact 1: _____

fact 2: _____

Kingdom: _____

example: _____

fact 1: _____

fact 2: _____

School-Home Connection: Have students take this page home to share with family members. They can use it to tell them about the five kingdoms.

How Do Scientists Name Organisms?

① Build Background

Access Prior Knowledge

When to Use	Proficiency Levels
Before introducing the lesson 15 minutes	✔ Beginning ✔ Intermediate ✔ Advanced

Write *system* on the board. Tell students that a system is a way to arrange or classify things. Ask them to give examples of systems they have seen. *(filing systems for records, libraries, rulebooks, departments in stores, photo albums)* Ask students to tell what they already know about how scientists classify organisms. Ask volunteers to define *kingdom* and *subgroup*.

Preteach Lesson Vocabulary

genus, species

List the vocabulary words on the board.

- Remind students that scientists group organisms into kingdoms, and then divide kingdoms into smaller subgroups. Refer students to page 92. Read the title of the chart. Have students read aloud with you: *Kingdom, Phylum, Class, Order, Family, Genus, Species.* Point out that the *ph* in *phylum* is pronounced as an *f*.

- Explain that the classifications are listed from general to specific. *Kingdoms* are the largest with the most organisms; species are smallest with the fewest organisms.

- Have students find *genus* and *species.* Explain that genus and species names give an organism a unique scientific name. Define a species as a group that has a unique characteristic. Its members can only reproduce among themselves.

- Have students turn to page 94 and find *dichotomous key.* Explain that this type of key unlocks how to correctly name an organism. Say that the prefix *di-* means two. Ask students why they think this key is called "dichotomous."

Build Fluency

To begin learning the seven levels of classification, have students chant the following:

- K-P-C-O-F-G-S
- Kingdom-Phylum-Class-Order-Family-Genus-Species

Let students experiment with different rhythms.

② Scaffold the Content

When to Use With pp. 88–94	Proficiency Levels
⏱ 15 minutes	✔ Beginning ✔ Intermediate ✔ Advanced

Preview the Lesson

- Refer students to page 88 and have a volunteer read the title. Say that the lesson explains how scientists name all organisms on Earth.

- Ask volunteers to explain in their own words what a kingdom is. Then refer students to the chart on page 91 to show how the animal kingdom is subdivided into phyla and even smaller groups. Point out that all kingdoms are divided into many phyla.

- Use the chart on pages 92 and 93 to preview the seven levels of classification.

- Allow students to preview the pictures and chart on page 94 to see that an organism's genus and species names are used to give it a unique scientific name.

Investigate, p. 89

- Before students begin the Investigate, explain that they will be classifying different kinds of beans.

- Point out the identification key and explain that the term *dichotomous* comes from the word *dichotomy*. Say that dichotomy is the division of something into two parts.

- Explain that this system starts with two questions. The answer leads to another two questions and so on. Eventually the answers lead to a single answer or conclusion.

- Ask students to preview the key and name some of the characteristics they will use to identify beans.

Modify Instruction—Multilevel Strategies

Language and Vocabulary This lesson builds on students' understanding of the levels of classification. These activities will further develop the vocabulary of classification.

Beginning Have students copy and answer the following statements with *true* or *false*: You ask two questions at a time with a dichotomous key. *(true)*

Kingdom is the most specific group of organisms. *(false)*

An organism's name gives you information about its characteristics. *(true)*

Intermediate Have students choose two of the seven levels of classification. Have them look up the words in the dictionary and write the definition. Then have them write one sentence using each of the words.

Advanced Have students choose five animals and find their two-part scientific names. Have them make a chart with three columns: common name, scientific name, and picture.

For All Students Ask students to define as many of the following words on separate index cards as they can: *organism, dichotomous, mammal, genus, species.* Have them complete the other definitions as they work through the lesson.

Extend

Have the students complete the **Show What You Know** activity on page 33 to demonstrate their understanding of naming organisms.

③ Apply and Assess

Make a Class Book of Organism Pictures and Names

When to Use With Reading Review p. 95 20 minutes	Proficiency Levels ✔ Beginning ✔ Intermediate ✔ Advanced

Materials: magazines, markers, glue, art paper

- Have students create a class book of organisms and their scientific names.
- Ask each student to find three pictures of animals, plants, or other organisms. Have them cut them out and glue the pictures onto a piece of art paper.
- Then have students find the two-word name for the organism and write it next to the picture. Ask them to arrange the pictures and labels attractively on the page. Have students present their work to the group.
- When all the pages are complete, assemble and bind them into a class book. Let the students choose a title for the book.

Informal Assessment

Beginning	Intermediate	Advanced
Have students name the seven levels of classification in any order. (*Answers: kingdom, phylum, class, order, family, genus, species*)	Have students write the seven levels of classification in order from largest to smallest groups. (*Answers: kingdom, phylum, class, order, family, genus, species*)	Ask students to explain the seven-level system of classification and the naming system for organisms. Be sure they include the seven levels of classification in their answer. (*Answers: The system groups all organisms into kingdoms, then into smaller and smaller subgroups called phylum, class, order, family, genus, species. The scientific name combines the genus and species names.*)

The Classification Pyramid

Fill in the upside-down pyramid with the names of the seven levels of classification. Write the most general at the top and the most specific at the bottom.

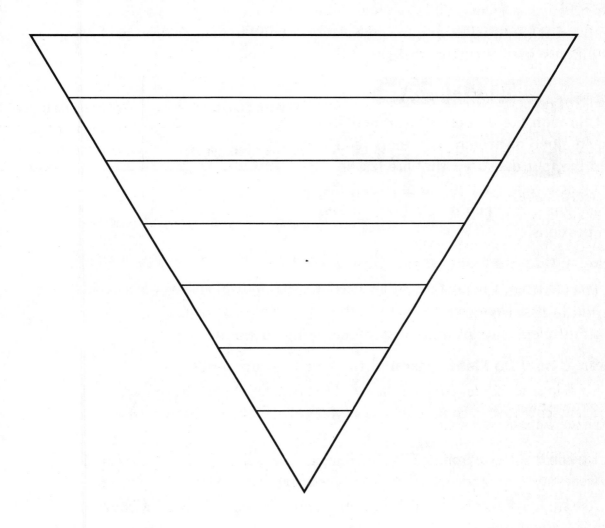

School-Home Connection: Have students take this page home to share with family members. They can use this page to tell about the seven levels of classification.

3 Plants and Plant Growth

Develop Scientific Concepts and Vocabulary

In this chapter, students will learn about different kinds of plants and how they reproduce. Students will also learn how plants respond to their environment and how different plant structures help meet the needs of plants.

Preview Scientific Principles

Walk through the chapter with students, reading aloud or having volunteers read aloud the four questions that are lesson titles. Encourage students to tell what they already know that might help them answer the questions.

When to Use With Chapter Opener	Proficiency Levels
🕐 30 minutes	✔ Beginning ✔ Intermediate ✔ Advanced

Lesson 1: How Do Plants Meet Their Needs?

- Ask students to name things they need in order to live, such as water, food, and shelter. Then have them name things they think a plant needs.
- Ask students to explain or pantomime caring for a potted plant.

Lesson 2: How Do Plants Respond to Their Environment?

- To help students understand the word *respond*, tell them that you will read a few sentences. Each time they hear you say *plants*, they should respond by clapping.
- Explain that an environment is everything around a living thing. Display outdoor scenes and have students call out words describing the environments shown.
- Ask students to pantomime how they might respond to a cold environment.

Lesson 3: What Are Some Types of Plants?

- Have students draw their favorite plants. Then, help the class classify all the drawings into groups, such as trees or flowers.
- Show students pictures of a pine tree and a wildflower. Have them compare and contrast the plants.
- Write *nonflowering* on the board. Have a volunteer underline the prefix *non-* and explain its meaning. Discuss other words that begin with this prefix.

© Harcourt

Lesson 4: How Do Angiosperms Reproduce?

- Show pictures of flowering plants. Explain that all are *angiosperms*. Then, display pictures of angiosperms (in bloom), gymnosperms, nonvascular plants, and vascular plants that do not produce seeds. Help students identify the angiosperms.

- Tell students that the word *reproduce* means "to make a copy." When animals reproduce, they make young animals; plants make young plants. Ask why it is important for plants to reproduce. (*Plants die, so new plants must replace them.*)

Practice

Have students cut out pictures of plants from old magazines. Write these headings or similar ones on the board: *Plants We Eat, Plants Used for Medicine, Flowering Plants.* Ask students to arrange the pictures by category on large sheets of paper. Encourage them to describe the categories and the plants in words or sentences.

Apply

Tell students that most plants can be grouped into three categories: plants that do not make seeds, nonflowering plants that make seeds, and flowering plants. Copy the following chart on the board. Have students use the textbook or other reference sources to find out the category for each plant listed.

Plant	Category
apple tree	flowering plant
cactus	flowering plant
fern	plant that does not make seeds
ginkgo tree	nonflowering plant that makes seeds
horsetail	plant that does not make seeds
moss	plant that does not make seeds
pine tree	nonflowering plant that makes seeds
rose	flowering plant
sago palm	nonflowering plant that makes seeds

© Harcourt

1 Build Background

Access Prior Knowledge

When to Use	Proficiency Levels
Before introducing the lesson	✔ Beginning
🕐 15 minutes	✔ Intermediate
	Advanced

Invite students to share any experiences they have had in caring for plants, such as working in the yard at home, planting a garden, or tending potted plants. Then, display a diagram of a plant. Have students identify the leaves, roots, and stem.

Preteach Lesson Vocabulary

vascular plant, xylem, phloem, nonvascular plant

List the vocabulary words on the board.

Say each vocabulary word and have students repeat it after you. Then:

- Tell students that the word *vascular* comes from a Latin word that means "vessel." Have students find the blood vessels on their inner wrists. Point out that vascular plants have vessels like these. These vessels carry water and other materials throughout the plant.

- Remind students that the prefix *non-* means "not." What would the word *nonvascular* mean? (*not vascular* or *not with vessels*)

- Underline the *x* in *xylem*. Tell students that when a word starts with *x* in English, this sound is pronounced /z/.

- Underline the *ph* in *phloem*. Explain that the letters *ph* in an English word are pronounced /f/.

Build Fluency

Have students name plant parts for you to list on the board. (*roots, leaves, stems, trunks, vessels, flowers, seeds*) Then, invite volunteers to use these parts to complete the following sentence:

Plants have _____.

© Harcourt

② Scaffold the Content

Preview the Lesson

Materials: wax paper, plants, scissors, hand lenses

Read the lesson title and ask students what they think they will learn. Then, have them look at page 104 and explain why seeds might have a hard time growing in the desert.

Have students form pairs. Distribute the materials and have each pair lay the wax paper on their desk and put the plant on it.

- Tell students to use the hand lens to look for different parts on their plants.
- Have students carefully make a vertical cut along the plant's stem and use the lens to observe the inside of the stem.
- Ask students to scan the lesson and find pictures of the plant parts they found.

Investigate, p. 105

Before students begin the Investigate:

- Hold up a bean seed and explain that the word *germinate* comes from a Latin word that means "seed." The word *germinate* means "to begin to grow."
- Say: *The seed is beginning to grow.* Have a volunteer repeat the sentence using *germinating* instead of *beginning to grow.* Explain that another word that means the same as *germinate* is *sprout.* Ask students to use *sprout* in the same sentence.
- Review the steps in the Procedure and make sure students understand them. Ask volunteers to explain each step in their own words.

Modify Instruction—Multilevel Strategies

Background/Experience In this lesson, students will learn a great deal about a subject that is probably already familiar to them. Help them relate this new knowledge to their previous experiences.

Beginning Have students draw a vascular plant and a nonvascular plant and label the main parts (leaf, stem, roots). You might provide lists of plants to choose from.

Intermediate Ask students what plants need in order to stay healthy. *(water, light, carbon dioxide, oxygen, nutrients)* Display a picture of an outdoor plant. Ask how this plant gets each of the five things it needs. For example: Where does this plant get water? *(rain)*

Advanced Ask students to think of a time when they have seen a plant in distress, such as a withered plant during a drought. Discuss why the plant was having problems. Which of its needs was not being met? *(water)*

For All Students Display pictures of familiar plants and ask students whether each one is vascular or nonvascular. If students say it is vascular, ask how they know. *(The plant has xylem and phloem tissue to carry food and water. It is larger than nonvascular plants.)*

Extend

Have the students complete the **Show What You Know** activity on page 39 to demonstrate their understanding of plants and their needs.

③ Apply and Assess

Make a Model of a Vascular Plant

When to Use	Proficiency Levels
With Reading Review p. 111	✔ Beginning
🕐 15 minutes	✔ Intermediate
	✔ Advanced

Materials: pipe cleaners, construction paper, string, markers, and so on

- Ask pairs of students to make a model of a vascular plant. Their models should include chloroplasts, xylem, and phloem.
- Have the pairs label their models, using words or sentences to describe the function of each plant part.
- Have pairs exchange models. Ask pairs to study the models they received and find the plant part that changes light energy into sugars *(chloroplasts)*, the part that carries water *(xylem)*, and the part that carries sugar *(phloem)*.

Informal Assessment

Beginning	Intermediate	Advanced
Show students pictures of various plants and have them point to vascular plants and nonvascular plants. *(Answers will vary.)*	Have students list the five main needs of plants. *(water, light, carbon dioxide, oxygen, nutrients)*	Have students write a sentence or two explaining how to take care of a plant. *(Possible answer: You should water it and make sure it gets enough sunlight and nutrients.)*

Name _____

Date _____

Plant Match-Up

Match each clue below with a word on the right. Write the letter of the correct word on the line.

1. _____ plants with vessels

2. _____ carries water through the plant

3. _____ carries sugar to plant cells

4. _____ captures sunlight

5. _____ gas needed by plants

6. _____ plants without vessels

7. _____ when a plant sprouts

8. _____ source of a plant's energy

A. chlorophyll

B. germinates

C. nonvascular

D. carbon dioxide

E. phloem

F. sunlight

G. vascular

H. xylem

 School-Home Connection: Have students take this page home to share with family members. They can use this page to tell what they have learned about the needs of plants.

How Do Plants Respond to Their Environment?

① Build Background

Access Prior Knowledge

When to Use	Proficiency Levels
Before introducing the lesson 15 minutes	✔ Beginning ✔ Intermediate Advanced

Tell students that all organisms, including humans, respond to their environment. For example, how do they respond to a hot day? *(by wearing shorts, drinking lots of water, and so on)* Ask how they think a lizard would respond to a cool day *(by sitting in the sun)*, how a cat would respond when summer approaches *(by shedding hair)*, and how a frog would respond when its pond dries up *(by finding another pond)*.

Preteach Lesson Vocabulary

> **tropism, phototropism, gravitropism**

List the vocabulary words on the board.

Underline the letters *tropism* in each word. Then:

- Explain that tropisms are ways that plants respond to their environments. Tropisms are growth toward or away from something. Have students stand up and move *away* from their desks. Then, have them move *toward* their desks.

- Write the words *photograph* and *photosynthesis* under *phototropism* on the board. Have a volunteer underline the part of each word that is the same. *(photo)* Ask what *photo* means. *(light)* Explain that *phototropism* is a response to light. Tell students that humans also respond to light. In a dark room the center part of our eyes, the iris, gets larger to let in more light. In bright light the iris gets smaller to protect our eyes from too much light.

Build Fluency

Read each word in the following list to students. Have them repeat the word and clap out its rhythm with one clap for each syllable. Demonstrate how to pause after the clap for a stressed syllable in each of the following words: *annual, dormant, environment, gravitropism, negative, perennial, phototropism, positive, respond, tropism.*

© Harcourt

② Scaffold the Content

Preview the Lesson

When to Use
With pp. 112–116

🕐 20 minutes

Proficiency Levels
✔ Beginning
✔ Intermediate
✔ Advanced

- Ask students to follow along as you read the lesson title on page 112. Encourage them to answer the question in the title. Write their responses on the board.

- Ask how the students respond to their environment. For example, what do they do when it begins to rain or when the sun is in their eyes?

- Have students turn to page 116. Explain that the word *rhythm* has several meanings, but in this lesson it means "patterns or cycles that are repeated over and over." Plant rhythms may take place during a day or a year. Have students name or pantomime some daily or yearly rhythms people follow, such as getting up, getting dressed, and brushing their teeth.

Investigate, p. 113

Before students begin the Investigate:

- Read the following list of directional prepositions and have students pantomime the direction each one indicates: *above, across, against, behind, below, beneath, beside, between, by, down, inside, on, toward, under, up, within.*

- Have a volunteer demonstrate each step in the Procedure as you read it aloud. Remind students to use the photographs as a guide.

- Review the meaning of *hypothesize*, "to make a prediction based on what you know and what you observe." When you *hypothesize* (verb), you make a *hypothesis* (noun).

- After the activity, discuss students' conclusions.

Modify Instruction—Multilevel Strategies

Comprehensible Input Ask students how plant tropisms and rhythms affect gardening and farming. For example, what could you do if the leaves on a houseplant keep turning toward the sunlight coming in a window? *(put the plant in a brighter place, turn the plant periodically)*

Beginning Display seed-catalog pictures of an annual, a perennial, a short-day plant, and a long-day plant. Ask students to find the one you name. (Some plants can have two labels, such as *perennial* and *short-day*.) Also, have students pantomime how a plant would respond to the sun overhead and to water in the soil below its roots.

Intermediate Write the terms *annual*, *perennial*, *short-day*, *long-day*, *phototropism*, and *gravitropism* on the board. Read the terms aloud and have students echo you. Then, ask them to use each word in a simple sentence.

Advanced Have students use the words listed under Intermediate in sentences describing plants they have seen growing (or tended themselves) and tropisms they have observed. Invite volunteers to read their sentences to the class.

For All Students Have students name their favorite plants and help each other figure out whether they are annuals or perennials.

Extend

Have the students complete the Show What You Know activity on page 43 to demonstrate their understanding of tropisms.

③ Apply and Assess

Planning Plants

Materials: seed catalogs, scissors, large sheets of paper, drawing materials, paste

When to Use With Reading Review p. 117 🕐 25 minutes	Proficiency Levels ✔ Beginning ✔ Intermediate ✔ Advanced

- Organize groups of four and distribute the materials. Tell students to design a garden that includes annuals, perennials, short-day plants, and long-day plants. They will cut out pictures of the plants they choose or draw the plants, using the pictures as a guide.

- Have groups arrange their garden on a large sheet of paper and label the different plants by name and by type of plant. Some plants will be two types, such as *long-day* and *annual*.

- Ask each group to share its garden with the class. Discuss how the different plants respond to their environment.

Informal Assessment

Beginning	Intermediate	Advanced
With the classroom lights off, use a flashlight to represent the sun. Have students pantomime a plant using phototropism to meet its needs. *(Students should bend their bodies toward the light.)*	Ask students why some plants are called *long-day* and some are called *short-day*. *(Long-day plants bloom in summer; short-day plants bloom in fall or winter.)*	Have students write sentences explaining the difference between phototropism and gravitropism and between annuals and perennials. *(Phototropism means "growing toward light"; gravitropism means "growing toward pull of gravity." Annuals live for one growing season, perennials live through several growing seasons.)*

Name _____

Date _____

Illustrating Tropisms

Plants respond to their environments in many ways. Show how plants move in response to light and to gravity.

Draw a plant that is using phototropism to meet its needs. Use arrows to show the direction the plant is moving.	
Draw a plant that is using gravitropism to meet its needs. Use arrows to show the direction the plant is moving.	
Draw a picture of your favorite flowering plant. Label it as a long-day plant or a short-day plant.	

© Harcourt

School-Home Connection: Have students take this page home to share with family members. They can use this page to explain how plants respond to their environments.

What Are Some Types of Plants?

① Build Background

Access Prior Knowledge

When to Use	Proficiency Levels
Before introducing the lesson 15 minutes	✔ Beginning ✔ Intermediate Advanced

Ask students to list broad categories of plants, such as trees, bushes, and flowers. Write these categories as headings on the board. Then, have students list specific plants under each category. For example, under *trees* students could list oaks, maples, evergreens, palms, cedars, junipers, sumacs, elms, and so on.

Preteach Lesson Vocabulary

List the vocabulary words on the board.

> **moss, asexual reproduction, spore, fern, gymnosperm, conifer, angiosperm**

Have students scan the lesson to find where the words *moss* (p. 120), *fern* (p. 122), and *conifer* (p. 124) are explained and pictured. Then:

- Write the word *sexual* on the board. Explain that this word means "having to do with sex." Tell students that sexual reproduction occurs when a male sex cell (a sperm) joins with a female sex cell (an egg).

- Write *a-* on the board. Tell students that the prefix *a-* is like the prefix *non-* because both mean "no" or "not." Underline the *a-* in the word *asexual* on the board. Ask students what *asexual* means. *(not having to do with sex)* Explain that organisms that reproduce asexually do not use sperm or eggs. They use *spores*.

- Tell students that *gymnosperms* and *angiosperms* are both vascular plants that produce seeds. However, only angiosperms produce flowers.

Build Fluency

Have students list as many kinds of plants as they can, such as apple tree, fern, moss, rosebush, yucca, cactus, and orchid. Ask volunteers to use those kinds of plants to complete this sentence:

There is a(n) _____ in the garden.

② Scaffold the Content

Preview the Lesson

When to Use
With pp. 118–126

🕙 10 minutes

Proficiency Levels
✔ Beginning
✔ Intermediate
✔ Advanced

- Have students follow along as you read the lesson title on page 118. Ask what types of plants they can name.
- Have students skim the lesson and see where these types of plants are first mentioned: *angiosperm* (p. 118), *vascular* (p. 120), *nonvascular* (p. 121), plants using *sexual reproduction* (p. 121), plants using *asexual reproduction* (p. 121), and *gymnosperms* (p. 124).
- Instruct students to make a chart with the following headings: *Nonvascular plants*, *Vascular plants without seeds*, *Gymnosperms*, and *Angiosperms*. Have them list plants under the correct heading as they progress through the lesson.

Investigate, p. 119

Before students begin the Investigate:

- Review the steps in the Procedure, modeling any instructions that might be confusing for students. Ask volunteers to describe what they will do during the activity. Remind students to use the photographs for guidance.
- If necessary, model how to write a description of an observation.
- Review the meaning of *adaptation*, "a way that plants and animals change to survive in a certain environment."
- After students complete the activity, discuss what they observed and concluded.

Modify Instruction—Multilevel Strategies

Comprehensible Input Collect many small pictures of different kinds of plants. On the board or chart paper, create a chart like the one below.

Type of Plant	Examples
1. nonvascular 2. vascular 3. without seeds 4. gymnosperms (seeds in cones) 5. angiosperms (seeds in fruit)	

Beginning Read each kind of plant in the chart aloud and have students echo you. Then, hold up a small picture of a plant and name it. Ask students to repeat its name. Then, have a volunteer tape the picture in the correct category on the chart.

Intermediate Repeat the activity under *Beginning*, but help students explain their choice in a short sentence. Example: *This pine tree is a gymnosperm.*

Advanced Show students an example of a dichotomous key. Have students develop a dichotomous key that could help somebody identify a nonvascular plant, a vascular plant that does not produce seeds, a gymnosperm, and an angiosperm.

For All Students Challenge students to bring in pictures and descriptions of different types of plants. Work together to label each plant by its type.

Extend

Have the students complete the **Show What You Know** activity on page 47 to demonstrate their understanding of different kinds of plants.

③ Apply and Assess

What Am I?

When to Use With Reading Review p. 127 ⏱ 15 minutes	Proficiency Levels ✔ Beginning ✔ Intermediate ✔ Advanced

- Organize groups of five and give each group a set of cards with the following words written on separate cards: *moss, spore, liverwort, hornwort, fern, conifer, seed, fruit, gymnosperm,* and *angiosperm.* Each group will place its cards in a pile, face down.

- Have one student in each group select a card and hide the word from the other group members. They will ask the student yes-or-no questions about the word, such as, "Are you a nonvascular plant?"

- Have group members ask questions until they guess the word on the card. Then, another student will select a card to continue the game. Have groups play until they have guessed the words on all of the cards.

Informal Assessment

Beginning	Intermediate	Advanced
Ask students to draw a nonvascular plant, a vascular plant that does not produce seeds, a gymnosperm, and an angiosperm. *(Answers will vary.)*	Display pictures of moss, a fern, a conifer, and a flowering plant. Give students four cards with the following labels: *nonvascular plant, vascular plant that does not produce seeds, gymnosperm,* and *angiosperm.* Have students match the cards with the pictures.	Have students write a paragraph explaining whether they think ferns are more like nonvascular plants or more like gymnosperms. *(Answers will vary, but students should offer clear reasons for their opinions.)*

Name _____

Date _____

Making Connections

Draw lines between the terms that go together. One set has been done for you as an example. As you can see, some terms can be matched with more than one term.

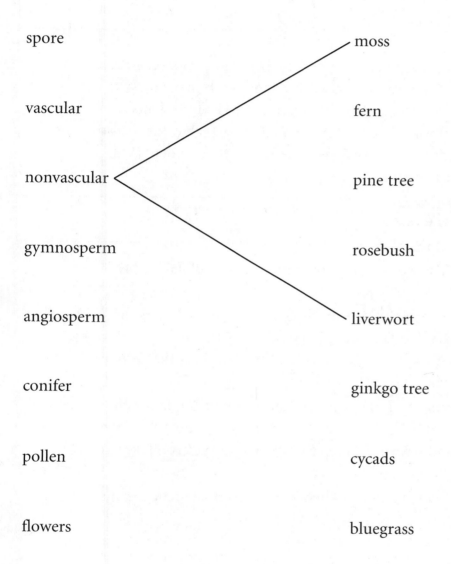

spore	moss
vascular	fern
nonvascular	pine tree
gymnosperm	rosebush
angiosperm	liverwort
conifer	ginkgo tree
pollen	cycads
flowers	bluegrass

School-Home Connection: Have students take this page home to share with family members. They can use this page to tell what they have learned about kinds of plants.

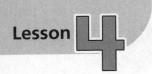
① Build Background

Access Prior Knowledge

When to Use	Proficiency Levels
Before introducing the lesson 15 minutes	✔ Beginning ✔ Intermediate Advanced

Materials: drawing materials, flowers, hand lenses

Ask each student to draw a flower, including details. Then, distribute the real flowers to partners or groups. Have students compare them with their drawings. What parts does the real flower have that they omitted? Have students use the hand lens to examine the flower. Ask them to name the parts they know and explain their function. Note any misconceptions and explain that students will learn more about flowers in this lesson.

Preteach Lesson Vocabulary

> **pollination, fruit**

List the vocabulary words on the board.

Ask students to clap the number of syllables in *fruit* (1) and *pollination* (4). Then:

- Add the word *pollen* to the board. Have students underline the letters that *pollen* and *pollination* share. Explain that pollen contains the male sex cells of plants. Pollination occurs when pollen reaches the plant part that contains female sex cells.

- Point to the word *pollination* and underline the suffix, *-tion*. Explain that this suffix means "the process of." *Pollination* is "the process of pollinating." Write *education* on the board and have a volunteer underline the suffix. Have students define this word. *(the process of educating)*

- Have students list fruits they like to eat. Then, explain that all angiosperms make fruit, but not all of these fruits are eaten by people.

Build Fluency

Have students list as many fruits as they can, such as apples, bananas, pineapples, oranges, and pears. Invite volunteers to use the fruits to complete this sentence:

I like to eat _____.

© Harcourt

② Scaffold the Content

Preview the Lesson

Invite students to answer the title question on page 128. Help them recall a seed's role in the reproduction. *(A seed contains a tiny plant that is produced when pollen joins with an egg cell. The seed can grow into a plant.)* Then:

- Direct students to page 134. Tell them seeds are either monocots or dicots. Write the terms on the board, underlining the prefixes. Discuss their meanings. Explain that monocots have one seed leaf, while dicots have two.

- Review the captions on page 135. Help students realize that fruits contain the seeds of angiosperms. Fruits protect seeds and provide their nutrients.

Investigate, p. 129

Before students begin the Investigate:

- Have volunteers demonstrate or explain the Procedure in their own words.

- Be sure students understand that *structure* means "part of something."

- After students complete the Investigate, have them compare their drawings with those they made in the *Access Prior Knowledge* activity. How are the drawings different? *(Their first drawings are likely less detailed than their second ones.)*

- Have students compare their Investigate drawings to the photo on page 131. Ask them to use the illustration to label as many parts of their drawings as they can.

Modify Instruction—Multilevel Strategies

Comprehensible Input Expose students to as many different types of flowers as possible, through samples or pictures, so they can begin to recognize the variations in the shapes of the parts.

Beginning Have students turn to p. 131. Ask them to point to the part of the flower that makes pollen. *(anthers)* Where are the egg cells? *(in the ovary)* Where does pollen enter to reach the ovary? *(stigma)* Which part becomes a fruit? *(ovary)*

Intermediate Have pairs make a flipbook to show an animated version of how a plant becomes pollinated and how its fruit develops. Encourage students to use words and sentences to share their flipbooks with the class.

Advanced Have students write a paragraph describing how a certain plant in a meadow becomes pollinated.

For All Students Have students work together to make posters showing the parts of a flower and different kinds of fruits and their seeds. Ask them to label each part.

Extend

Have the students complete the Show What You Know activity on page 51 to demonstrate their understanding of angiosperm reproduction.

③ Apply and Assess

Presentations on Angiosperms

When to Use With Reading Review p. 137 ⏱ 30 minutes	Proficiency Levels ✔ Beginning ✔ Intermediate ✔ Advanced

Materials: seed catalogs, reference books or access to the Internet, drawing materials

Have small groups look through seed catalogs to find an angiosperm that interests them.

- Ask each group to research that plant's life cycle and plan how to share what they learn in a two-minute presentation. The presentations should explain how the plant reproduces, how it is pollinated, and what kind of fruit it produces.
- Encourage students to create a large drawing of their plant to use during the presentation.
- Allow time for groups to make their presentations to the class.

Informal Assessment

Beginning	Intermediate	Advanced
Have students draw a flower and color the part that makes pollen yellow and the part that contains eggs green. *(The anthers should be yellow and the ovary should be green.)*	Give students a line drawing of a flower. Have them label the anther, pistil, stigma, and ovary. Next to each label, students should write words and phrases that tell the function of that part.	Have students write a short paragraph describing how angiosperms reproduce. *(The anthers produce pollen. Wind carries the pollen to the stigma of other plants. The pollen travels down to the ovary and pollinates the eggs. The ovary develops into a fruit with seeds inside. The seeds germinate and grow into new plants.)*

Putting Steps in Order

The steps below tell how an angiosperm produces fruit. However, the steps are out of order. Put them in the correct order. Write *1* next to the first step, *2* next to the second step, and so on.

_____ The fertilized egg cell develops into a fruit with seeds.

_____ The fruit drops from the plant.

_____ Pollen reaches the ovary.

_____ Pollen enters the stigma.

_____ The seeds in the fruit sprout.

_____ The anthers make pollen.

_____ Pollen joins with an egg cell.

School-Home Connection: Have students take this page home to share with family members. They can use this page to tell what they have learned about angiosperm reproduction.

4 Ecosystems

Develop Scientific Concepts and Vocabulary

In this chapter, students will learn about ecosystems, how energy flows through ecosystems, and how organisms interact within and between ecosystems. Students will also learn about large groups of similar ecosystems known as biomes.

Preview Scientific Principles

Walk through the chapter with students, pausing to read aloud or to have volunteers read aloud the four questions that are lesson titles. Encourage students to briefly discuss each question and to tell what they already know that might help them answer the questions.

When to Use With Chapter Opener	Proficiency Levels
⏱ 25 minutes	✔ Beginning ✔ Intermediate ✔ Advanced

Lesson 1: What Are Ecosystems?

- Write the term *ecosystem* on the board. Underline *eco-* and explain the prefix is derived from the Greek word for "house." Other words include *ecology* and *ecosphere*. Tell students that all of these words have to do with places where organisms, or living things, live. The prefix *eco-* refers to places where organisms are housed.

- Circle *-system*. Have students look up the word *system* in the dictionary. Ask students to give examples of some systems they are familiar with (e.g.; a stereo system, an alarm system, a computer system, the cardiovascular system, and so on). Then tell students that an ecosystem is a group of related organisms and the places where those organisms live.

Lesson 2: How Do Organisms Get Energy?

- Make sure students recall the meaning of the word *organism*. Show students various photographs with at least one kind of organism in them. Have students point to all of the organisms they see. Ask students to try to name the organisms as well.

- Have students stand up. Ask the students to demonstrate for you that they have energy. Explain that energy comes in many forms. Movement is a form of mechanical energy, light is a form of electromagnetic energy, and wood contains chemical energy that is released when it is burned.

- Ask students where they get their energy from *(food)*. Then ask students where the energy in their food comes from. Help students understand that the energy in the food they eat comes from the sun.

Lesson 3: How Do Organisms Interact?

- Write the word *interact* on the board. Underline the prefix *inter-* and tell students that it means "between." Therefore, *interact* in the lesson title means "the actions taking place between" organisms.

Lesson 4: What Are Biomes?

- Write the word *biome* on the board. Underline the prefix *bio-* and tell students that it means "life." Have students use a dictionary to find other words with this prefix.

Practice

- Have students choose a particular region of the world that they are interested in. Students should research the types of plants and animals that live there, as well as the physical features found in the area such as landforms and bodies of water.
- Have students make dioramas that show a natural scene from their chosen region. Explain that the dioramas are depicting different ecosystems.

Apply

Tell students that biomes are large groups of similar ecosystems. Write on the board the names of the biomes in the chart below. If possible, also have pictures of each of the biomes for students to look at. Have students describe what they think the biome may be like and list some of the plants and animals living in each biome.

Major Biomes of the World

Biome	Description
Desert	dry with only a few plants and animals; snakes, scorpions, cacti
Grassland	warm area with few to no trees; gophers, buffalo, grass
Tropical Rain Forest	warm, wet area with many different kinds of organisms; monkeys, frogs, jaguars
Tundra	cold area with frozen ground; polar bears, caribou, small plants

What Are Ecosystems?

① Build Background

Access Prior Knowledge

When to Use	Proficiency Levels
Before introducing the lesson	✔ Beginning
🕐 15 minutes	✔ Intermediate
	✔ Advanced

Materials: drawing paper, pencils

Have students draw pictures of what the natural environment looks like in the countries they were born in. Have intermediate and advanced students show their drawings to the class and describe the natural environment they drew. Then have students discuss how the environments in their countries of origin differ from the environment they live in now.

Preteach Lesson Vocabulary

ecosystem, population, community, habitat, niche, diversity

List the vocabulary words on the board.

- Have students write the vocabulary words down in their notebooks in alphabetical order.

- Tell students that the word *habitat* has a very similar meaning to the prefix *eco-*. *Eco-* can mean "place where organisms are found." *Habitat* means "a place where an organism lives." Have students write a sentence using the words *ecosystem* and *habitat*.

- Write the word *niche* on the board. Pronounce the word slowly and have students repeat the word back to you. Remind students that the combination of the letters *ch* is usually pronounced with a hard sound like in the words *church*, *chain*, and *such*. However, in some English words that are derived from foreign languages such as French, the *ch* is pronounced as *sh*. Examples of these words include *chandelier*, *chaise*, and *machete*.

Build Fluency

Have students find a word that has the same last syllable as *ecosystem*. Then have students take turns saying the word they chose. Repeat this for the other four vocabulary words in the lesson. Example: *ecosystem, stem*; *population, gravitation*; *community, pretty*; and *diversity, university*.

② Scaffold the Content

Preview the Lesson

Write the following words on the board: *coral reef*, *desert*, and *forest*. Tell students to look at the pictures on pages 150–153 and use the words on the board to identify the type of ecosystem in each picture by using the pattern, "This is a _____ ecosystem."

Investigate, p. 149

Before the students begin the Investigate, ensure students understand weather terms.

- Show students a national weather map with illustrations such as a sun to show sunny weather and a rain cloud to show rainy weather. Point to different areas on the map and have students describe the weather there.

- Tell students that weather is the condition of the atmosphere in a certain place at a certain time. Have students call out adjectives that can describe the weather, such as windy, rainy, sunny, warm, and cold.

- Explain to students that climate is average weather conditions in an area over a long period of time.

Modify Instruction—Multilevel Strategies

Background/Experience Show students a large globe. Have students put map stickers on the globe indicating places they have visited. Then have students take turns describing the ecosystems that they saw while visiting each of those places.

Beginning Have students draw pictures of a population, a community, and an ecosystem that can be found in a place they have visited.

Intermediate Students should make a graphic organizer that shows the types of groupings of organisms in an ecosystem (individual, population, and community). Next to each grouping, students should give an example.

Advanced Have students write a postcard to a friend. The postcard should have a picture of a place that they have visited. The message on the postcard should describe organisms that belong to that community and some of the nonliving parts of the environment that affect that community.

For All Students Organize students into groups of four. Two of the students should find pictures of ecosystems with a great amount of diversity. The other two students should find pictures of ecosystems with little diversity. The groups should compare the two sets of pictures and describe the differences they see.

Extend

Have the students complete the **Show What You Know** activity on page 57 to demonstrate their understanding of environmental organization.

③ Apply and Assess

Biography of an Organism

When to Use	Proficiency Levels
With Reading Review p. 155 ⏱ 30 minutes	✔ Beginning ✔ Intermediate ✔ Advanced

Have students choose an organism that interests them. Students should research the organism's community, ecosystem, niche, and habitat. Instruct students to put together a presentation that includes all of this information. Students' presentations can be in the form of a poster, slideshow, speech, or diorama.

Informal Assessment

Beginning	Intermediate	Advanced
Ask students to draw a picture showing an example of the following terms: *community, ecosystem, population*. (*Answers will vary.*)	Show students a drawing of several organisms of the same species, a drawing of several different kinds of organisms, and a drawing of several different kinds of organisms along with their nonliving environment. Have students label each picture using terms from the following word bank: *community, ecosystem, population*. (*Answers will vary.*)	Have students write a short paragraph describing the difference between populations, communities, and ecosystems. (*Answers will vary.*)

Environmental Classification

Organisms can be grouped in many ways in an ecosystem. Place the following terms in the graphic organizer below, from the largest grouping on top to the smallest grouping on the bottom.

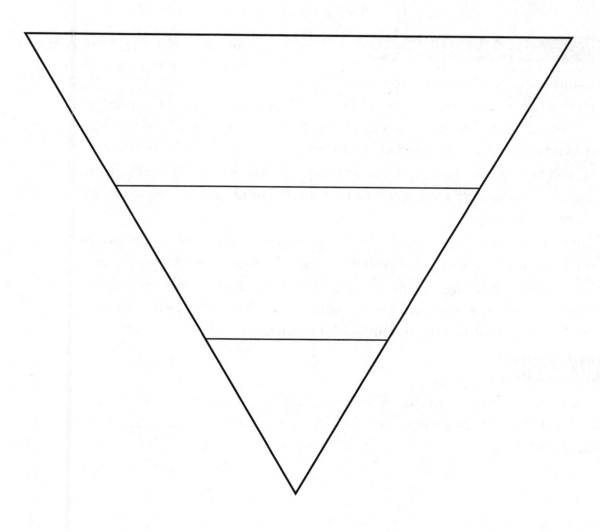

community   population   individual organism

School-Home Connection: Have students take this page home to share with family members. They can use this page to tell about how organisms are grouped in an ecosystem.

How Do Organisms Get Energy?

① Build Background

Access Prior Knowledge

When to Use	Proficiency Levels
Before introducing the lesson 15 minutes	✔ Beginning ✔ Intermediate ✔ Advanced

Show students a picture of a hamburger. Explain that all of the ingredients in a hamburger contain energy. Then ask the following questions, "Where does the beef in a hamburger come from? Where does the cow get energy from? Where does the energy in the grass come from? How does grass make energy from sunlight?"

Preteach Lesson Vocabulary

> producer, consumer, food chain, food web, energy pyramid

List the vocabulary words on the board.

- Have students examine the vocabulary words for the lesson. Ask students to identify the terms or parts of a term that they already know. For example, students may already know *food* and *energy*.

- Write the word *produce* on the board. Explain that *produce* is another word for *make*. Producers are organisms that "make" food using sunlight or inorganic chemicals.

- Write the word *consume* on the board. Explain that *consume* means "to use up." Consumers are organisms that "use up" the food made by producers.

- Tell students that three of the vocabulary terms include words that identify a particular shape. Show students a picture of a chain, web, and pyramid and have them match the picture with the correct word.

Build Fluency

Tell students that most producers are plants and most consumers are animals. Have students take turns completing the following sentence: A _____ is a producer, and a _____ is a consumer.

© Harcourt

② Scaffold the Content

Preview the Lesson

When to Use
With pp. 156–162

⏱ 20 minutes

Proficiency Levels
✔ Beginning
✔ Intermediate
✔ Advanced

Materials: paper, colored pencils

Have students think of their favorite breakfast food. Ask them, "What organism is used to make this food?" Breakfast cereal could be from wheat. Sausage could be from pigs. Have students draw a picture of the organism and a picture of themselves. Have them draw an arrow from the organism to themselves. Explain that they have just drawn a food chain.

Investigate, p. 157

Before the students begin the Investigate, review some terms.

- Write the word *diet* on the board. Ask if students have heard the word before, and if so, in what context. Most students will say that a person goes on a diet to lose weight.

- Explain to students that in science the word *diet* means the things eaten by an organism on a regular basis. Have students make a list of the foods that they eat regularly. Tell them that they have just described their diet.

- Make sure students know what kind of bird an owl is by showing them pictures of several different types of owls, including the picture on page 156. Each time you hold up a picture, slowly pronounce the word *owl*.

Modify Instruction—Multilevel Strategies

Background/Experience Have each student write the name of an animal on a piece of paper. Collect the papers. Read a name of an animal from one of the papers and have students use their previous knowledge of the animal to call out what foods that animal eats. List the foods on the board. After several foods have been listed, have the class classify the animal as a producer, herbivore, carnivore, both herbivore and carnivore, or scavenger.

Beginning Have students draw a diagram illustrating how energy flows from the sun to producers and then to consumers in an ecosystem. Students should use specific examples of producers and consumers that are already familiar to them.

Intermediate Have students complete the activity above. In addition, students should label their diagrams. Afterwards, ask students to verbally explain why there is less energy available in the ecosystem as you move up a food chain.

Advanced Have students draw a food web that they belong to. Then have students write a short paragraph explaining what might happen if all of the producers were removed from the food web.

For All Students Ask students, "Are humans producers? Are humans herbivores? Are humans carnivores? Are humans scavengers? Are humans decomposers?"

Extend

Have the students complete the **Show What You Know** activity on page 61 to demonstrate their understanding of how energy moves through an ecosystem.

③ Apply and Assess

Cooking Up Producers

When to Use	Proficiency Levels
With Reading Review p. 163	✔ Beginning
⏱ 15 minutes	✔ Intermediate
	✔ Advanced

- Instruct students to come up with a recipe for a healthy meal or snack that only uses products made from producers.
- Allow students to make their recipes at home and bring them to class to share.

Informal Assessment

Beginning	Intermediate	Advanced
Have students draw a food chain and label the producer and consumer. *(Answers will vary.)*	Ask students the following questions: Where does all the energy in most of Earth's ecosystems come from? *(the sun)* What is at the bottom of a food pyramid? *(producers)*	Have students write a sentence explaining the difference between a food chain and a food web. *(Possible answer: a food chain is a sequence of connected producers and consumers, and a food web is a group of interconnected food chains.)*

Name _____

Date _____

Complete the Food Chain

In the empty boxes, draw pictures of organisms that will correctly complete the food chains below.

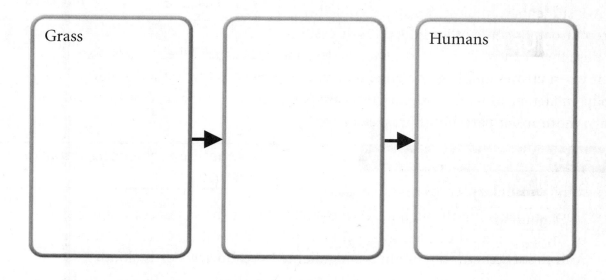

Grass → ☐ → Humans

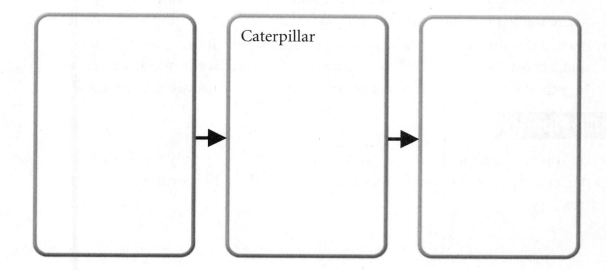

☐ → Caterpillar → ☐

School-Home Connection: Have students take this page home to share with family members. They can use this page to tell about food chains.

How Do Organisms Interact?

① Build Background

Access Prior Knowledge

When to Use	Proficiency Levels
Before introducing the lesson 20 minutes	✔ Beginning ✔ Intermediate ✔ Advanced

Ask students who have ever had a cold, flu, strep throat, or some other infectious disease to raise their hands. Then ask students to describe what caused their illness. Explain that when viruses and bacteria enter a person, they interact with that person's body. In fact, viruses and some bacteria are parasites. Tell students that they will learn more about parasites in this lesson.

Preteach Lesson Vocabulary

> **competition, symbiosis, parasite, host**

List the vocabulary words on the board.

- Have students flip through pages 166–168 to locate the sentences where each of the lesson vocabulary words is first introduced in the text. Have volunteers read the sentences containing the highlighted vocabulary words aloud.

- Write the word *symbiosis* on the board and underline the *y*. Ask students how the *y* is pronounced in this word. Have students list other words they know where the *y* is pronounced like an *i*.

- Break down the word *symbiosis* into its prefix, *sym-*, and its root, *bio*. Remind students that *bio* means "life." Tell students that the prefixes *sym-* and *syn-* mean "together" or "with." Explain that organisms living in symbiosis "live together."

Build Fluency

Have students use the dictionary to write a sentence using only words that contain the letter *y*. Then have each student stand up and read his or her sentence to the class.

© Harcourt

② Scaffold the Content

Preview the Lesson

Explain to students that they will learn about different ways organisms interact with each other in this lesson. Organize students into pairs. Have each pair of students pantomime likely interactions between the following organisms: butterfly and flower; lion and zebra; bird and tree; and dog and flea.

Investigate, p. 165

Before the students begin the Investigate, ensure students know about the organisms.

- Show students pictures of a hydra and a *Daphnia* before students start the lab. Hold up both pictures at the same time. Instruct students to point to the hydra. Repeat this for the *Daphnia*.

- Show students a picture of green algae. Ask students what color the algae are. Explain to students that a hydra's body is translucent, meaning you can see through it. Have students identify other objects that are translucent.

Modify Instruction—Multilevel Strategies

Comprehensible Input Help students to understand the differences between predator-prey relationships and parasite-host relationships. Explain to students that predators eat, and usually kill, their prey. Parasites feed off of, but usually don't kill, their hosts. Have students classify the following relationships as predator-and-prey or parasite-and-host:

- snake and field mouse
- tick and dog
- strep throat bacteria and human
- bird and worm

Beginning Have students draw examples of a competitive relationship, a symbiotic relationship, and a predator-prey relationship.

Intermediate Organize students into groups of five or six. Instruct students to write a five minute play that illustrates a competitive relationship, a symbiotic relationship, or a predator-prey relationship. Students should perform their plays for the rest of the class. The class should try to identify what type of relationship is being represented in the play.

Advanced Have students research an example of mutualism that is not discussed in the text. Students should give a brief oral report about the example they chose and explain how both organisms benefit from the relationship.

For All Students Lead students in a discussion about why it is not beneficial for a parasite to kill its host. Help students to understand that if the host dies, the parasite will lose its food source.

Extend

Have the students complete the **Show What You Know** activity on page 65 to demonstrate their understanding of interactions between animals.

③ Apply and Assess

Relationship Web

When to Use	Proficiency Levels
With Reading Review p. 171	✔ Beginning
	✔ Intermediate
⏱ 20 minutes	✔ Advanced

Materials: paper, colored pencils

Explain to students that the relationships between animals often determine how energy flows through an ecosystem. Have students draw several animals that live in an ecosystem in your area. Students should draw arrows between organisms that interact with one another and write what kind of relationship the organisms share.

Informal Assessment

Beginning	Intermediate	Advanced
Show students a picture of a predator such as a lion hunting down its prey. Ask students if the picture shows a parasite-host relationship. *(no)*	Have students give examples of the following types of relationships: a competitive relationship, a symbiotic relationship, or a predator-prey relationship. *(Answers will vary.)*	Have students list three types of symbiotic relationships. Then tell students that some species of ants protect a type of insect called an aphid from predators. In return, the aphid secretes a sugary substance that the ants use for food. Ask students to identify what type of relationship exists between the ants and aphids. *(parasitism, mutualism, and commensalism; mutualism)*

Which Organism Benefits?

Look at the chart below that lists different kinds of relationships between animals and examples of each relationship. Put a check mark (✔) in the box of each organism that benefits from the relationship.

Relationship	Examples	
Predation	lynx	snowshoe hare
Parasitism	heartworm	dog
Mutualism	bee	flower
Commensalism	barnacle	mussel

© Harcourt

School-Home Connection: Have students take this page home to share with family members. They can use this page to tell about relationships between animals.

What Are Biomes?

① Build Background

Access Prior Knowledge

When to Use	Proficiency Levels
Before introducing the lesson 20 minutes	✔ Beginning ✔ Intermediate ✔ Advanced

- Write the word *forest* on the board. Have students describe what a forest is. Then have students describe different forests that they have seen.

- Repeat this activity with the words *grassland* and *desert*. Encourage students to use drawings or descriptive adjectives to describe these different types of ecosystems.

Preteach Lesson Vocabulary

biome

Write the vocabulary word on the board.

- Pronounce the word *biome* and have students repeat the word back to you. Then ask students how many syllables are in the word *biome*.

- Have students make a two-columned chart in their notebooks with the title, "Different Kinds of Biomes." Have students turn to the map on pp. 174–175. Students can use the map key to list the different kinds of biomes in the first column of their chart. Instruct students as they read to fill in the second column in their chart with specific details about each of the listed biomes.

- Remind students that the root of the word *biome* is *bio*, which means "life." Have students use a dictionary to list other words with the root *bio*. Answers may include *biology*, *bionic*, and *biography*.

Build Fluency

Have students use the names of biomes shown on the map key on p. 175 to complete the following sentence: A _____ is a type of biome. Students can take turns completing the sentence until all of the biomes have been named.

② Scaffold the Content

Preview the Lesson

- Have students turn to p. 174–175 and examine the world biome map. Ask students to place their finger on the area where they live. Have students use the map key to identify the name of the type of biome that is found in their community.

- Read students a description of the biome found in your area. Then have students compare the description with the ecosystems found around their community. Does the description match all of your area or are there some differences between the description and your local ecosystems? If so, what are they?

- Use this discussion to help students understand that a biome is a generalization of a large group of similar ecosystems.

Investigate, p. 173

Before the students begin the Investigate, ensure students understand *latitude* and *longitude*.

- Show students a globe and indicate where the lines of latitude and longitude are found.

- Have students make a drawing of Earth. Then have students draw three lines of latitude across the drawing. Make sure the lines are running horizontally.

- Have students draw a second picture of Earth. Have students draw three lines of longitude across the drawing. Make sure the lines are running vertically.

- Give students a globe and then call out different latitude, longitude coordinates. Instruct students to find the location of those coordinates on the globe.

Modify Instruction—Multilevel Strategies

Comprehensible Input Organize students into pairs. Assign at least one pair to read pp. 176–177 of the text together. Assign another pair to read pp. 178–179 of the text together. And assign a third pair to read p. 180 of the text together. After students have read their assigned pages, have each pair give a short presentation to the other pairs of students summarizing the information they read. The presentations can be oral or in the form of drawings, diagrams, or graphic organizers.

Beginning Instruct students to draw pictures of three different biomes. Students should exchange the pictures with a partner. The partner should try to guess which biome is represented in each picture.

Intermediate Have students research a type of biome. Students should use their research to make a poster that illustrates three organisms that live in that biome. The posters should give information about the adaptations of the organisms that make them suited to live in that particular environment.

Advanced Have students choose their favorite biome and write a short paper explaining why they like the biome and why they think it would be a nice area to live in.

For All Students Show students several different pictures of grasslands, forests, tundra, and deserts. Hold up the picture and ask students to call out what type of biome they think the picture is of.

Extend

Have the students complete the **Show What You Know** activity on page 69 to demonstrate their understanding of biomes.

③ Apply and Assess

Build a Biome

When to Use With Reading Review p. 181 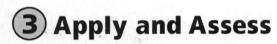 15 minutes	Proficiency Levels ✔ Beginning ✔ Intermediate ✔ Advanced

Materials: various materials to build dioramas

Have students choose a type of biome and then build a diorama that illustrates the major characteristics of that biome. Their dioramas should show different organisms that live in the biome, and each organism should be labeled. Students should also include note cards with their dioramas that identify the biomes they chose to model and briefly describe the climate of that biome.

Informal Assessment

Beginning	Intermediate	Advanced
Show students a picture of a grassland. Ask: Is this a picture of a grassland biome? *(yes)*	Ask students which type of biome is the driest type of biome. *(a desert)*	Have students list at least four types of biomes. *(Possible answers: forest biome, desert biome, tundra biome, and grassland biome.)*

Draw a Biome

Each box below has a name of a biome in it. Draw a picture of the named biome inside the box.

Grassland Biome	Hot Desert Biome
Forest Biome	**Tundra Biome**

 School-Home Connection: Have students take this page home to share with family members. They can use this page to tell about biomes.

5 Resources in Ecosystems

Develop Scientific Concepts and Vocabulary

In this chapter, students will learn about different kinds of natural resources. Students will also learn how some natural resources cycle through ecosystems and how human activities can affect an ecosystem.

Preview Scientific Principles

Walk through the chapter with students, pausing to read aloud or to have volunteers read aloud the three questions that are lesson titles. Encourage students to briefly discuss each question and to tell what they already know that might help them answer the questions.

When to Use With Chapter Opener	Proficiency Levels
⏱ 20 minutes	✔ Beginning ✔ Intermediate ✔ Advanced

Lesson 1: What Are Natural Resources?

- Ask students to make a drawing of something that is "natural." Then explain to students that when scientists say something is natural, they mean that it can be found occurring in nature. In other words, something that is natural is not man-made.

- Hold up a piece of paper and ask students what the paper is made of. *(wood)* Repeat this task with several other objects such as a paperclip *(metal)*, a glass *(sand)*, or plastic *(petroleum)*. Explain to students that wood, metal, sand, and petroleum are all natural resources. Then have students try to think of a product that is *not* made from natural resources. *(All products are made from natural resources.)*

Lesson 2: How Do Natural Cycles Affect Ecosystems?

- Show students a picture of a bicycle. Explain to students that it is called a bicycle because it has two *(bi-)* wheels *(cycle)*. The wheels move round and round. Then tell students that a cycle in nature is something that occurs again and again.

- Ask students to suggest some natural cycles they already know about. Students may list familiar cycles such as the seasons of the year and the cycle between day and night.

Lesson 3: How Do Humans Affect Ecosystems?

- Write the words *affect* and *effect* on the board. Tell students that *affect* is a verb and *effect* is a noun. Have students write a sentence using the word *affect*. Then have students write a sentence using the word *effect*. Check to make sure students used the words correctly.

Practice

Have each students choose products, such as toothpaste, paper plates, or aluminum foil, that they use every day. Encourage students to suggest what natural resources are used to make their products. Students can use their combined findings to make a list of natural resources consumed by the class on a daily basis.

Apply

Copy the chart below on the board. Have students work together to make a list of the resources used to make each of the listed products.

Uses of Natural Resources

Product	Materials Needed to Make It
book	wood, ink dyes from plants
soda can	aluminum
plastic wrap	petroleum
hamburger	various plants, cows
t-shirt	cotton plant

What Are Natural Resources?

① Build Background

Access Prior Knowledge

When to Use	Proficiency Levels
Before introducing the lesson 15 minutes	✔ Beginning ✔ Intermediate ✔ Advanced

Ask students what resources people use today that may not be available in the future. Students may suggest some nonrenewable resources such as petroleum or fossil fuels. Then have students suggest things that people could do to make these resources last longer.

Preteach Lesson Vocabulary

> **natural resource, conservation, recycle, reuse**

List the vocabulary words on the board.

Read the list of vocabulary words aloud to students and have students repeat them. Then:

- Write the words *resource*, *recycle*, and *reuse* on the board. Underline the prefix *re-* in each word. Explain to students that the prefix *re-* means "again." Ask students to use this knowledge to describe the meaning of the word *reuse. (to use again)*

- Explain to students that when a material is *re*cycled, it is sent through the manufacturing cycle again to be made into a new product.

- Tell students that the word *resource* comes from the Latin word *resurgere*, which means "to rise again." A resource is often a material, such as trees, that can be used and then will naturally be replenished. In other words, the resource will "rise again."

Build Fluency

Write the following list of words on the board: *build*, *create*, *do*, *join*, *new*, *read*, *think*, and *use*. Have students add the prefix *re-* to each word and use the word in a sentence.

② Scaffold the Content

Preview the Lesson

When to Use
With pp. 190–198

30 minutes

Proficiency Levels
✔ Beginning
✔ Intermediate
✔ Advanced

- Have students read the title on page 192. Then have them look at the graph and pictures on pages 192–193 and identify several resources used by people.
- Have students read the title on page 194. Tell students to look at the pictures on pages 194–195. Have students suggest several natural resources.
- Have students read the title on page 196. Ask students to look at the subtitles on pages 196–197 and suggest several ways that humans manage resources.

Investigate, p. 191

Have a volunteer read the title of the Investigate aloud. Ask:

- "What do you think you will be doing in this Investigate?" *(Possible answer: using old paper to make new paper)*
- "Do you think making new paper from old paper could be considered a form of recycling?" *(Lead students to understand that they will be recycling the newspaper in this activity.)*
- "What are some ways you could reuse newspaper without having to first make it into new paper?" *(Possible answer: Use the paper for gift wrap.)*

Modify Instruction—Multilevel Strategies

Comprehensible Input Have students work together as a class to choose a resource to monitor. For example, students could choose soda cans. Students should keep a list of how many soda cans (or any other resource) they use up over the course of a week. Then students can compare and compile their data. Students should then suggest some ways that they can reduce their use of their chosen resources.

Beginning Have students use old magazines to make collages of many different types of natural resources. Students should include at least two renewable resources and two nonrenewable resources.

Intermediate Have students research some of the resources found in their native countries. Students should make posters listing the resources, showing what sort of products are made from the resources, and showing some ways the resources can be conserved.

Advanced Have students decide what they think the most important natural resource is. Students should write several paragraphs naming the resource, explaining why they think it is so important, and describing ways in which the resource can be conserved.

© Harcourt

For All Students Have students take turns listing a resource they used today and how it was used. For example, a student could say, "I used water to brush my teeth."

Extend

Have the students complete the **Show What You Know** activity on page 75 to demonstrate their understanding of natural resources.

③ Apply and Assess

Conserve a Resource

When to Use With Reading Review p. 199 ⏱ 15 minutes	Proficiency Levels ✔ Beginning ✔ Intermediate ✔ Advanced

- Organize students into groups of three or four. Tell students to suppose that the whole class would only have 100 sheets of paper per year with which to do their schoolwork on. Explain that they must think of ways to *conserve* the paper.

- Have the groups brainstorm ideas about how they could divide the resource (paper) fairly among the students and steps students could take to ensure that the paper would last them the whole school year.

- After the groups finish their brainstorming session, have them share their ideas with the class.

Informal Assessment

Beginning	Intermediate	Advanced
Instruct each student to draw a picture of a natural resource and then to draw a second picture of how people use that resource. *(Drawings will vary.)*	Show students a handful of soil. Ask: Is this a natural resource? *(yes)* What is this resource called? *(soil)* How do people use soil? *(to grow crops)*	Instruct each student to write a short paragraph describing lifestyle changes he or she can make to conserve resources. *(Paragraphs will vary.)*

Drawing Natural Resources

In each box below there is a sentence describing a natural resource. Draw a picture of a resource that matches the description.

This is a **renewable resource**.	This is a **nonrenewable resource**.
This resource can be **recycled**.	This resource can be **reused**.

School-Home Connection: Have children take this page home to share with family members. They can use this page to tell about natural resources.

How Do Natural Cycles Affect Ecosystems?

① Build Background

Access Prior Knowledge

When to Use	Proficiency Levels
Before introducing the lesson 15 minutes	✔ Beginning ✔ Intermediate ✔ Advanced

Show students a picture of a forest. Tell them to suppose that the forest burned down. Ask them what would most likely happen to the ecosystem during the next 200 years. Many students may understand that it is likely a forest community will establish itself again in the area after a certain amount of time. Explain to students that ecosystems often develop in cycles that include death and rebirth.

Preteach Lesson Vocabulary

> **succession, carbon cycle, nitrogen cycle**

List the vocabulary words on the board.

Have volunteers take turns reading the definitions of each vocabulary word in the glossary. Then:

- Write the word *succession* on the board. Explain that it comes from the Latin word *succedere*, which means "to go after." Something that succeeds another thing goes after it. Ask students what succeeds winter. *(spring)* What succeeds day? *(night)* Explain the difference between this meaning (*sucesión* in Spanish) and "succeeding" at a task (*tener éxito* in Spanish). Tell students that *succeed* is used for both meanings in English, but may be different in other languages.

- Write the word *cycle* on the board. Have students list terms that they already know that contain the word *cycle. (Possible answers: bicycle, motorcycle, recycle, and water cycle)* Point out that all of the words refer to something that "goes around."

Build Fluency

Have students turn to SCIENCE UP CLOSE: The Carbon Cycle on pp. 204–205. Begin by reading a caption of one step in the cycle. After you read the step, have students ask you, "What succeeds that?" Respond by reading the next step in the cycle. Students should continue repeating the question until you have read all the steps in the cycle.

© Harcourt

② Scaffold the Content

Preview the Lesson

When to Use
With pp. 200–208

⏱ 15 minutes

Proficiency Levels
✔ Beginning
✔ Intermediate
✔ Advanced

Direct students to point to each heading in the section as you read it aloud.

- Have students study the carbon cycle diagram on pages 204–205 and the nitrogen cycle diagram on pages 206–207.
- Ask: What do the two diagrams have in common? *(The steps show how something cycles through an ecosystem.)* How are the diagrams different? *(One describes how carbon cycles through an ecosystem and the other describes how nitrogen cycles.)*

Investigate, p. 201

Show students a stem of elodea. Pronounce the word *elodea* slowly and write the word on the board. Then:

- Show students a picture of a plant. Have students point to the plant's stem. Then have students repeat the word *stem* after you.
- Have students use an object to pantomime different ways they can observe something (sight, smell, touch, hearing, and taste). Remind students that smell and taste are rarely, if ever, used during a science experiment for safety reasons.
- After the activity, work with students to make inferences and predictions.

Modify Instruction—Multilevel Strategies

Comprehensible Input Lead students in a discussion about why it is important to life on Earth that chemicals such as carbon and nitrogen cycle through ecosystems. Students should demonstrate an understanding that organisms need a constant flow of carbon and nitrogen to carry out their life processes.

Beginning Have students draw a diagram of the carbon cycle and the nitrogen cycle.

Intermediate Have students complete the Beginning activity. In addition, ask students to label each step in both cycles.

Advanced Have students write short stories about a carbon or nitrogen atom that gets carried through an ecosystem during its natural cycle. Stories should include information about how the atom moves from one place to the next in the cycle.

For All Students Have students make flipbooks that illustrate an ecosystem going through different stages of ecological succession.

Have the students complete the **Show What You Know** activity on page 79 to demonstrate their understanding of natural cycles.

③ Apply and Assess

Changing a Cycle

When to Use With Reading Review p. 209	Proficiency Levels
🕐 20 minutes	✔ Beginning ✔ Intermediate ✔ Advanced

Materials: jar with a lid, 2 small plants

Have students use what they have learned about the carbon cycle to hypothesize what would happen to a plant that is placed in a sealed jar.

- After students write their hypotheses, organize them into groups and have them carry out experiments to test their hypotheses. (Students should place a plant in a sealed jar, and place another identical plant outside of the jar as a control group.) Note: If students are going to give water to the plants, they should devise a way to water the plant in the jar without letting air in.

- Ask the groups to compare their results and explain their findings. *(The plant in the sealed jar will become stressed after a short period of time.)*

Informal Assessment

Beginning	Intermediate	Advanced
Write the steps of the nitrogen cycle on index cards. Have students arrange the cards into a correct nitrogen cycle. *(Check students diagrams by comparing them to the illustration on pages 206–207.)*	Ask students: What gas is released into the atmosphere when fossil fuels are burned? *(carbon dioxide)* What gas is released into the atmosphere when plants perform photosynthesis? *(oxygen)* What gas is released into the atmosphere when animals respire? *(carbon dioxide)*	Have students draw examples of ecological succession. Each illustrated step should be accompanied by a caption. *(Illustrations and captions will vary.)*

Describing Natural Cycles

Choose a natural cycle and write or draw five successive steps of the cycle in the boxes below.

1.

2.

5.

3.

4.

School-Home Connection: Have children take this page home to share with family members. They can use this page to tell about natural cycles.

How Do Humans Affect Ecosystems?

① Build Background

Access Prior Knowledge

When to Use	Proficiency Levels
Before introducing the lesson 15 minutes	✔ Beginning ✔ Intermediate Advanced

Ask students how they are affecting the ecosystem in the classroom right now. (*They are breathing.*) Invite volunteers to suggest other ways in which humans affect ecosystems. After the discussion, you may want to take students on a walk through the school's neighborhood and point out different ways that human activity has affected the ecosystem in your area.

Preteach Lesson Vocabulary

Materials: a match

> **extinction, endangered species, wetland**

List the vocabulary words on the board.

Say each of the vocabulary words one syllable at a time. Then repeat the word at a normal speed. Have students repeat the words back to you slowly. Then:

- Light a match, then blow it out. Tell students that when you blew the match out, you *extinguished* it. *Extinguish* means "to put out, to put an end to, or to destroy," and is related to the Spanish word *extinguir*. Write the word *extinction* on the board (*extinción* in Spanish) and explain that a species that becomes *extinct* is extinguished, or no longer in existence.

- Write the term *endangered* on the board, and underline *danger*. Ask students to describe what the word *danger* means. (*something that is not safe*) Explain that a species that is endangered is in danger of extinction.

Build Fluency

Write the following list of animals on the board: *bighorn sheep, black rhinoceros, blue whale, elephant, gorilla, gray wolf, grizzly bear, leopard, musk deer, spider monkey, tiger,* and *whooping crane*. Explain that all of the listed animals are endangered species. Have students use the list to complete the following sentence until they have used all of the animals in the list: "The _____ is an endangered species."

② Scaffold the Content

When to Use With pp. 210–216	Proficiency Levels
30 minutes	✔ Beginning ✔ Intermediate ✔ Advanced

Preview the Lesson

- Have students locate the section title on page 212. Invite a volunteer to read it aloud. Then have students look at the pictures on pages 212–213 and suggest ways in which humans affect their environment.

- Have students locate the section title on page 214. Invite a volunteer to read it aloud. Then have students study the pictures on pages 213–215. Ask students what kinds of ecosystems are in danger (*ecosystems involving water*). Have students suggest some ways in which humans affect water ecosystems.

Investigate, p. 211

Have students read through the list of materials and the procedure. Answer any questions students might have.

- Ask students how water might become polluted. If necessary, show students pictures of polluted areas. For example, you could show an oil spill, a factory dumping its waste into a lake or stream, or erosion from a farm field. Repeat the word *pollution* every time you indicate a pollutant.

- Tell students that the word *pollute* means "to make dirty" or "to make unfit for living things."

- After the activity, help students work through the steps of designing an experiment.

Modify Instruction—Multilevel Strategies

Background/Experience Ask students if they have ever seen a place that was polluted. Have them draw pictures of what the places looked like or have them orally describe the places. Students should describe how the pollution made the area look and how they felt seeing it.

Beginning Have students draw pictures of animals they know are extinct. Students should do research to find out when and why the animal became extinct. Have students label their pictures with this information.

Intermediate Have students make dioramas of a wetland. (If possible, the students should use wetlands that they have visited.) Students should include a story cards with their dioramas that explain why wetlands are important.

Advanced Have students research endangered species that they have seen at a zoo or in the wild. Students should make fact sheets about the organisms. The fact sheets should include information about where the organisms live, why they are endangered, and what people can do to help the organisms.

For All Students Have students draw maps or pictures showing how communities they have lived in have changed over a period of time due to human activities.

Extend

Have the students complete the **Show What You Know** activity on page 83 to demonstrate their understanding of how humans affect ecosystems.

③ Apply and Assess

Species Count

When to Use	Proficiency Levels
With Reading Review p. 217 🕐 20 minutes	✔ Beginning ✔ Intermediate ✔ Advanced

- Take students to the schoolyard or another landscaped area. Have students stand in one place and count the different types of organisms they see. Then take students to a natural area. Have them repeat the exercise.
- Most likely, students will be able to count more organisms (both plants and animals) in the natural area than in the landscaped area.
- Lead students in a discussion about their results and what this indicates about human activity. Help students realize that human activities often result in a decrease in the variety of species in an area. This can lead to species becoming endangered or even extinct.

Informal Assessment

Beginning	Intermediate	Advanced
Show students a picture of a dodo. Explain that there are no more dodos alive today. Ask: Is the dodo an endangered species? *(no)* Is the dodo extinct? *(yes)* Then show a picture of a tiger. Explain that tigers have been hunted for their fur. There are only a few tigers left in the world today. Ask: Is the tiger an endangered species? *(yes)* Is the tiger extinct? *(no)*	Show students a picture of the Everglades. Ask: What type of land is this? *(a wetland)* Show students a picture of a prairie. Ask: What type of land is this? *(a grassland)*	Have students write short paragraphs describing three ways in which humans affect their environment. *(Answers will vary.)*

Human Activities and Ecosystems

Use the terms in the word bank below to complete the sentences. Terms may be used only once, and not all terms are used.

acid precipitation	**exotic**	**fossil fuel**	**grassland**
endangered species	**laws**	**pollution**	**wetlands**

1. People often drain _____ so that they can build homes and businesses there.

2. When people burn fossil fuels, _____ is released into the air.

3. Hunting an animal too much can cause it to become a(n)

   _____.

4. In the United States, many _____ have been passed to protect ecosystems.

5. People have turned large areas of _____ into farmland.

6. Air pollution can lead to _____, which can kill the fish in lakes.

School-Home Connection: Have children take this page home to share with family members. They can use this page to tell about how humans affect ecosystems.

Changes to Earth's Surface

Develop Scientific Concepts and Vocabulary

In this chapter, students will learn about the different ways that Earth's surface can change, including changes caused by weathering, erosion, and deposition and by the movement of Earth's plates. They will also learn about the causes of earthquakes and volcanoes.

Preview Scientific Principles

Walk through the chapter with students, pausing to read aloud or to have volunteers read aloud the three questions that are lesson titles. Encourage students to briefly discuss each question and to tell what they already know that might help them answer the questions.

When to Use With Chapter Opener	Proficiency Levels
🕐 20 minutes	✔ Beginning ✔ Intermediate ✔ Advanced

Lesson 1: How Does Earth's Surface Change?

- Tell students that the word *surface* means "the outer or topmost part of an object." Have students point to the surface of their desks. Make sure students understand that an object's surface is on the outside of the object.

- Show students a globe and then ask them what covers most of Earth's surface. *(water)*

Lesson 2: What Are Plates and How Do They Move?

- Display pictures of different kinds of plates, such as a dinner plate, a printing plate, a plate of sheet metal, a glass plate, and a baseball home plate to the class. Explain to students that all of the objects are plates. Ask students to identify the characteristics that all of the plates have in common. *(They are all relatively smooth, flat, thin, and rigid.)*

- Explain to students that a plate is an object that is relatively smooth, flat, thin, and rigid. Then tell students that Earth's surface is made up of many large plates. Ask students what they think Earth's plates are made of. *(rocks)*

© Harcourt

Lesson 3: What Causes Earthquakes and Volcanoes?

- Write the word *earthquake* on the board and underline *quake*. Explain to students that the verb *quake* means "to shake." Have students pantomime the meaning of *quake*. Then ask students to describe what they think happens during an earthquake.

- Have students who have seen an earthquake or volcanic eruption in person or on television describe what they saw or draw a picture of what they saw.

Practice

Write "Earth's Surface" on the board. Have students describe or draw a picture of different formations they have seen, such as mountains, valleys, islands, plateaus or mesas, deserts, oceans, lakes, or rivers. Ask volunteers to suggest how some of these features may have formed or may have changed over time. Encourage students to discuss, draw, or pantomime what they already know about these processes.

Apply

Write the sentences on the chart below on the board. Provide students with modeling clay. Have students use the clay to make a model of the underlined word. Then have students choose an adjective to complete each sentence. (If students are unfamiliar with the underlined words, show them photos of the described landform and have them look up the landform in the dictionary.) *(Adjectives will vary.)*

Describing Surface Features

A <u>mountain</u> is _____.
A <u>plateau</u> is _____.
A <u>hill</u> is _____.
A <u>volcano</u> is _____.
A <u>plain</u> is _____.
A <u>cliff</u> is _____.

How Does Earth's Surface Change?

① Build Background

When to Use	Proficiency Levels
Before introducing the lesson 25 minutes	✔ Beginning ✔ Intermediate ✔ Advanced

Access Prior Knowledge

Materials: A rock with sharp edges, a rock with smooth edges

Show students a rock that has sharp, rough edges. Tell students to suppose that you throw the rock into a river. Have students draw a picture of what they think the rock will look like if it stays in the river for several years. Then show students a rock with smooth edges and have students compare the rock to their pictures. Explain that wind and water can change the shape and size of rocks by breaking off and carrying away tiny pieces of rock.

Preteach Lesson Vocabulary

crust, mantle, core, weathering, erosion, deposition, glacier

List the vocabulary words on the board.

Draw a three-column chart on the board. In the first column, write *crust*, *mantle*, and *core*. In the second column, write *weathering*, *erosion*, and *deposition*. In the third column, write *glacier*. Explain to students that each column contains related terms. Then:

- Write the words *corps* and *corpse* next to the word *core* on the board. Pronounce each word, making sure students realize that *core* and *corps* have identical pronunciations. Then ask a volunteer to use a dictionary to read the definitions of the words. Have students write sentences in which they use each word correctly.

- Underline *weather* in the word *weathering*. Have a volunteer describe what weather is. Then explain that *weathering* is a process that is caused by weather.

Build Fluency

Have students turn to pp. 230–231 and use the illustration of Earth's layers to complete the sentences below. After students have completed the sentences, have them take turns reading their sentences aloud to a partner.

The _____ is above the mantle. *(crust)*

The _____ is below the crust. *(mantle)*

The _____ is below the mantle. *(core)*

The _____ surrounds the core. *(mantle)*

② Scaffold the Content

When to Use	Proficiency Levels
With pp. 228–236	✔ Beginning
	✔ Intermediate
🕐 30 minutes	✔ Advanced

Preview the Lesson

- Have students read the section title on page 230 and look at the illustration and captions in the **Science Up Close** on pages 230–231. Ask how many layers the illustration shows. *(six)*

- Have students read the title on page 232 and look at the pictures on pages 232–233. Ask, *"Which picture shows earth changes caused by wind?"* *(the sand dune)*

- Have students read the section title and look at the pictures on pages 234–235. Ask students what landform is being caused by the glacier shown at the bottom of page 235. *(a valley)*

Investigate, p. 229

Show students pictures of various objects that have layers. For example, you could show a picture of a layer cake, an onion sliced in half, layers of sedimentary rock, or a fashion model wearing layers of clothing. Point out the layers to the students. Then:

- Explain that a *layer* is a single thickness or coating of a material spread out over or covering a surface.

- Have students turn to pp. 230–231 and help them identify the different layers of Earth that are shown in the illustration. Explain that each of Earth's layers is made of different materials.

Modify Instruction—Multilevel Strategies

Comprehensible Input Show students pictures of the Himalayan Mountains and the Appalachian Mountains. Use a globe to indicate to students where each mountain range is found. Explain to students that long ago, the Appalachians looked very similar to the Himalayas. Have volunteers suggest why they think the Appalachians changed over time. Then have students hypothesize what they think the Himalayas might look like 500 million years from now.

Beginning Have students use construction paper to make a model of Earth's layers. After they have completed their models, have them point to the layer of Earth that is affected by weathering. *(Students should point to the crust.)*

Intermediate Students should draw a picture of what a local landform looks like now, and what it might look like if it underwent weathering or an impact by a meteorite. Students should label their drawings with the type of change they are illustrating.

Advanced Have students research the geologic history of one area of the United States. Students should write a short paper describing how the area has changed over time. Encourage students to include illustrations in their paper.

For All Students Have students make an animated flipbook showing a mountain range like the Himalayas being slowly weathered until it resembles the Appalachians.

Extend

Have the students complete the **Show What You Know** activity on page 89 to demonstrate their understanding of how Earth's surface changes.

③ Apply and Assess

Modeling River-Bed Erosion

When to Use	Proficiency Levels
With Reading Review p. 237	✔ Beginning
🕐 20 minutes	✔ Intermediate
	✔ Advanced

Materials: aluminum baking pan, sand of two different colors, blocks, pitcher of water

Have students use the aluminum baking pan and sand to build a model of a river bed. Students should use one color of sand on one end of the pan and another color of sand at the other end of the pan.

- Have students prop one end of their models up by placing the end on one or two small blocks.
- Students should slowly pour water near the top end of their modeled river beds. Instruct students to observe how the water moves the sand.
- Ask students to hypothesize how the sand would move differently if wind was the primary agent of erosion in their model.

Informal Assessment

Beginning	Intermediate	Advanced
Give students a pile of small pebbles or dried beans. Tell them that the pile represents a boulder sitting on top of a mountain. Ask students to pantomime eroding the boulder. *(Students should take some of the pebbles away.)* Then ask students to pantomime depositing the eroded materials. *(Students should set the pebbles down somewhere else.)*	Have students draw and label a diagram of Earth's layers. *(The diagram should resemble the illustration on pp. 230–231.)*	Show students a picture of the Grand Canyon. Ask students to explain how the canyon formed. *(Possible answer: Over time, water carried away material, causing the river bed to sink further and further down through the layers of rock.)*

How Earth's Surface Changes

Each of the boxes below has a title describing a landform. Draw a picture that matches the description.

A Cave Formed by Erosion	A Hill Deposited by a Glacier
A Meteorite Impact	A Sand Dune Deposited by Wind

© Harcourt

School-Home Connection: Have children take this page home to share with family members. They can use this page to tell about Earth's surface changes.

2 What Are Plates and How Do They Move?

① Build Background

Access Prior Knowledge

When to Use	Proficiency Levels
Before introducing the lesson	✔ Beginning
⏱ 20 minutes	✔ Intermediate
	Advanced

Materials: globe

Show students a globe. Point to the continents on the globe and have students repeat the word *continent* after you. Then ask students if they think the continents have always been in the same place. Point out to students how South America and Africa seem to fit together like a jigsaw puzzle.

Preteach Lesson Vocabulary

> **plate tectonics, mid-ocean ridge, rift, sea-floor spreading**

Materials: globe

List the vocabulary words on the board.

Point out that two of the terms contain compound words.

- Underline *mid-* in *mid-ocean ridge.* Explain to students that the prefix *mid-* comes from the word *middle.* Draw a circle on the board and ask a volunteer to place a dot in the middle of the circle. Then hold up a globe and point to the Atlantic Ocean. Ask students where they think a mid-ocean ridge might be found.

- Write the term *sea-floor spreading* on the board. Ask students to use their hands to pantomime the meaning of the verb *spread.* Then have students point to the room's floor. Explain to students that sea-floor spreading occurs when the floor of a sea spreads.

Build Fluency

Organize students into pairs. Have each pair write two sentences using the word *spread.* Then instruct each pair to read to the rest of the class the sentences they wrote.

© Harcourt

② Scaffold the Content

Preview the Lesson

When to Use With pp. 238–244	Proficiency Levels
⏱ 35 minutes	✔ Beginning ✔ Intermediate ✔ Advanced

Materials: tissue paper, colored pencils

Have students turn to pages 240–241 in their textbooks and examine the illustrations of Earth's plates. Give each student a sheet of tissue paper, and instruct students to use the tissue paper to outline the borders of the plates in one color and the edges of the continents in another color. Have students close their books and use their tissue paper to answer the following questions:

- North America is made up of how many plates? *(two)*
- Is India on the same plate as the rest of Asia? *(no)*

Investigate, p. 239

- Give students time to read the materials list and the procedure. If students have difficulty understanding the procedure, suggest that they look at the pictures.
- Have students look at a globe. Point out how North and South America form a single land mass and how Europe and Africa form another land mass.
- As students do the activity, help them with any steps that might confuse them.
- If necessary, help students demonstrate the other types of plate movement in the Draw Conclusions section.

Modify Instruction—Multilevel Strategies

Background/Experience Ask students to list places that often get earthquakes. Many students will list California, or other states along the west coast of the United States. Tell students that earthquakes often happen near plate boundaries. Show students a picture of the San Andreas Fault in California. Explain to students that earthquakes in California often occur along the San Andreas Fault. Have students use the map on page 240 of their textbooks to identify the two plates that border each other in California.

Beginning Have students use the map on page 240 to identify which plate the country they were born in sits on. Then have students turn to page 244 and find where their birth country was located 220 million years ago.

Intermediate Have students draw a map that includes the country they were born in, the country they are living in now, and the plates that these countries sit on. The map should include arrows showing the direction that the plates are moving.

Advanced Have students choose a continent and write a story describing how the plate on the continent is moving. Tell students to include information about the types of boundaries the plate has with its neighbors.

For All Students Have students stand together in a circle with their hands pressed up against their neighbor's hand. Tell students that they each represent a plate. Have students act out different ways that plates can move.

Extend

Have the students complete the Show What You Know activity on page 93 to demonstrate their understanding of how Earth's plates move.

③ Apply and Assess

Modeling Plate Movement

When to Use	Proficiency Levels
With Reading Review p. 245	✔ Beginning
🕐 25 minutes	✔ Intermediate
	✔ Advanced

Materials: modeling clay

Give students modeling clay and have them perform the following steps:

- Students should make two "plates" out of clay. Have students use the plates to model the movements that occur at a transform fault boundary. Have students describe what happens to the clay.

- Students should make two "plates" out of clay. Have students use the plates to model the movements that occur at a convergent fault boundary. Have students describe what happens to the clay.

Informal Assessment

Beginning	Intermediate	Advanced
Ask: Is a mid-ocean ridge found at a transform fault boundary? *(no)* Is a mid-ocean ridge found at a convergent boundary? *(no)* Is a mid-ocean ridge found at a divergent boundary? *(yes)*	Ask students to draw a diagram that illustrates what happens at a divergent boundary. *(Illustrations should show two plates pulling apart and molten rock rising up to fill the gap.)*	Have students write a brief paragraph explaining the different ways that Earth's plates can move. *(Answers will vary.)*

Name _____

Date _____

Plate Boundary Movements

Draw a simple diagram of each of the plate boundaries below. Include arrows indicating the direction of the movement.

Divergent Boundary	
Convergent Boundary	
Transform Fault Boundary	

School-Home Connection: Have children take this page home to share with family members. They can use this page to tell about how Earth's plates move.

© Harcourt

What Causes Earthquakes and Volcanoes?

① Build Background

Access Prior Knowledge

When to Use	Proficiency Levels
Before introducing the lesson 25 minutes	✔ Beginning ✔ Intermediate ✔ Advanced

Have students examine the picture of a volcano erupting on p. 246 of their textbooks. Ask students why they think the materials in the picture are different colors. *(Students will probably know that the lava is much hotter than the cooled rock.)*

Preteach Lesson Vocabulary

> **fault, earthquake, focus, epicenter, volcano**

List the vocabulary words on the board.

Read each word in the vocabulary list and have students repeat the word after you. Then:

- Point to the word *fault* on the board. Explain that this word has many meanings. The usual meaning of *fault* is "mistake or error." *Fault* can also mean "weakness or defect." It is this meaning of *fault* that relates to the geological term *fault*, which is a break in Earth's crust. *Fault* is also used in the common idioms *at fault*, which means "deserving blame," and *to a fault*, which means "excessively."

- Tell students that, like the word *fault*, the word *focus* has many meanings. *Focus* is both a verb and a noun. Its common meaning as a verb is "to concentrate." Point out that when stresses build up or are "concentrated" at a point inside Earth, it can trigger an earthquake. In photography, *focus* means "to make the image clear." If possible, bring a camera, a microscope, or binoculars to class and have students focus the lens.

Build Fluency

A related meaning of *focus* is "the main subject." Have students flip through the pages of this lesson. As they do, they should complete the following sentence for each page: The focus of page _____ is _____. For example, they could say, "The focus of page 246 is volcanoes."

② Scaffold the Content

Preview the Lesson

When to Use
With pp. 246–254

 30 minutes

Proficiency Levels
✔ Beginning
✔ Intermediate
✔ Advanced

Use the italicized words in the lesson, as well as the captions on the pictures and table on pages 249–250 to identify and clarify difficult terms, such as *seismograph*, *magnitude*, and *tsunami*. Point out that, just as a bathroom scale and a ruler measure two different properties of a person, the Richter scale and the moment magnitude scale measure two different properties of an earthquake. Relate the up and down movement in the seismograph picture to the size of the waves measured on the Richter scale. Place your palms together to model a fault. Slide your hands back and forth. Point out that the moment magnitude scale is based on the distance the plates slide along the fault.

Investigate, p. 247

Ask students what the word *locate* means. Then:

- Lead students in an "I-spy" game using the word *locate*. For example, you could say, "Locate something green in the room."
- Give students a map of the United States. Review with them how to use the scale on the map. Then have them use the compass to calculate the distances between several major cities across the United States. For example, you could have students calculate the distance between Chicago and Dallas, Los Angeles and New York, and Miami and Boston.

Modify Instruction—Multilevel Strategies

Language and Vocabulary Bring to class photocopies of newspaper or magazine articles about actual earthquakes and volcanoes. Give students highlighters and have them highlight any of the lesson vocabulary terms that they find in the articles. Ask each student to read a sentence from his or her article with a highlighted word aloud to the class.

Beginning Have students build a model of a fault. Students should use their models to demonstrate how an earthquake occurs. After they demonstrate an earthquake, have them point to where the focus and the epicenter of the earthquake were.

Intermediate Have students use modeling clay to make models of the three different types of volcanoes. Students should label their models.

Advanced Have students write a short radio news announcement about an earthquake. Instruct students to use as many of the lesson vocabulary words as possible. Have students perform their announcements for the rest of the class.

© Harcourt

For All Students Have students go through the articles about earthquakes that you brought to class. Students should identify the magnitude of each of the described earthquakes and make a list of the earthquakes from weakest to strongest.

Extend

Have the students complete the **Show What You Know** activity on page 97 to demonstrate their understanding of volcanoes.

③ Apply and Assess

Earthquake or Volcano Documentary

When to Use With Reading Review p. 255　⏱ 20 minutes	Proficiency Levels ✔ Beginning ✔ Intermediate ✔ Advanced

Organize students into groups. Have the groups choose a volcanic eruption, earthquake, or tsunami that occurred in the past.

- Students should work together to research their chosen events and write a short documentary or reenactment of the event.

- Have students perform their documentary or reenactment for the rest of the class. During their performance, encourage students to use as many of the lesson vocabulary terms as possible.

- Give students the option to videotape their documentaries or reenactments, and bring a tape to show to the class.

Informal Assessment

Beginning	Intermediate	Advanced
Have students draw a diagram of an earthquake occurring. The diagram should show the fault, focus, and epicenter of the earthquake. *(Diagrams will vary, but should resemble the illustration on p. 248 of the text.)*	Ask students: Where does an earthquake begin? *(at the focus)* What causes a tsunami? *(an earthquake under the sea)* What are mountains formed from cooled magma called? *(a volcano)* What type of volcano is formed only from explosive eruptions? *(a cinder cone volcano)*	Have students write a short paragraph explaining, in their own words, how the Hawaiian islands formed. *(Paragraphs will vary, but should include the information given in the text on p. 254.)*

© Harcourt

Identifying Volcano Shapes

The drawings below are simple diagrams of the shapes of three different kinds of volcanoes. Write the name of the volcano type underneath the correct shape.

_____

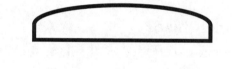

_____

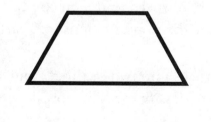

_____

School-Home Connection: Have children take this page home to share with family members. They can use this page to tell about how different types of volcanoes form.

7 Earth's Rocks

Develop Scientific Concepts and Vocabulary

In this chapter, students will study the physical properties of minerals. They will also learn about the three rock types and how these forms relate to each other in the rock cycle. Finally, students will learn about how soil forms and why it is an important resource.

Preview Scientific Principles

Walk students through the chapter, pausing to read the questions that are lesson titles or have volunteers read them aloud. Allow time for students to tell what they know that might be helpful in answering the questions. Ask students to identify and describe pictures they recognize in the chapter.

When to Use With Chapter Opener	Proficiency Levels
30 minutes	✔ Beginning ✔ Intermediate ✔ Advanced

Lesson 1: How Are Minerals Identified?

- Display examples of minerals for students to observe, such as carbon, salt, or talc. Ask students to describe the properties of the minerals.

- Explain that minerals are rated by how hard they are. Have students choose three objects, order them from softest to hardest, and explain how they ranked the objects.

Lesson 2: How Are Rocks Classified?

- Have students collect a variety of rocks, and then compare and contrast the rocks. Direct them to describe their observations to a partner or record them in a table.

- Ask students to classify the rocks into two or three groups and explain their system. Explain that scientists classify rocks by how they form—as igneous, sedimentary, or metamorphic. Help students pronounce each term.

Lesson 3: What is the Rock Cycle?

Explain that rocks can change from one form to another. Review the three kinds of rocks and ask volunteers to name the six possible changes, such as igneous to sedimentary or metamorphic to igneous. Explain that these changes make up the *rock cycle*.

© Harcourt

Lesson 4: How Do Soils Form?

Allow time for students to observe and describe soil samples. Define *soil* as broken-down bits of rock mixed with water, air, leaves and other organic material.

Practice

- Write *compound word* on the board. Explain to students that a compound word is made of two separate words. Point out that there are many in this lesson.
- Write the following terms on the board: *bedrock, topsoil, sandpaper, fingernail, underground, sandstone, limestone, mudstone, chalkboard.*
- Have students take turns writing a word, dividing it into its two components, and using the two parts to define it.
- Students may consult a dictionary to find the meaning or check their answers.

Apply

- Write the two columns of words shown below on the board. Explain how to play *I'm Thinking of Something...*
- Have students form two lines. The first student in one line will say, "I'm thinking of something..." and read one of the phrases on the left. The first person in the second line will complete the phrase by finding and saying the correct word on the right.

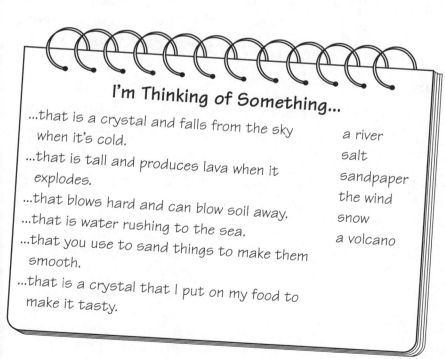

I'm Thinking of Something...

...that is a crystal and falls from the sky when it's cold.

...that is tall and produces lava when it explodes.

...that blows hard and can blow soil away.

...that is water rushing to the sea.

...that you use to sand things to make them smooth.

...that is a crystal that I put on my food to make it tasty.

a river
salt
sandpaper
the wind
snow
a volcano

Lesson 1 — How Are Minerals Identified?

① Build Background

Access Prior Knowledge

When to Use	Proficiency Levels
Before introducing the lesson 15 minutes	✔ Beginning ✔ Intermediate Advanced

Ask students to describe a gemstone they have seen, either "in person" or in a picture. Discuss the properties of these minerals and where they come from. Ask the students to name other minerals they have seen. Tell them that in this lesson they will define *mineral* and learn about the physical properties of minerals.

Preteach Lesson Vocabulary

> **mineral**

Write the vocabulary word on the board.

- Have students find the word *mineral* on page 266 and locate its definition. Then ask a volunteer to read the definition aloud.

- Review that one of the properties of minerals is that they grow as *crystals*. Tell students that crystals are solids with regular patterns of growth. They grow in different shapes depending on how the particles are arranged.

- Refer students to the pictures on page 267 to see examples of different crystal forms. Ask students for other examples of crystals. *(salt, snowflake)*

Build Fluency

Model the following sentence. Then read the words in italics, one-by-one, and have students repeat them with you. Then show them how to replace words to fill in the blank.

You can identify a mineral by its _____. *(streak, fluorescence, crystal structure, cleavage, hardness)*

② Scaffold the Content

Preview the Lesson

When to Use
With pp. 264–270

⏱ 15 minutes

Proficiency Levels
✔ Beginning
✔ Intermediate
✔ Advanced

- Divide students into seven groups and assign each group one of the properties of minerals: *streak, fluorescence, crystal structure, cleavage, hardness.*

- Have each group find its assigned term in the lesson and prepare a short presentation to explain the term to the class. The presentation should include the page reference in the lesson, a definition, and any appropriate pictures if they are available.

- Have groups take turns presenting their information to the other students. The other students should make notes about the name and meaning of each term.

Investigate, p. 265

- Before students begin the Investigate, explain that they will have the chance to observe the properties of different minerals.

- Review aloud the names of the minerals they will be testing.

- Ask a volunteer to hold up a streak plate, a magnet, a nail, and a penny.

- Remind students that they will be recording, or writing down, adjectives for the minerals. Preview some terms students might use to describe the texture, hardness, color, and other properties of minerals.

Modify Instruction—Multilevel Strategies

Background/Experience The ability to correctly identify minerals involves understanding their different properties. The following exercises provide opportunities for students to discover more about the physical properties of minerals, such as the structure of the crystals, how they break apart, and how shiny they are. Write the seven physical properties of minerals on the board: *streak, fluorescence, crystal structure, cleavage, hardness, luster, fracture.*

Beginning Have each student copy the terms and pronounce each one.

Intermediate Have students write the names of the properties on seven different index cards. Have partners work together to write definitions for streak, hardness, and luster.

Advanced Have students make their own set of seven flashcards, with one term on each side and a definition on the other. Students may want to work in pairs or small groups. Encourage them to use their books to find the definitions.

For All Students Have students make a table or other visual organizer to record the physical properties of the minerals salt (halite), talc, and graphite. They can extend or edit the tables as they work through the lesson. They can create new tables for other minerals as well.

Extend

Have the students complete the Show What You Know activity on page 103 to demonstrate their understanding of minerals.

③ Apply and Assess

Make a Mineral Poster

When to Use	Proficiency Levels
With Reading Review p. 271 ⏱ 20 minutes	✔ Beginning ✔ Intermediate ✔ Advanced

Materials: markers or colored pencils, butcher paper

- Divide the students into small groups. Assign each group a different mineral and ask them to draw and label it on the butcher paper.
- Then have students write a brief description of their mineral. This description should include at least two physical properties of the mineral.
- Students may want to use their textbooks, encyclopedias, or other resources to find the information for their posters.
- Display the posters on a bulletin board.

Informal Assessment

Beginning	Intermediate	Advanced
Ask students to name three of the properties of minerals. *(Possible answers: streak, fluorescence, crystal structure, cleavage, hardness)*	Ask partners to read their three definitions. *(streak: the color of a mineral's powder; hardness: the ability to resist being scratched)*	Read aloud the definitions on one side of students' flashcards and have them tell you which word is being defined. Then ask students to read aloud all of the words on their flashcards. *(streak: the color of a mineral's powder; fluorescence: ability to glow in ultraviolet light; crystal structure: the pattern of the crystals; cleavage: how a mineral breaks along planes; hardness: the ability to resist being scratched)*

Name _____

Date _____

Minerals Word Web

In each box, write a physical property that can be used to identify minerals.

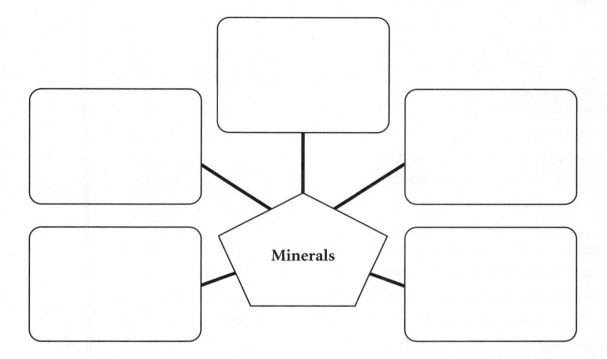

School-Home Connection: Have students take this page home to share
with family members. They can use this page to tell about the physical properties
of minerals.

© Harcourt

How Are Rocks Classified?

① Build Background

Access Prior Knowledge

When to Use	Proficiency Levels
Before introducing the lesson 20 minutes	✔ Beginning ✔ Intermediate ✔ Advanced

Ask students if they have ever collected rocks and give them the opportunity to share what they know about different kinds. Tell students that geologists, or scientists who study the earth, have classified the rocks found on Earth into three categories, including *igneous rock*. Ask them if they can name the other two categories. Tell students that they will learn more about these classifications in this lesson.

Preteach Lesson Vocabulary

> **igneous rock, magma, lava, sedimentary rock, metamorphic rock, metamorphism**

List the vocabulary words on the board.

- Define for students that a rock is a natural, solid object found on Earth. It is made of one or more minerals.
- Have students review the vocabulary list to find the three main kinds of rocks, and then find these vocabulary terms in the section heads in the lesson.
- Explain that rocks first form when *magma* or *lava* cools. Ask students to find these terms on page 274. Point out that magma and lava both refer to melted rocks. Then ask students to search the page to identify the main difference between magma and lava.

Build Fluency

Review the derivation of the terms igneous, sedimentary, and metamorphic, then do the following call-and-response activity with two groups. Help them develop a chant rhythm for each sentence, emphasizing the words in bold type.

Your name means "**fiery**." I am an **igneous rock**. Your name means "**from sediment**." I am a **sedimentary rock**. Your name means "**change**." I am a **metamorphic rock**.

② Scaffold the Content

Preview the Lesson

- Allow time for students to work in small groups to preview the three sections on igneous, sedimentary, and metamorphic rocks (pages 274–279).
- Ask them to use the pictures to describe the features of each type of rock.
- Ask them to explain the main way that each rock type forms. Suggest that they scan the sections for captions, charts, and boldface or italic type for clues about how each rock type forms.

Investigate, p. 273

Materials: safety goggles

- Before students begin the Investigate, explain that they will be examining and classifying rocks. Remind them that *texture* refers to the look or feel of the surface of the rock. Ask volunteers to name some adjectives to describe texture.
- Write the word *grains* on the board. Tell students that *grains* refers to particles or crystals in rocks, not cereal grains used to make bread.
- Write *safety goggles* on the board. Display a pair and then discuss with students how and why to wear them.

Modify Instruction—Multilevel Strategies

Language and Vocabulary Rocks are classified into three main categories by how they form. The names of the three groups are long and often unfamiliar to students. These activities will provide additional practice helping students pronounce and write the terms.

Beginning Have students correctly pronounce and spell the three kinds of rocks.

Intermediate Have students write the names of the three kinds of rocks. Check for the correct spelling.

Advanced Have students write a sentence about each of the three kinds of rocks, using the name for the rock type in each sentence.

For All Students Have students write the name of each rock type at the top of a separate piece of paper. As they work through the lesson, have them add phrases that describe features of the rocks. Students may also want to add the names of rocks that belong in that category.

Have the students complete the **Show What You Know** activity on page 107 to demonstrate their understanding of the different types of rocks.

③ Apply and Assess

That Old Time Rock and Roll

When to Use With Reading Review p. 281 ⏱ 20 minutes	Proficiency Levels ✔ Beginning ✔ Intermediate ✔ Advanced

- Assign one student to be the "teacher."
- Give the "teacher" a list of all the students in the group and have him or her call roll.
- When each student's name is called, he or she should say the name of a rock category or tell one fact about rocks. Allow students to consult their books for this activity.
- Give several students the chance to be the "teacher."

Informal Assessment

Beginning	Intermediate	Advanced
Write the name of a rock category on the board. Ask students to read it. (*Possible answers: igneous, sedimentary, metamorphic*)	Ask students to name all three rock types. (*igneous, sedimentary, metamorphic*)	Ask students to write the names of all three rock categories. (*igneous, sedimentary, metamorphic*)

Name _____

Date _____

Rocky Words

For each letter, write as many words as you can that relate to rocks and begin with that letter.

 School-Home Connection: Have students take this page home to share with family members. They can use this page to tell about rock categories.

© Harcourt

What Is the Rock Cycle?

① Build Background

Access Prior Knowledge

When to Use	Proficiency Levels
Before introducing the lesson	✔ Beginning
🕐 20 minutes	✔ Intermediate
	✔ Advanced

Ask students if they have ever seen sand blowing in a storm or a river rushing through a canyon. Ask them to tell you about these experiences and to describe what happens to the land during these storms. Tell students that the Earth is constantly changing, even though the changes are often very slow. Then ask them to guess how one kind of rock can change into another.

Preteach Lesson Vocabulary

> **rock cycle**

Write the vocabulary words on the board.

- Have students look at page 284 to introduce the *rock cycle*.
- Discuss the idea of a *cycle* as something that goes around and around. Students may think about the wheels on a bicycle turning around and around. They may also recall other cycles they have studied, such as the water cycle, or know the meaning of recycling because they do it at home.
- Explain that the rock cycle tells about how rocks are made, changed, and remade as a result of natural forces.
- Have students find *plate boundaries* in the heading on page 286. Reintroduce the idea of Earth's plates by relating them to the pieces of a broken dinner plate that can move around, but fit back together. Review the meaning of a boundary as a place where objects meet.

Build Fluency

Model these chant-sentences aloud and accent the words in bold:

Any rock can become an **igneous rock**.

Any rock can become a **sedimentary rock**.

Any rock can become a **metamorphic rock**.

Have students read them and stand whenever they say the name of the rock type.

© Harcourt

② Scaffold the Content

When to Use With pp. 282–286	Proficiency Levels
⏱ 20 minutes	✔ Beginning ✔ Intermediate Advanced

Preview the Lesson

- Ask students to look at the picture on page 282. Read the caption and explain that *erosion* breaks down rocks over time. Ask students what kind of rock might form when these broken bits of sediment form together into a rock. (*sedimentary rock*)

- Allow time for students to preview the rock cycle chart (p. 284) and identify some of the ways different rock types can change to other types and how.

Investigate, p. 283

- Before students begin the Investigate, point out that they will be making a model of sedimentary rock. Allow time for students to review what they know about sedimentary rocks.

- Tell students that they will be using different colors of clay and foam pellets to represent the way sedimentary rock forms.

- Remind them that sediments are pressed down to form sedimentary rock, and that they will use a rolling pin to apply pressure to their model. Ask a volunteer to draw a rolling pin on the board and tell how it is usually used.

Modify Instruction—Multilevel Strategies

Comprehensible Input For students to understand the rock cycle, they must have a firm understanding of the meaning of the three types of rocks and how each forms. These activities will reinforce the definitions of igneous, sedimentary, and metamorphic by relating them to root or related words. Write *ignite*, *sediment*, and *morph* on the board.

   Beginning Review the meanings of the terms on the board (to set fire; bits of rock; to change) and ask students to use the source words to review definitions of igneous, sedimentary, and metamorphic rocks.

   Intermediate Have students research the meanings of the terms and use them to define igneous, sedimentary, and metamorphic.

   Advanced Have students write definitions of igneous, sedimentary, and metamorphic by relating the terms to ignite, sediment, and morph.

   For All Students Have students begin their own diagram of the rock cycle without using the textbook as a reference. Have them fill in any missing steps as they work through the lesson.

© Harcourt

Extend

Have the students complete the **Show What You Know** activity on page 111 to demonstrate their understanding of the rock cycle.

③ Apply and Assess

Visualize the Rock Cycle

| When to Use With Reading Review p. 287 🕐 25 minutes | Proficiency Levels ✔ Beginning ✔ Intermediate ✔ Advanced |

Materials: poster board, paints, bits of fabric, shiny ribbon, other textured items

- Divide students into three groups. Assign each group one of the following topics to represent visually:

  1. Magma cools and becomes igneous rock.

  2. Erosion forms layers of sediment that become sedimentary rock.

  3. Heat and pressure make metamorphic rock.

- Provide each group with poster board, paints, and textured materials. Ask them to produce a poster showing their "part" of the rock cycle.

- Put the posters on the bulletin board and label them *The Rock Cycle*.

Informal Assessment

Beginning	Intermediate	Advanced
Ask students to define one of the types of rock by explaining how that type forms. *(Igneous rocks form when magma or lava cools. Sedimentary rocks form when sediments press together. Metamorphic rocks form under heat and pressure.)*	Ask students to define two of the types of rock by explaining how they form. *(Igneous rocks form when magma or lava cools. Sedimentary rocks form when sediments are pressed together. Metamorphic rocks form under heat and pressure.)*	Ask students to read all of their definitions. *(Answers will vary.)*

© Harcourt

Name _____

Date _____

Rock Cycle Diagram

Fill in each box with the names of the three kinds of rocks. Describe how each kind forms.

The Rock Cycle

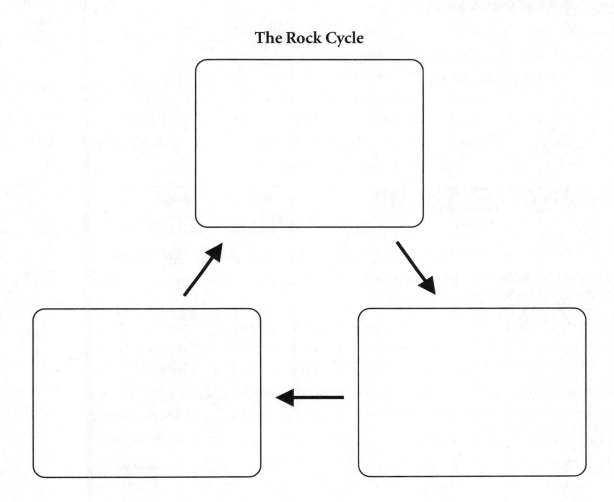

School-Home Connection: Have students take this page home to share with family members. They can use it to tell about the rock cycle.

© Harcourt

How Do Soils Form?

① Build Background

Access Prior Knowledge

When to Use	Proficiency Levels
Before introducing the lesson ⏱ 20 minutes	✔ Beginning ✔ Intermediate ✔ Advanced

Materials: a scoop of soil

Point out to students that soil is more than just dirt that people walk on. It takes many, many years to form and provides a place for food to grow. Have students look at and touch the soil sample. Allow time for them to use adjectives to describe it. Make a list of those adjectives on chart paper. Ask students to describe the soil where they live and any experiences they have had using soil, perhaps with gardening.

Preteach Lesson Vocabulary

> **bedrock, topsoil**

List the vocabulary words on the board.

- Post the list of adjectives students compiled to describe soil. Ask students to use the list, their prior knowledge, and further observations of the soil sample to identify the components of soil.

- Guide them to the understanding that soil is made up of broken pieces of rock, water, air, and many kinds of organic material. Organic material comes from living things, such as rotting plant parts, animals, and insects.

- Have students find the vocabulary words on page 290. Explain that there are three main layers of soil called topsoil, subsoil, and bedrock. Draw a diagram or stack books to model these three layers. Write the words on the board.

- Point out that topsoil is on "top." Subsoil is "sub," or below the topsoil. Bedrock is at the bottom—the bed that the other layers rest on. Encourage students to use these word clues to help remember the soil layers.

Build Fluency

Ask students: *What is topsoil made of?* Have them chant and clap to the following:

Topsoil's made of *bits of rock.*
Topsoil's made of *bits of plants.*
Topsoil's made of *rotting insects.*
Topsoil's made of *water and air.*

© Harcourt

② Scaffold the Content

Preview the Lesson

When to Use	Proficiency Levels
With pp. 288–292	✔ Beginning
⏱ 15 minutes	✔ Intermediate
	✔ Advanced

- Preview the picture and caption on page 288. Review the meaning of erosion and ask students to discuss ways they might slow erosion on a farm or hillside.

- Review the order of soil layers—bedrock, subsoil, and topsoil—by referring students to page 290. Have students help you draw and label these soil layers on the board.

- Ask students how bits of rock and organic matter in soil might form. Point out that two ways—physical and chemical weathering—are explained on pages 290 and 291.

- Preview the section head *Conserving Soil* on page 292. Ask students what it means to conserve a natural resource and discuss how and why soil might be conserved.

Investigate, p. 289

- Before students begin the Investigate, explain that they will create erosion and study ways to stop it.

- Review the meaning of erosion, the forces that cause it, and possible ways to stop or slow it. Discuss why it is important to reduce topsoil erosion and conserve this natural resource.

- Point out that during the Investigate, students will conduct three *trials*. Explain that this means that they will do the same experiment three times and then compare the results. Summarize that a trial is one run of an experiment.

Modify Instruction—Multilevel Strategies

Background/Experience Students can practice using their textbook as a reference and preview some of the information about soil by completing the following activities. Remind them that the title of this lesson is *How Do Soils Form?* Write the following questions on the board and read them aloud:

What is topsoil?

Why do rocks break down?

How is physical weathering different from chemical weathering?

Why is it important to conserve soil?

Beginning Have students copy one of the questions from the board and write a short answer on a sheet of paper.

© Harcourt

Intermediate Have partners copy and answer two of the questions on a sheet of paper using complete sentences. Encourage partners to discuss the questions and write the answers together.

Advanced Ask students to write an answer for each question. Allow them to consult encyclopedias or other reference materials for additional information. Let them share their information with the entire group in an informal presentation.

For All Students Have students continue to ask and answer questions about soil as they work though the lesson. They can post the questions and answers on a bulletin board as a reference for the entire class.

Extend

Have the students complete the **Show What You Know** activity on page 115 to demonstrate their understanding of soil.

③ Apply and Assess

Soil Models

When to Use With Reading Review p. 293 ⏱ 30 minutes	Proficiency Levels ✔ Beginning ✔ Intermediate ✔ Advanced

Materials: modeling clay, index cards

- Have students work in small groups to make a model of the three layers of soil using modeling clay or other classroom objects to represent bedrock, subsoil, and topsoil.

- Have them write the names of the layers on index cards or self-stick notes and use the notes to correctly label each layer.

- Have groups take turns presenting their models and telling what they know about each layer of soil in the model.

Informal Assessment

Beginning	Intermediate	Advanced
Ask students to read their question and answer. *(Answers will vary.)*	Ask partners to share their two questions and answers with the group. *(Answers will vary.)*	Ask yes/no questions about the subject matter in the questions to evaluate student understanding. *(Answers will vary.)*

Topsoil Word Web

Complete the word web. On the line that makes each spoke, write the name of something that makes up topsoil. At the end of the spoke, draw a small picture of it.

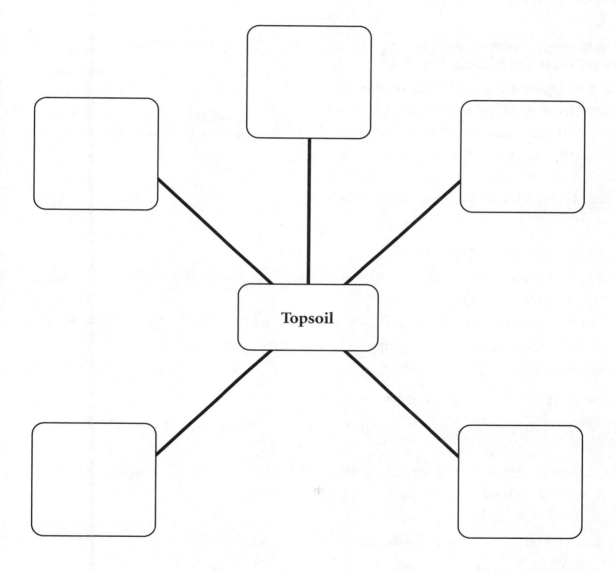

School-Home Connection: Have students take this page home to share with family members. They can use it to tell what they know about topsoil and why it is important.

8 Fossils

Develop Scientific Concepts and Vocabulary

In this chapter, students will learn about fossils and what they tell us abut life in the past.

Preview Scientific Principles

Walk through the chapter with students, pausing to read aloud or to have volunteers read aloud the three questions that are lesson titles. Encourage students to briefly discuss each question and to tell what they already know that might help them answer the questions.

When to Use With Chapter Opener	Proficiency Levels
20 minutes	✔ Beginning ✔ Intermediate ✔ Advanced

Lesson 1: How Do Fossils Form?

- Preview the pictures in the lesson with students. Point out that there are many types of fossils.
- Explain that fossils are created in different ways and by different natural forces.
- Call on volunteers to give examples of fossils they have seen in nature or in museums.

Lesson 2: What Do Fossils Tell Us About Earth?

- Ask students how it could be that fossils of sea creatures can be found high in the mountains.
- Explain to students that if students know the time during which the organism lived that formed a fossil, they can determine the age of the rock that the fossil was found in.
- Briefly review with students the theory of continental drift.
- Ask students what fossils might tell us about continental drift.

© Harcourt

Lesson 3: What Do Fossils Tell Us About Life in the Past?

- Ask for volunteers to define the word *ecosystem*. Discuss and clarify their ideas about ecosystems.
- Ask for volunteers to describe the La Brea Tar Pits.
- Ask for volunteers to explain the concept of mass extinction. Discuss and clarify their ideas about mass extinction.
- Briefly explain the concept of adaptation to students.

Practice

- To help students use vocabulary from the chapter's topic, involve them in contributing to a giant word web around the word *FOSSIL* on the board. Encourage students to dictate or write related words around the focus word. Words might include types of fossils, things fossils tell us about Earth, and things fossils tell us about life in the past.
- Have students choose words from the web to use in sentences about fossils.

Apply

Copy the simple chart below on the board. Then, work with students to complete it.

Fossils

How They Are Formed	What They Tell Us About Earth	What They Tell Us About Life in the Past

1 How Do Fossils Form?

① Build Background

Access Prior Knowledge

When to Use	Proficiency Levels
Before introducing the lesson 15 minutes	✔ Beginning ✔ Intermediate Advanced

Give students an opportunity to use sentences as they talk about their ideas about how fossils form. Ask them to give examples of fossils they have seen. Ask them what natural forces might cause fossil formation.

Preteach Lesson Vocabulary

fossil, mold, cast, fossil fuel

Materials: rocks without fossils, rocks with fossils, fossils removed from rocks

List the vocabulary words on the board.

Have students look at page 304 and find the words on the board.

- Place on a desk several pieces of rock with no fossil presence, a few pieces of rock with fossil imprints, and some fossils that have been removed from rock.

- Allow students time to examine the samples.

- Introduce the concept of *fossil formation* by explaining that the fossil imprints and individual fossils are naturally formed casts of once living organisms.

- Ask students for their ideas about how fossils could be formed.

Build Fluency

Have students work in pairs. Model sentences by completing pairs of sentence frames such as the following:

1. A fossil is a —————— of a once living organism. *(cast)*

2. Fossils are formed in ————. *(rocks)*

Ask students to use sentences like these to further clarify the fossil formation process.

② Scaffold the Content

Preview the Lesson

When to Use With pp. 302–310	Proficiency Levels
🕐 30 minutes	✔ Beginning ✔ Intermediate Advanced

- Ask students to point to the title on page 302 as you read it aloud. Explain to them that they will find the answer to this question in the lesson. Have students examine the photo.

- Ask students to look at the pictures on pages 304–310 and to tell what they show.

- Explain that the pictures on pages 304 through 307 show various types of fossils. The pictures on pages 308 through 310 deal with the formation of fossil fuels.

- Point out the importance of the three types of fossil fuels (coal, petroleum, and natural gas) in meeting our energy needs.

- Write *tissues* on the board and have students find it on page 306.

- Invite discussion of the concept of tissue.

- Ask students to give examples of hard and soft tissues on or in their own bodies.

Investigate, p. 303

Before the students begin the Investigate, allow time for students to examine the various objects to be used in the activity at close hand.

To further develop the lesson concepts, you may want to build comprehension and provide meaning for some of the important technical words, such as *sediment, impression, petrified, amber, decompose, scavenger,* and *protist*. Read aloud the words you choose, using each in a context sentence, and provide its meaning.

Modify Instruction—Multilevel Strategies

Background/Experience The formation of fossils, the focus of this lesson, involves understanding the concepts of decomposition and rock formation. Learners will benefit by associating these concepts with their own daily activities. The following activities provide opportunities for students to recognize examples of decomposition and rock formation in their own daily lives.

Beginning Have students use tracing paper to recreate the pictures of fossils in the text. Then, have them add labels naming the various fossils.

© Harcourt

Intermediate Have students copy from the board simple sentences about fossil formation and fossil fuels. Read each sentence aloud, having students read along or echo the sentences. Invite partners to choose one sentence to copy and illustrate.

Advanced Ask students to turn to page 304 and examine the illustration. Call on volunteers to read the captions. Then, call on volunteers to summarize the process depicted in their own words.

For All Students Direct the students to the world map on page 310. Ask students to give their ideas about what the map shows about the locations of ancient oceans and swamps.

Extend

Have the students complete the **Show What You Know** activity on page 121. Students will demonstrate their understanding of different kinds of fossils.

③ Apply and Assess

Make a Cast

When to Use With Reading Review p. 311 20 minutes	Proficiency Levels ✔ Beginning ✔ Intermediate Advanced

Materials: plaster of Paris

- Extend the Investigate by having students work in groups of three to five to find out more about molds and casts.
- Provide them with plaster of Paris to create casts from molds.
- Ask the groups to duplicate the Investigate activity, and then carry it to conclusion by pouring plaster into the molds and allowing it to harden, thereby creating casts. Have groups share their finished casts.

Informal Assessment

Beginning	Intermediate	Advanced
Have each student give an example of a type of fossil. *(Answers will vary.)*	Have each student give an example of a way a fossil could be formed. *(Answers will vary.)*	Have each student write two sentences about fossil fuels. *(Answers will vary.)*

Identifying Fossils

Draw lines to match the first part of the fossil name on the left with the rest of its name on the right. Then, draw a picture of a "three-lobed" fossil in the box.

cor-   -tom

trilo-   -pod

dia-   -oid

brachio-   -al

crin-   -bite

School-Home Connection: Have students take this page home to share with family members. They can use it to show what they have learned about fossils.

What Do Fossils Tell Us About Earth?

① Build Background

Access Prior Knowledge

When to Use	Proficiency Levels
Before introducing the lesson ⏱ 15 minutes	✔ Beginning ✔ Intermediate Advanced

Give students an opportunity to use sentences as they talk about their ideas about what fossils tell us about Earth. Ask them to give examples of things fossils can tell us about Earth. Ask them how scientists might glean information from fossils.

Preteach Lesson Vocabulary

index fossil

Materials: sand, clear plastic bowl or pan, small rock

Write the vocabulary words on the board.

Have students look at page 314 and find the words on the board.

- Pour about an inch of sand into a clear plastic bowl or pan.
- Put a small rock on top of the sand, touching one of the sides of the bowl or pan.
- Pour about another inch of sand on top of the rock, taking care not to change its position.
- Explain to students that the rock is like an index fossil, showing that the sand below it is "older" than the sand above.

Build Fluency

Have students work in pairs. Model sentences by completing pairs of sentence frames such as the following:

1. Fossils that are _____ make the best index fossils. *(common)*
2. _____ rocks often form layers. *(Sedimentary)*

Ask students to use similar sentences to tell how fossils can be used to date rock layers.

© Harcourt

② Scaffold the Content

Preview the Lesson

- Ask students to point to the title on page 312 as you read it aloud. Explain to them that they will find the answer to this question in the lesson. Have students discuss the picture.
- Ask students to look at the pictures on pages 314 through 316 and to tell about what the illustrations depict.
- Explain that each of the pictures shows how the location of a fossil can give clues about changes to Earth's landforms over time.
- Ask students what the pictures on page 314 show.
- Write *diatoms* on the board and have students find it on page 312.
- Ask students how diatoms help scientists determine the temperatures of ancient oceans.

Investigate, p. 313

Before the students begin the Investigate, pass out activity materials to each student pair. Briefly review the procedure with students to reinforce comprehension.

To further develop the lesson concepts, you may want to build comprehension and provide meaning for some of the other important technical words, such as *radioactive*, *relative age*, *trilobite*, and *continental drift*. Read aloud the words you choose, using each in a context sentence, and provide its meaning.

Modify Instruction—Multilevel Strategies

Comprehensible Input The concept of what fossils tell us about Earth involves understanding that the age of a fossil is related to the age of the rock in which it is found. Learners will benefit by associating this concept with their own daily activities.

Beginning Have students imagine three shirts. One is faded and stained, the second is missing just one button, the third is in perfect shape. Tell students that they could infer from the appearance of the shirts that the one with the most wear is the oldest, while the one with no wear is the newest.

Intermediate Have students copy from the board simple sentences about what fossils tell us about Earth. Read each sentence aloud. Invite partners to choose one sentence to copy and illustrate.

© Harcourt

Advanced On the board, draw a central circle surrounded by three other circles and connected to them by lines. In the central circle, write "What Fossils Tell Us About Earth." Have students complete the web by naming a type of information fossils can give for each of the three outer circles.

For All Students Direct the students to the world map on page 316. Encourage class discussion of the map.

Extend

Have the students complete the Show What You Know activity on page 125. Students will demonstrate their knowledge of what fossils tell us about Earth.

③ Apply and Assess

Make a Mural

When to Use With Reading Review p. 317 ⏱ 20 minutes	Proficiency Levels ✔ Beginning ✔ Intermediate Advanced

Materials: poster or butcher paper, art media, such as crayons, colored pencils, or paints

- Have students work in groups of three to five to find out more about continental drift.
- Then, have them create murals that show, in stages, how Earth's original giant landmass broke apart and spread out over time.
- Display the finished murals on the classroom walls and discuss their similarities and differences.

Informal Assessment

Beginning	Intermediate	Advanced
Have each student give one example of information a fossil can give about Earth. (Answers will vary.)	Have each student give an example of how fossil information can help scientists learn about Earth. (Answers will vary.)	Have each student write two sentences about how fossils tell us about Earth. (Answers will vary.)

Name _____

Date _____

Stories That Fossils Tell

Find out more about trilobites. Write six trilobite facts on the lines below. Then, draw a picture of a trilobite in the box.

TRILOBITES

_____

_____

_____

_____

_____

_____

School-Home Connection: Have students take this page home to share with family members. They can use it to show what they have learned about what fossils tell us about Earth.

3 What Do Fossils Tell Us About Life in the Past?

① Build Background

Access Prior Knowledge

When to Use	Proficiency Levels
Before introducing the lesson	✔ Beginning
⏱ 15 minutes	✔ Intermediate
	Advanced

Give students an opportunity to use sentences as they discuss their ideas of what fossils tell us about life in the past. Ask them to define the word *ecosystem* and to give examples of ecosystems they have seen. Ask them if they know the names of some ecosystems.

Preteach Lesson Vocabulary

> **mass extinction**

Write the vocabulary words on the board.

Have students look at page 320 and find the board words on the page. Then:

- Ask for a volunteer to stand with you in front of the group.
- Have the volunteer read the words on the board out loud.
- Invite students to offer definitions of the board words.
- Call on other volunteers to expand upon the definition of the two-word terms.

Build Fluency

Have students work in pairs. Model sentences by completing pairs of sentence frames such as the following:

1. Changes in _____ cause changes in ecosystems. *(climate)*
2. Fossils show that different living organisms have lived in different _____. *(ecosystems)*

Ask students to use similar sentences to clarify what fossils tell us about life in the past.

② Scaffold the Content

When to Use	Proficiency Levels
With pp. 318–324	✔ Beginning
	✔ Intermediate
🕐 20 minutes	Advanced

Preview the Lesson

- Ask students to point to the title on page 318 as you read it aloud. Explain to them that they will find the answer to this question in the lesson. Ask students to give their ideas about how the *dunkleosteus* shown resembles a modern shark.

- Ask students to look at the pictures on pages 320 through 324 and to summarize what they see.

- Explain that most of the pictures show various types of extinct organisms, while the picture on page 321 shows the La Brea Tar Pits.

- Write *mass extinction* on the board and have students find it on page 323.

- Explain that the fossil record shows that there have been many mass extinctions throughout Earth's history.

Investigate, p. 319

Before the students begin the Investigate, review the meanings of the words *classify*, *observe*, and *compare* with students.

To further develop the lesson concepts, you may want to build comprehension and provide meaning for some of the other important technical words, such as *ecosystem*, *climate*, *deciduous*, *extinct*, *species*, and *hypothesize*. Read aloud the words you choose, using each in a context sentence, and provide its meaning.

Modify Instruction—Multilevel Strategies

Language and Vocabulary To explore and clarify how words in the English language work, introduce the concept of scientific language, using the word *archaeopteryx* (page 324) as an example. Explain that many scientific words may be difficult to pronounce and understand because they were formed from Greek and Latin root words when scientists began classifying fossils.

Beginning Have students look up the word *trilobite* in the dictionary to find that it is a word of Greek origin meaning "three-lobed." Have students look at the picture of a trilobite on page 324 and discuss why scientists might have given this organism that name.

© Harcourt

Intermediate Write several scientific words on the board. Read the words aloud and give their meanings as students repeat after you. Have student pairs choose a word to write down and illustrate its meanings. Then, have students define the words in their own terms.

Advanced Ask students to think of other scientific words. Encourage them to do research to find out the meanings of the words. Have them pick a word and write it in a sentence.

For All Students Call on volunteers to share their ideas on why scientists continue to use such difficult terminology in modern-day fossil classification. Encourage discussion of the ideas presented.

Extend

Have the students complete the **Show What You Know** activity on page 129. Students will demonstrate their understanding of what fossils tell us about life in the past.

③ Apply and Assess

Make a Graphic Organizer

When to Use	Proficiency Levels
With Reading Review p. 325	✔ Beginning
⏱ 20 minutes	✔ Intermediate
	Advanced

Materials: poster or butcher paper, pencils

- Have students work in groups of three to five to create a graphic organizer about mass extinction.
- Have groups begin by drawing a large circle and writing "Mass Extinction" inside it.
- Then, have them draw four smaller circles around the main circle, connected to it by lines.
- Ask students to search the text to find four possible reasons for mass extinction and to write and illustrate one reason in each of the four small circles.
- Have students compare and discuss their completed graphic organizers.

Informal Assessment

Beginning	Intermediate	Advanced
Have each student give an example of an organism that has changed a great deal over time. *(birds)*	Have each student give an example of an organism that has changed very little over time. *(sharks)*	Have each student write two sentences that summarize the ways in which mass extinction could occur. *(Answers will vary.)*

Name _____

Date _____

Fossils and the Past

Match each word on the left with its definition on the right. Write the number of the word on the line.

1. ecosystem

2. climate

3. deciduous

4. extinct

5. species

6. hypothesize

_____ no longer living

_____ the average weather over a period of years

_____ to develop a theory

_____ falling off, as in shedding leaves

_____ a category used in classifying organisms

_____ an ecological unit in nature

School-Home Connection: Have students take this page home to share with family members. They can share what they have learned about what fossils tell us about life in the past.

9 The Water Planet

Develop Scientific Concepts and Vocabulary

In this chapter, students will study the water cycle, and then learn about oceans. They will find out about the different regions, or zones, of the ocean, and will discover how they differ from each other. Students will also find out about the amazing variety of organisms that inhabit Earth's oceans.

Preview Scientific Principles

Walk through the chapter with students, pausing to read aloud or to have volunteers read aloud the three questions that are lesson titles. Encourage students to briefly discuss each question and to tell what they already know that might help them answer the questions.

When to Use With Chapter Opener	Proficiency Levels
35 minutes	✔ Beginning ✔ Intermediate ✔ Advanced

Lesson 1: What Is the Water Cycle?

- Using a large map of the world, have volunteers point to the different large bodies of water on Earth. Say the names of the bodies, and for each one, ask students whether they think the water is salt water or fresh water. Ask students how they decide.

- Put 8–10 ice cubes in a large drinking glass, and fill it with water. Have students observe the outside of the glass. Explain that this is an example of *condensation.*

Lesson 2: What Are the Characteristics of the Ocean?

- Draw the outline of the ocean floor on the board. Include the shoreline and the three main regions of the ocean: the continental shelf, the continental slope, and the abyssal plain. Label them and have students repeat the words aloud.

- Tell students that a continent is defined as *any of the main large land areas of Earth.*

- Ask students why they think it's important for scientists to be able to map the ocean floor.

Lesson 3: What Lives in the Ocean?

- Display photographs or slides of various organisms that live in the ocean. Explain that each region of the ocean has its own ecosystem that supports a huge variety of life.

- Write the word *intertidal* on the board. Ask students to tell what the prefix *inter* means. *(between or among)* Explain that *intertidal* refers to the area between high tide and low tide. Ask students to think of other words that begin with the prefix *inter*.

Practice

Help students think about the variety of organisms living in the ocean by having them complete the following word puzzle. Write the term CONTINENTAL SLOPE *vertically* on the board, and have them copy it onto their papers. Then ask them to think of as many sea creatures beginning with each letter as they can, and write the names next to the letter, separated by commas. Students may use encyclopedias or online resources to find names of animals. *(Examples: C: crab, clam, cod, coral; O: octopus, oyster, otter; S: seaweed, shark)*

Apply

Copy the following call/response pairs on the board. Divide students into two groups and have them say the verses as a call-and-response. Have them begin by reading the verses, and then ask them to memorize the calls or the responses.

Have You Seen a Coral Reef...?

Call: Have you seen a **coral reef**? Tell me what you saw!

Response: I saw parrotfish, surgeonfish, and butterfly fish! I saw sponges and I saw seaweed, but mainly I saw coral!

Call: Have you seen the **intertidal zone**? Tell me!

Response: I saw crabs and barnacles, seahorses and rays, sand dollars and mussels, sea anemones and lots and lots of seaweed!

Call: Have you seen the **near-shore zone**? Tell me!

Response: I saw shrimp and jellyfish, and even a shark. There were dolphins and porpoises, and even some whales!

What Is the Water Cycle?

① Build Background

Access Prior Knowledge

When to Use	Proficiency Levels
Before introducing the lesson 25 minutes	✔ Beginning ✔ Intermediate ✔ Advanced

Ask volunteers to explain where rain comes from and how water in the ocean is different from water in a lake or river. Ask students if they have ever lived where their water came from a well. Have volunteers suggest how well water differs from the water they get in cities. Explain that in this lesson, they will learn all about how water gets "recycled" in the Earth's *water cycle.*

Preteach Lesson Vocabulary

> **water cycle, evaporation, condensation, precipitation, groundwater**

List the vocabulary words on the board.

- Have students turn to pages 338 and 339 and find the term *water cycle.* Have them point to the terms on the illustration of the water cycle as you describe *evaporation* and *condensation.* Explain that evaporation and condensation are reverse processes. In evaporation, liquids change to gases. In condensation, gases change to liquids.

- Point out that the word *precipitate* has several meanings, such as to cause something to happen. In earth science, precipitation is something that falls from the sky, such as rain, snow, sleet, or hail. Ask students what those four forms of precipitation have in common. *(They are all forms of water.)* Have students find the term in the water cycle.

- Explain to students that *groundwater* is water found under Earth's surface. It collects in holes and pores in rock and in underground formations called *aquifers.* Ask students to identify the root of the word *aquifer. (aqua = water)*

Build Fluency

Have students repeat the following phrases for word practice.

Condensation: water vapor changing to liquid water

Evaporation: liquid water changing into water vapor

Precipitation: solid or liquid water falling from the air to the ground

Groundwater: water found in rocks and aquifers under Earth's surface

© Harcourt

② Scaffold the Content

Preview the Lesson

- Have students read the three section heads on pages 338, 340, and 342. Ask students what three things they expect to learn about in the chapter. *(the water cycle, where fresh water is found, and how to protect water resources)*
- Have students look at the pictures on page 340. Ask them how the water in a glacier differs from the water in the ocean. *(glaciers are fresh water, the ocean is saltwater)*
- Ask students to find a picture that shows how water can be recycled after it is used by people. *(page 342)*

Investigate, p. 337

- Display the materials students will use in the activity. As you name the items, have students point to them.
- Give students time to read through the procedure and look at the pictures. Answer any questions students might have.
- Write the following words on the board: *clay soil, gravel, sand, potting soil.* Tell students that these are different types of soil or materials found in soil. Explain that they will be observing how water moves through each of these types of soil.
- Remind students what a model is and how to "model" a pond.

Modify Instruction—Multilevel Strategies

Language and Vocabulary The concept of the water cycle, the focus of this lesson, involves understanding that Earth's water goes through several processes as it recycles. Learners will better understand this concept if they understand and can use the terms correctly. Ask students to imagine that the water they drink could have come from the other side of the world, or from an ancient body of water. Tell students that energy from the sun is responsible for the process known as the *water cycle*, because it provides energy for water on Earth to evaporate.

Beginning Have students copy the vocabulary words and their definitions onto index cards. Encourage students to illustrate each term.

Intermediate Have students say *true* or *false* as you read each of the statements. 70% of Earth is covered in water. *(true)* Most of Earth's fresh water is groundwater. *(false)* Precipitation returns water to Earth's surface and into rivers and lakes. *(true)* Aquifers are the same as glaciers. *(false)* Hail and snow are types of transpiration. *(false)* Energy from the Sun causes water in rivers to evaporate. *(true)*

Advanced Have students write a story about the travels of a drop of water through the water cycle.

For All Students Provide students with world atlases. Have them find the oceans and seas, and help them locate the major rivers on all of the continents.

Extend

Have the students complete the **Show What You Know** activity on page 135 to demonstrate their understanding of the processes in the water cycle.

③ Apply and Assess

Visualize the Water Cycle

When to Use With Reading Review p. 343 🕐 25 minutes	Proficiency Levels ✔ Beginning ✔ Intermediate ✔ Advanced

Materials: a sheet of art paper for each student, paints, markers or colored pencils, scrap-booking materials, such as ribbon, fabric, glitter, etc.

- Invite students to create their own version of Earth's water cycle.
- First, review the vocabulary words, and remind students how each one fits into the water cycle. Then ask students to represent the water cycle with various materials, color, arrows, and labels on their piece of art paper.
- Challenge students to be original in their representations. When students have completed the assignment, hold an "art fair." Display the students' work and invite parents or other classes to view the display. Have students explain their posters to visitors and answer questions.

Informal Assessment

Beginning	Intermediate	Advanced
Ask students to work with a partner to read the words and their definitions that they made in the Multilevel Strategies aloud. Then have students put the cards away. Read the definitions to students and ask them to identify each word. Write the words *groundwater, transpire, aquifer, vapor, glacier,* and *salt water* on cards. As you give the definitions/descriptions, have students point to the correct card. *(Answers will vary.)*	Read statements about lesson content aloud to students and have them tell you whether the statements are true or false. For the ones that are false, ask students to give you a version of the statement that is true. Then ask them to look in the lesson and write several more *true/false* statements to ask a fellow classmate. *(Answers will vary.)*	Ask students to write a simple quiz on the water cycle appropriate for the class. Allow time for each student to give the quiz to other students and then review the questions and answers with the group, as a teacher would. *(Answers will vary.)*

The Water Cycle

Read each definition and then fill in the other letters of each word.

1. The process in which liquid water changes into water vapor is

   __ __ __ __ __ __ __ TION.

2. The process in which water vapor changes into liquid water is

   __ __ __ __ __ __ __ __ TION.

3. Solid or liquid water that falls from the air to the Earth is

   __ __ __ __ __ __ __ __ __ TION.

4. The process in which plants release water vapor into the air through their leaves is

   __ __ __ __ __ __ __ __ __ TION.

 School-Home Connection: Have students take this page home to share with family members. They can use the page to talk about the water cycle.

What Are the Characteristics of the Ocean?

① Build Background

Access Prior Knowledge

When to Use	Proficiency Levels
Before introducing the lesson	✔ Beginning
🕐 25 minutes	✔ Intermediate
	✔ Advanced

Ask students where they think the highest mountains in the world are located. If students don't mention the mountains in the oceans, remind them that much of Earth's surface is covered in water. Ask if they think there may be taller mountains in the ocean. Ask volunteers to give definitions for *valley* and *plain*. Give students a chance to describe which oceans and beaches they are familiar with. As a group, compare their examples. Ask students to give words that describe the ocean. Write their words on the board.

Preteach Lesson Vocabulary

> **continental shelf, continental slope, abyssal plain, currents**

List the vocabulary words on the board.

- Have students look at the diagram of the ocean floor on pages 346 and 347. Remind students that *continental* refers to something on or near a large land mass. Tell students that the *continental shelf* extends out from land. Remind them that people can sometimes walk out a long way into the ocean at the beach before the water gets very deep. They are walking on the continental shelf.

- At the end of the continental shelf, the land *slopes* downward quickly. Have students point to the *continental slope*.

- Write the word *abyss* on the board. Tell students that the word *abyss* means "bottomless," but that the ocean isn't really bottomless. Tell students that the *abyssal plain* is the floor of the deep ocean at the bottom of the continental slope.

- Have students look on page 348 and find the word *currents*. Explain that *currents* are streams of seawater moving in different directions through the ocean.

Build Fluency

Have students say the correct term as you point to each sentence on the board.

The _____ is the part of the ocean floor closest to land. *(continental shelf)*

The _____ begins at the bottom of the continental slope. *(abyssal plain)*

Along the _____, ocean water continues to get deeper. *(continental slope)*

The _____ is the floor of the deep ocean. *(abyssal plain)*

② Scaffold the Content

Preview the Lesson

When to Use With pp. 344–350	Proficiency Levels
⏱ 35 minutes	✔ Beginning ✔ Intermediate ✔ Advanced

- Have students read the lesson title on page 344. Ask students what *characteristics* means.
- Have students read the section title on page 346. Point out that a *floor* is usually a flat surface, but that the ocean floor is the surface of Earth that is under ocean water and that it isn't always flat.
- Have students read the section title on page 348 and look at the picture of ocean currents. Ask students why they think the ocean water off California might be colder than the ocean water off Florida.

Investigate, p. 345

- Have students read through the steps of the procedure and look at the picture. Explain to students that they will be making a model of the ocean floor, representing such features as mountains, canyons, slopes, and plains.
- Demonstrate to students what is meant by *cut a slit* in number 2 of the Procedure.
- Draw an example of a cross section on the board. Ask for other examples of things that you can view in a cross section.
- Ask students how they might use the chopstick to measure the depth.

Modify Instruction—Multilevel Strategies

Comprehensible Input The concept of the ocean characteristics and how the ocean affects climate, the focus of this lesson, involves understanding that Earth's water goes through several processes as it recycles. Learners will better understand this concept if they can visualize features within the ocean and the interaction of the sun, wind, land, and ocean in shaping climate. Ask students to picture an island in their minds. Explain that an island is really a huge mountain that has risen from the abyssal plain, and tall enough to be outside of the water. Then tell students that earthquakes are common in the ocean, and that they occur when one tectonic plate slides beneath another.

Beginning Have students use clay to build a model of the ocean floor. Students should label the parts of the model.

Intermediate Have students write *surface currents, warm water currents,* and *cold water currents* on three index cards. As you say, "caused by winds," "begin near the equator," and "begin near the poles," have students hold up the matching card.

Advanced Have students draw a graphic organizer around the term *salt water*. Encourage students to include the resources found in the oceans, as well as the use of desalination to provide fresh water in some regions.

For All Students Have students suggest ways that they use resources from the ocean. Discuss how the ocean can be harvested and mined, as well as ways to preserve the natural resources found in oceans.

Extend

Have the students complete the **Show What You Know** activity on page 139 to demonstrate their understanding of ocean characteristics.

③ Apply and Assess

Ocean Resources Collage

When to Use With Reading Review p. 351 🕐 25 minutes	Proficiency Levels ✔ Beginning ✔ Intermediate ✔ Advanced

Materials: paints or markers, poster board, scrap-booking papers and supplies, magazines, scissors, glue

- Divide students into groups. Have each group create a collage showing the different resources found in the ocean. Encourage students to come up with an interesting, colorful, and clear way to show the different types of resources, such as water, salt, pearls, fish, and petroleum. Their collages should contain labels or words as well as pictures.

- Students may want to consult online resources or encyclopedias to find information or ideas that are not in their book. When they are finished, have each group display their collage and answer any questions from other students.

Informal Assessment

Beginning	Intermediate	Advanced
Have students use the clay model they built. Students should point to each section of the model and explain in a complete sentence what it is. They should then add one interesting piece of information about each section. *(Answers will vary.)*	On an outline map that shows the oceans, have students draw a surface current, a warm water current, and a cold water current. Students should show the direction of the currents with arrows and write a sentence about each type of current at the bottom of the map. *(Answers will vary.)*	Have students turn their graphic organizer into a story. The story should include all of the items they showed on the graphic organizer. Have students read or tell their story to a group of students. They should be prepared to answer questions about their story. *(Answers will vary.)*

The Ocean: Key Terms

Read each definition. Below the definition, write the letters of the term that was described or defined.

1. the steady, stream-like movements of the ocean's water

   __ __ __ __ __ __ __

2. the gradually sloping portion of the ocean's floor that you wade into at the beach

   __ __ __ __ __ __ __ __ __ __ __ __   __ __ __ __ __

3. the part of the ocean floor that steeply plunges to the deepest part of the ocean

   __ __ __ __ __ __ __ __ __ __ __ __   __ __ __ __ __

4. the deepest and flattest part of the ocean floor

   __ __ __ __ __ __ __   __ __ __ __ __ __

5. the cause of surface currents

   __ __ __ __ __ __   __ __ __ __ __ __

6. where the tectonic plates of the Earth's crust are being split apart

   __ __ __ __ __ __ __ __ __   __ __ __ __ __ __

7. these are valued for the pearls that sometimes form in their bodies

   __ __ __ __ __ __ __

8. where salt and other minerals are removed from seawater

   __ __ __ __ __ __ __ __ __ __ __ __   __ __ __ __ __ __

School-Home Connection: Have students take this page home to share with family members. They can use this page to tell about ocean characteristics.

What Lives in the Ocean?

① Build Background

Access Prior Knowledge

When to Use	Proficiency Levels
Before introducing the lesson 25 minutes	✔ Beginning ✔ Intermediate ✔ Advanced

Ask students if they have ever been "tide pooling." If so, ask them to describe the types of organisms they saw in the tide pools. Tell them that in this lesson, they will learn more about tidal areas, as well as the other areas, or zones, of the oceans. Ask them to name their favorite animal that lives in or near the ocean. Encourage them to describe the animal's appearance and behaviors. Ask students if they think the same kind of organisms live in the other parts of the ocean.

Preteach Lesson Vocabulary

> **intertidal zone, near-shore zone, open-ocean zone, coral reefs**

List the vocabulary words on the board.

- Ask students if they have ever seen the size of a beach change over the course of a day. At times, the waves wash very far onto the beach and leave behind debris, such as driftwood, shells, and bits of seaweed. The highest line of debris on the beach marks the high tide. The beach is bigger at low tide when the water level is lowest. Explain that the *intertidal zone* is the area between the high-tide mark and the low-tide mark.

- Encourage students to describe where they think the near-shore zone and open-ocean zone are. Explain that the *near-shore zone* is the area over the continental shelf. The *open-ocean zone* is the area over the continental slope and abyssal plain. Ask students how they think the amount of sunlight varies in these zones.

- Tell students that *coral reefs* are made up of the bony outer skeletons of tiny animals called corals that live in the shallow waters of the near-shore zone. The reef grows as new corals attach themselves to the skeletons of dead coral.

Build Fluency

Have students make up a rap song about the four vocabulary words. Each line of the song should tell some characteristics of the three zones or the coral reef. Have students present their songs to the rest of the group, while the group claps along to the rhythm. Students may have the group say the name of the zone when it is repeated in the song.

② Scaffold the Content

When to Use
With pp. 352–360

⏱ **30 minutes**

Proficiency Levels
✔ Beginning
✔ Intermediate
✔ Advanced

Preview the Lesson

- Have students look at the picture on page 352. Do a choral reading of the caption. Then ask a volunteer to identify the word in the caption that also has a very different meaning. *(school)* Explain to students that the word can be used as a noun with several meanings, and as a verb.

- Have students skim the chapter and look at the pictures. Point out that, because each zone gets different amounts of sunlight, there are different types of ecosystems in the ocean. Explain that most organisms live close to the surface because there is more sunlight, therefore, more food available.

Investigate, p. 353

- Begin by asking students what the difference is between tap water and the pond water that they will be using in this Investigate. Make sure students understand that pond water contains many organisms that can be seen with a microscope.

- Ask students what factors might affect the ecosystems they will create. Discuss how light, temperature, and moisture might affect the organisms in an ecosystem.

- Have students look at samples of pond water under a microscope and then draw what they see. Ask them to come up with adjectives to describe each item, and then write them down. Help students look them up in a reference book.

Modify Instruction—Multilevel Strategies

Background/Experience The concept of the ocean ecosystems, the focus of this lesson, involves understanding the factors that organisms require to live. Learners will better understand this concept if they use what they already know about ecosystems and factors that affect plants and animals. Show students pictures or slides of ocean creatures. Include mammals, many different kinds of fish, etc. Then show students pictures of animals that live in the deepest part of the ocean. Ask them to compare the different animals. Tell students that the ocean can be as deep as 36,000 feet. Explain that scientists learn about this zone using vessels called *submersibles* or *ROVs* (remotely operated vehicles.)

   Beginning Have students make a list of as many organisms as they can find named in the lesson. Then ask students to draw some of them. *(Examples are: crabs, mussels, barnacles, plankton, coral, jellyfish, dolphins, shrimp, whales, krill, squid, fish, sponges.)*

© Harcourt

Intermediate As students read through the lesson, have them identify one organism that lives in each zone. Students should write a sentence about how the organism survives in that zone. *(Answers will vary. Example: Sand dollars live in the intertidal zone. They bury themselves in the sand when the tide goes out.)*

Advanced Have students research the following terms, and then find the kinds of organisms that live in each of the following parts of the ocean: *the sunlight zone, the twilight zone, the midnight zone, the abyssal zone,* and *the hadal zones.*

For All Students As a group, research the history of ocean exploration. Draw a group timeline to show the information students find.

Extend

Have the students complete the Show What You Know activity on page 143 to demonstrate their understanding of life in the ocean.

③ Apply and Assess

What Does It Look Like?

Materials: paints or markers, sheets of art paper for each student, scrap-booking materials of various textures, tag board sentence strips

When to Use With Reading Review p. 361  30 minutes	Proficiency Levels ✔ Beginning ✔ Intermediate ✔ Advanced

- Write the following list on the board: *deep-ocean vents, fish from the midnight zone, poisonous sea creatures, camouflage and sea creatures, kelp beds, life in coral reefs, sea organisms with shells, "jet-propelled" sea creatures, mythical ocean creatures.*
- Have students choose one topic and do a visual representation of it.
- Then have students provide several descriptive sentences about their topic, written on sentence strips. Ask students to label their drawings.
- Hold a class "seminar" entitled *What Does It Look Like?*, asking each student to present his or her work. Then display students' work on the bulletin board.

Informal Assessment

Beginning	Intermediate	Advanced
Have students return to the list of organisms they made in the Multilevel Strategies. Have students select one organism from each zone and tell several facts about the organism and how it survives in that zone. *(Answers will vary.)*	Draw a cross section of the ocean zones on the board. Point to a zone and ask students to describe the characteristics of that zone and name several organisms in the zone's ecosystem. *(Answers will vary.)*	Have students compile information on *the sunlight zone, the twilight zone, the midnight zone, the abyssal zone,* and *the hadal zones* in outline form. Copy the outlines and pass them out to other class members. Encourage students to ask each other questions about the outlines. *(Answers will vary.)*

© Harcourt

Name _____

Date _____

What's Down In the Ocean?

Place numerals in the puzzle boxes to match the "Across" and "Down" clues with the words in the crossword puzzle.

Across   **1** Cracks in the ocean floor where hot water full of minerals gushes

2 It can be pink, white, yellow, or green, and it forms reefs

3 Ocean zone where most life is found

Down   **1** On the ocean's surface, these are driven by wind

2 This means "harbor wave," and it often follows an earthquake

3 Community of organisms and their non-living environment

4 The rise and fall of sea level twice a day

	W											
	A				T							
	V	E	N	T	S							
	E				U							
	S	E			N							
		C	O	R	A	L						
		O			M							
		S		I	N	T	E	R	T	I	D	A	L
		Y			I							
		S			D							
		T			E							
		E			S							
		M										

School-Home Connection: Have students take this page home to share with family members. They can use it to talk about what lives in the oceans.

© Harcourt

10 Earth's Weather Patterns

Develop Scientific Concepts and Vocabulary

In this chapter, students will learn about weather patterns. They will explore the different layers of the atmosphere and study the different gases that make up the atmosphere. Students will also learn the different factors that affect weather, such as air masses, clouds, and fronts, and how different types of storms are formed.

Preview Scientific Principles

Walk through the chapter with students, pausing to read aloud or to have volunteers read aloud the three questions that are lesson titles. Encourage students to look at illustrations on the pages and briefly discuss each question. Have them tell what they already know about weather and weather patterns that might help them answer the questions.

When to Use With Chapter Opener	Proficiency Levels
20 minutes	✔ Beginning ✔ Intermediate ✔ Advanced

Lesson I: What Makes Up the Atmosphere?

- Ask students what the atmosphere is. Explain that, like Earth itself, the atmosphere is made up of layers. Ask students what purposes they think the atmosphere serves.
- Review the sun's role in providing energy to Earth.
- Have students think about where on Earth it is colder or warmer and why. Ask them if it is warmer or colder at the top of a mountain than at the foot and why.

Lesson 2: What Is Weather?

- Have students discuss weather by reviewing the four seasons, spring, summer, fall, and winter, and talking about the weather in each season.
- Explain the difference between weather and climate.
- Ask students how they think lightning occurs. Have them discuss what kind of energy a lightning bolt discharges.
- Ask students what they think causes wind and how wind affects weather.

© Harcourt

Lesson 3: How Can You Track Severe Storms?

- Conduct a class discussion on weather forecasts. Ask students how scientists can make predictions on what the weather will be like. Discuss equipment such as weather satellites, weather balloons, and Doppler radar.
- Ask students what they think thunderstorms are. Discuss what kinds of storms bring tornadoes or how different types of storms, such as hurricanes and blizzards, differ.

Practice

To help students use vocabulary from the chapter's topic, involve them in contributing to a giant word web around the central word *WEATHER* on the board. Encourage students to dictate or write related words around the focus word. Some words might be *atmosphere, storms, clouds, lightning, hurricanes, tornadoes,* etc. Then have students choose words from the web to use in sentences about weather. Encourage them to read their sentences aloud.

Apply

Write the lines from the following chart on the board and have students take turns echoing or reading a line aloud. You may wish to model how to pantomime some of the actions described in the lines. Have students search old newspapers or the Internet for weather maps for an entire month. Have them print, cut, and paste the maps on a sheet of construction paper to create a collage of weather maps.

Weather Stories

The atmosphere surrounds the Earth.
It contains the oxygen that we breathe.
The weather can be very hot in summer.
It can be very cold in winter.
It is hotter near the equator than near Earth's poles.
Thunderstorms and hurricanes can be dangerous.
Satellites in space track Earth's weather patterns.
Scientists use satellite data to make weather forecasts.
Blizzards have strong, cold winds.
If I need to go out in a blizzard, I must wear heavy clothing.

What Makes Up the Atmosphere?

1 Build Background

Access Prior Knowledge

When to Use	Proficiency Levels
Before introducing the lesson 15 minutes	✔ Beginning ✔ Intermediate Advanced

Give students an opportunity to use sentences as they talk about what they understand about Earth's atmosphere. Ask them how the atmosphere changes as astronauts leave Earth, go into orbit, and come back to Earth in their spacecraft. Remind students that when spacecraft return to Earth they must "reenter" the atmosphere. Ask students why returning to Earth through the atmosphere is a dangerous time for spacecraft. Remind them of how meteorites burst into flame when they enter the atmosphere.

Preteach Lesson Vocabulary

> atmosphere

Write the vocabulary word on the board.

Have students look at page 372 and locate the vocabulary word. Then:

- Divide the word *atmosphere* into syllables, and have students say each syllable with you. Then blend the syllables and say the whole word together.
- Tell students that the word *atmosphere* is made up of an ancient Greek word, *atmos*, which means gases or vapor, and the word *sphere*, which comes from Latin.
- Ask students what the word *sphere* means. Elicit that it means a globe or a globular body, such as the Earth, or a simple ball.
- Help students infer that *atmosphere* means the gases or vapors that surround the globe, or Earth.
- Explain that the *atmosphere* is a scientific term for what they usually call *air*. Air is made up of a number of gases, including water vapor. The atmosphere also contains tiny solid particles, such as dust and pollutants.

Build Fluency

Have students work in pairs. Model dialogues by completing questions and answers such as the following:

How does the word *atmosphere* describe what it means? *Atmos* means _____ and _____ is a sphere. *(gases, Earth)*

What is the _____? It is the layers of gases that surround the Earth. *(atmosphere)*

② Scaffold the Content

When to Use	Proficiency Levels
With pp. 370–374	✔ Beginning
	✔ Intermediate
20 minutes	✔ Advanced

Preview the Lesson

Ask students to point to the title on page 370 as you read it aloud. Explain to them that they will find the answer to this question in the lesson. Have students discuss the picture.

- Next, ask students to look at the pictures on pages 371–374 and tell what is happening in the pictured images.
- Review the process of photosynthesis and ask students which gas from the atmosphere plants use to create their food. Elicit or explain that plants need carbon dioxide.
- Ask students what they think the ozone gas is. Explain that this gas helps protect all living things from the damaging rays from the sun.

Investigate, p. 371

- Give students time to read the steps of the procedure.
- Draw a circle to represent Earth on the board. Label Earth. Write the words in Step 4 in a column above the circle, with troposphere closest to Earth and thermosphere farthest away.
- Explain that these are layers of the atmosphere. Pronounce each word and have students repeat the pronunciation.

Modify Instruction—Multilevel Strategies

Comprehensible Input Write the word *layer* on the board and ask students to read the word with you. Explain that the atmosphere is composed of five layers. Ask students what they think the word *layer* means. Explain that *layer* has several meanings. Ask volunteers to use the word in sentences that show different meanings. Tell students that in this lesson *layer* refers to a thickness of a gas that can be under or over another one. Each layer has different properties.

Beginning Ask students to point to words in the text such as *atmosphere*, *troposphere*, and *stratosphere* as you name them. Have them say the words with you.

Intermediate Ask students simple questions to elicit one-word answers, such as: What is the second layer of the atmosphere? *(the stratosphere)* Model how to answer in complete sentences, such as: The stratosphere is the second layer of the atmosphere.

Advanced Ask students to read aloud the section **The Atmosphere** on pages 372–373. Have them sum up each paragraph by describing the main idea and the most important details. Their descriptions should include the five layers of the atmosphere.

© Harcourt

ESL Support 147

For All Students Work with students to prepare a diagram showing why the sun doesn't heat Earth evenly. Have students draw illustrations on different parts of the diagram to represent temperature differences.

Extend

Have students complete the **Show What You Know** activity on page 149 to demonstrate their understanding of the gases that make up the atmosphere.

③ Apply and Assess

Make an Atmosphere Presentation and Display

When to Use	Proficiency Levels
With Reading Review p. 375 ⏱ 20 minutes	✔ Beginning ✔ Intermediate ✔ Advanced

Materials: magazines or other resources, construction paper, paste, markers

- Have students work together in groups of three to five to research and find illustrations and information on the different layers of the atmosphere in encyclopedias, magazines, or on the Internet.
- Have them organize the illustrations and the information by layer, such as troposphere, stratosphere, mesosphere, thermosphere, and exosphere.
- Ask the groups to paste the organized illustrations on construction paper and to label the layers with appropriate information.
- Have the groups present their findings and then display their work on the wall in an area titled: *The Five Layers of the Atmosphere.*

Informal Assessment

Beginning	Intermediate	Advanced
Ask individual students to say the word *sphere* by itself, having them blend each phoneme with you, if necessary. Emphasize the /f/ sound of the spelling *ph*. Then have them point to all the words with *sphere* in the text and help them pronounce each one.	Have each student complete a sentence or create a sentence that describes something about the layers of the atmosphere. *(Answers will vary but may include: It is very hot in the mesosphere.)*	Have each student describe why the ozone layer is important in the atmosphere. *(Answers will vary but may include: The ozone layer helps protect living things on Earth from radiation from the sun.)*

© Harcourt

Name _____

Date _____

Draw a Space Shuttle

Draw a space shuttle coming back to Earth as it speeds through each layer of the atmosphere. Include details of what is happening to the shuttle for each layer. **1.** Draw the space shuttle entering the exosphere. **2.** Draw the space shuttle entering the thermosphere. **3.** Draw the space shuttle entering the mesosphere. **4.** Draw the space shuttle entering the stratosphere. **5.** Finally, draw the space shuttle entering the troposphere and landing on a runway. Write a sentence or paragraph about your pictures on the back.

1.

2.

3.

4.

5.

School-Home Connection: Have students take this page home to share with family members. They can use this page to tell about the five layers of the atmosphere.

Lesson 2

What Is Weather?

1 Build Background

Access Prior Knowledge

When to Use	Proficiency Levels
Before introducing the lesson 15 minutes	✔ Beginning ✔ Intermediate Advanced

Give students an opportunity to use sentences as they talk about their personal experiences related to weather. Have them discuss rain and thunderstorms, snow and hail, and related phenomena such as tornadoes and hurricanes. Encourage them to consider how weather forecasters for newspapers or on TV predict the weather. Have them compare and contrast these forecasts to weather forecasts in their country of origin.

Preteach Lesson Vocabulary

> air pressure, relative humidity, front, climate

List the vocabulary words on the board.

Have students look at pages 379–384 and locate the vocabulary words. Then:

- Point to the words *relative humidity* on the board and have the class read the words with you. Explain that *relative humidity* compares how much water vapor is in the air to the total amount of water vapor that could be in the air.

- Point to the words *air pressure* and have students say the words with you. Explain that *air pressure* refers to the weight of the air pressing on a unit of area.

- Point to the word *front*. Have students suggest different meanings for the word *front*. Explain that a weather *front* is the boundary where two air masses collide.

- Finally, point to the word *climate* and have students say the word with you. Explain that *climate* refers to the average of all weather conditions, including temperature, wind speed, and precipitation, in an area over a period of time.

Build Fluency

Have students work in pairs. Model dialogues by completing questions and answers such as the following:

What is a _____? It's the boundary between two air masses that come together. (*front*)

What does _____ mean? It means all weather conditions in an area over a period of time. (*climate*)

© Harcourt

② Scaffold the Content

Preview the Lesson

Ask students to point to the title on page 376 as you read it aloud. Explain to them that they will find the answer to this question in the lesson. Have students discuss the picture.

- Next, ask students to look at the pictures on pages 377–384 and tell what is happening in the pictured images.
- Point out various things that influence the weather, such as ocean currents and winds blowing warm and cool air.
- Ask students what they know about types of clouds. Have them describe or draw the different types of clouds with which they may be familiar.

Investigate, p. 377

- Write the words *increase* and *decrease* on the board and ask for volunteers to read the words aloud. Then, have the rest of the class read the words with you. Ask students whether the words on page 377 are used as nouns or verbs. *(verbs)*
- Ask students to describe what the words *increase* and *decrease* mean. Elicit or explain that they mean *to become greater* and *to become smaller*. Remind students that properties other than size can increase and decrease.
- Have a volunteer read question 2 where both *increase* and *decrease* appear. After the activity help students conclude which term applies to their observations.

Modify Instruction—Multilevel Strategies

Background/Experience Direct students' attention back to the words *relative humidity*. Ask students if they remember the math term *ratio*. Elicit or explain that it is the relationship in amount or size between two or more things. Explain that the words *comparison* or *proportion* can also be used to describe *ratio*. Discuss that *relative humidity* is the ratio of the amount of water vapor in the air to the greatest amount possible.

Beginning Ask students to point to words in the text such as *air masses*, *weather*, and *humidity* as you name them. Have them say the words with you.

Intermediate Ask students simple questions to elicit one-word answers, such as: What is the boundary between two air masses? *(a front)* Model how to answer in complete sentences, such as: A front is the boundary between air masses.

Advanced Ask students to read aloud the section **Weather Fronts** on pages 380–381. Have them sum up each paragraph by describing the main idea using the most important details. Their summaries should include descriptions of warm fronts, cold fronts, and stationary fronts.

For All Students Work with students to develop a list of factors that influence global winds and climate.

Extend

Have students complete the **Show What You Know** activity on page 153 to demonstrate their understanding of the weather and weather patterns.

③ Apply and Assess

Mapping Weather Factors

When to Use With Reading Review p. 385 20 minutes	Proficiency Levels ✔ Beginning ✔ Intermediate ✔ Advanced

Materials: copies of Mercator projection maps of the world

- Have students work in groups of three to five to create a map showing weather factors in different regions on Earth.

- Suggest that each member of each group illustrate and/or label a different type of information, such as ocean currents, global winds, temperature ranges, and regions of heavy rainfall.

- Have students add labels that explain how the various factors influence weather in a region.

- Have the groups give their map a title and then display their work on the wall in an area titled: *Mapping Weather Factors.*

Informal Assessment

Beginning	Intermediate	Advanced
Say one of the weather-related terms from the lesson, such as fog or cirrus cloud. Ask individual students to point to illustrations in their text that show the term. Or you may point to some of these illustrations and ask students to identify them.	Have each student complete a sentence or create a sentence that describes one or more concepts of the lesson. *(Answers will vary but may include: A stationary front is a front that is not moving.)*	Have each student describe why thunderstorms occur. *(Answers will vary but may include: Thunderstorms are caused when cold air masses move very quickly and push up a lot of warm air.)*

Name _____

Date _____

Complete a Weather Word Web

Choose words from the box at the top of the page to complete the *Weather* word web. In each box, write a sentence that gives some information about the word in the box.

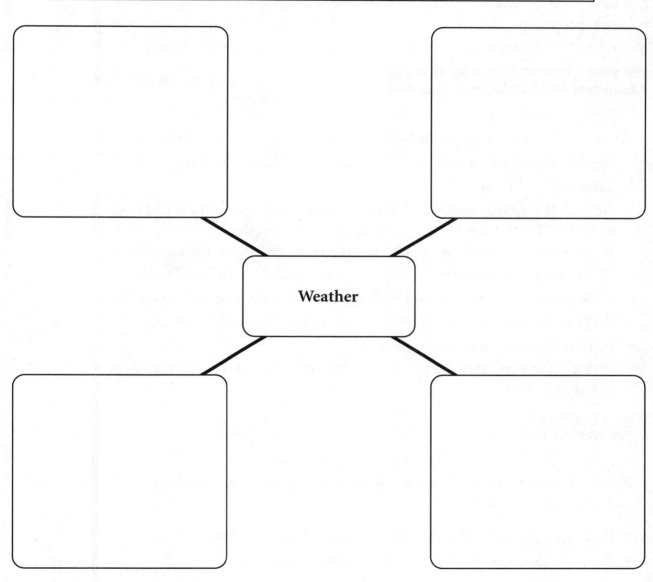

work	humidity	front	friction
thunder	magnetism	plants	air

Weather

School-Home Connection: Have students take this page home to share with family members. They can use this page to tell about weather and the factors that affect weather.

© Harcourt

How Can You Track Severe Storms?

① Build Background

Access Prior Knowledge

When to Use	Proficiency Levels
Before introducing the lesson 15 minutes	✔ Beginning ✔ Intermediate Advanced

Write the words *thunderstorm*, *hurricane*, *tornado*, and *blizzard* on the board. Give students an opportunity to tell what they know about each type of storm. List their ideas on the board below each word. Ask volunteers to suggest how weather forecasters know when a certain kind of storm will form. Some students may choose to draw pictures of instruments meteorologists might use.

Preteach Lesson Vocabulary

> thunderstorm, tornado, hurricane, blizzard

List the vocabulary words on the board.

Have students look at pages 390–394 and locate the vocabulary. Then:

- Point to the word *thunderstorm*. Explain that it is a strong storm with rain, lightning, and thunder.

- Point to the word *hurricane* on the board and ask for a volunteer to read the word aloud. Then have the rest of the class read the word with you. Ask students if they know the meaning of the word *hurricane*. Explain that it is a large storm with rotating winds that usually starts in tropical areas.

- Point to the word *blizzard* and have the class read the word with you. Explain that a *blizzard* is a winter storm with strong winds and blowing snow.

- Point to the word *tornado* and have the class say the word aloud with you. Explain that a *tornado* is a powerful spinning wind that usually forms from a thunderstorm.

Build Fluency

Have students write *thunderstorm*, *tornado*, *hurricane*, and *blizzard* on separate index cards. Give a definition of each term and have students hold up the matching card.

What is a strong storm with rain, lightning, and thunder? *(thunderstorm)*

What is a powerful tropical storm with rotating winds? *(hurricane)*

What is a winter storm with strong winds and blowing snow? *(blizzard)*

What is a powerful spinning wind that forms from a thunderstorm? *(tornado)*

© Harcourt

② Scaffold the Content

Preview the Lesson

When to Use	Proficiency Levels
With pp. 386–394	✔ Beginning
⏱ 20 minutes	✔ Intermediate
	✔ Advanced

Ask students to point to the title on page 386 as you read it aloud. Explain that they will find answers to this question in the lesson. Have students discuss the picture.

- Next, ask students to look at the pictures on pages 387–394 and tell what is happening in the pictures.
- Discuss with students the equipment that scientists, such as meteorologists, use to study the weather and make weather forecasts. Ask them if they have ever seen or heard of weather balloons or weather satellites.
- Use the images on page 394 to introduce the words *hypothermia* and *frostbite*.

Investigate, p. 387

- Give students the opportunity to read the materials list and the procedure.
- Focus your discussion on words with multiple meanings such as *plot* and *depression*. Be sure that students understand that in this instance *plot* is a verb meaning to use latitude and longitude information to mark locations on a graph. *Depression* refers to a type of weather disturbance.
- Ask students what they think *tropical* means. Model how to look up the word in a dictionary. Ask students to read the different meanings and ask which meaning applies more to how the word *tropical* is used on page 387.

Modify Instruction—Multilevel Strategies

Language and Vocabulary Write the word *thunderstorm* on the board and ask for a volunteer to read the word aloud. Then have students say the word with you. Ask whether the word is a noun or a verb. Elicit that it is a noun and that it is a compound word made up of the words *thunder* and *storm*. Use the word in a sentence and have volunteers come up with sentences of their own using the word *thunderstorm*. Discuss the different meanings of the word *track* as a noun (*railroad track, dirt track*), and as a verb (*track a storm*).

Beginning Ask students to repeat the words *meteorologists, thunderstorms,* and *cumulonimbus* after you. Then have them find the words in the text.

Intermediate Ask students simple questions to elicit one-word answers, such as: What is a strong storm with thunder, lightning, and rain? (*a thunderstorm*) Model how to answer in complete sentences, such as: A thunderstorm is a strong storm with thunder, lightning, and rain.

Advanced Ask students to read aloud the section **Blizzards** on page 394. Have them write a paragraph that summarizes the information. Their summaries should include descriptions of what *frostbite* and *hypothermia* are.

For All Students Continue the lesson by discussing the types of storms likely to occur in the students' region of the country, why it is important to pay attention to weather forecasts, and what precautions people can take in the event of an approaching storm.

Extend

Have students complete the **Show What You Know** activity on page 157 to demonstrate their understanding of storms.

③ Apply and Assess

Make a Storm Warning Book

When to Use	Proficiency Levels
With Reading Review p. 395	✔ Beginning
🕐 20 minutes	✔ Intermediate
	✔ Advanced

- Divide the class into four groups to produce a Storm Warning Book. Assign each group one type of storm—thunderstorm, tornado, hurricane, or blizzard. Each group should research and find illustrations and information on their type of storm in encyclopedias, magazines, or on the Internet.

- Each group should prepare four pages for the book: a page that describes the type of storm and the factors that cause it to form; a page containing a map showing where the type of storm is likely to form; a page of labeled images of the storm and its effects on people and objects; and a page of safety tips—what to do (and not to do) during such a storm.

- Assemble the pages produced by the groups. Have a volunteer create a cover.

Informal Assessment

Beginning	Intermediate	Advanced
Name a type of storm and have individual students point to illustrations or diagrams of tornadoes, thunderstorms, hurricanes, or blizzards depicted on some pages of their text. Or you may point to some of these illustrations and help students identify each one.	Have each student write or dictate one sentence to describe each type of storm. (*Answers will vary but may include: A blizzard is a large winter storm.*)	Have each student write a paragraph that compares and contrasts different types of storms. (*Answers will vary but may include: Tornadoes and hurricanes both have rotating winds, but hurricanes form in tropical areas.*)

Name _____

Date _____

Identify Storms

Draw a line from each definition on the left to its corresponding word on the right.

A violently rotating column of air   blizzard

A large rotating tropical storm   hurricane

A strong winter storm   tornado

A scientist who studies the weather   thunderstorm

A storm with rain and lightning   meteorologist

School-Home Connection: Have students take this page home to share with family members. They can use this page to tell about the different types of storms.

11 The Universe— Near and Far

Develop Scientific Concepts and Vocabulary

In this chapter, students will learn how the sun, moon, and Earth interact and what causes the phases of the moon. Students will also learn about celestial bodies in the solar system, and what is beyond our solar system.

Preview Scientific Principles

Walk through the chapter with students, pausing to read aloud or to have volunteers read aloud the four questions that are lesson titles. Encourage students to briefly discuss each question and to tell what they already know that might help them answer the questions.

When to Use With Chapter Opener	Proficiency Levels
🕐 25 minutes	✔ Beginning ✔ Intermediate ✔ Advanced

Lesson 1: What Are Some Earth-Moon-Sun Interactions?

- Have students draw a picture of Earth and of the sun. Lead students in a discussion about differences between Earth and the sun.
- Show students an illustration of the solar system. Invite volunteers to identify the sun, Earth, and Earth's moon.

Lesson 2: What Causes the Phases of the Moon?

- Have students draw pictures of different ways the moon can look in the night sky. Encourage students to share their pictures with one another.
- Explain that all of the different shapes of the moon, from a round circle to a small crescent, are called *phases*.

Lesson 3: What Is In the Solar System?

- Write the word *solar* on the board. Tell students that this word is derived from the Latin word *sol*, meaning "sun." Then explain that the word *solar* means "coming from or having to do with the sun."
- Show students a picture of a solar system. Explain that ours is not the only solar system. A solar system is one or more suns and the planets that move around the sun(s).

Lesson 4: What Is Beyond the Solar System?

- Point to the door of the classroom. Ask students to draw or describe what is *beyond* the door. Repeat this activity with another object until you are sure that all of your students understand the meaning of the word *beyond*.

Practice

Ask students to write the vocabulary words on large index cards, one term per card. Encourage a class discussion so students can talk about what they know about the terms. On the back of the cards, have them write or draw as much information as they can about that term. Ask them to include any questions they have about its meaning or use.

As students learn more about the terms during the chapter, they can update or correct the cards as needed. They can use the cards as a study guide or to create a vocabulary game.

Apply

Copy the poem and word bank from the chart below on the board. Tell students to fill in the blanks with a word from the word bank. They should choose words that rhyme with the last word in the previous line of the poem. After students have completed their poems, have a volunteer read his or her poem aloud to the class.

Solar System Poem

It would be fun
to go see the _____. (sun)
But I would just as soon
go see the _____, (moon)
and look at the girth
of my planet, _____. (Earth)

comet, Earth, moon, phase, planet, solar system, sun, star

What Are Some Earth-Moon-Sun Interactions?

① Build Background

Access Prior Knowledge

When to Use	Proficiency Levels
Before introducing the lesson 25 minutes	✔ Beginning ✔ Intermediate ✔ Advanced

Have students draw a picture of the sun, Earth, and moon on a piece of paper.

- Tell students that one of the bodies moves around another, and see if students know which body you are referring to. If students do not know, explain that Earth moves around the sun.
- Have students draw an arrow on their paper indicating Earth's movement. *(counterclockwise)*
- Repeat this activity with Earth and the moon.

Preteach Lesson Vocabulary

rotation, axis, revolution, eclipse, tides

Materials: video clip of the tide coming in and going out

List the vocabulary words on the board.

Read each word aloud to students. Ask students which two words sound most similar. *(rotation and revolution)* Then:

- Have a volunteer read the definitions of the words *rotation* and *revolution* to the class. Explain the difference between the two motions, using a pencil to show that an object can rotate and revolve at the same time. Then have students pantomime the two different movements described by the terms. Point out that they can rotate alone, but need a partner or another object to revolve.
- Tell students that the word *eclipse* comes from the Greek word *ekleipsis*, which means "to fail to appear." Have students use this information to explain what they think may happen during an eclipse of the sun. *(Students may say that the sun stops appearing in the sky during an eclipse.)*
- Use a video clip to explain what happens during rising and falling tides.

Build Fluency

Write the following sentence on the board: _____ revolves around _____. Instruct students to complete the sentence. Challenge students to write as many different versions of the sentence as they can. *(Sample answers: Earth revolves around the sun; the moon revolves around Earth; planets revolve around the sun.)*

② Scaffold the Content

Preview the Lesson

When to Use With pp. 404–412	Proficiency Levels
⏱ 35 minutes	✔ Beginning ✔ Intermediate ✔ Advanced

- Have students read the title of the section on page 406 and decide which of the images on pages 406–407 describes Earth's movement during a day and a year.

- Ask a volunteer to read the title of the section that begins on page 408. Tell students to look at the diagrams of the sun and Earth on pages 408–409 and write any questions they might have about what causes seasons.

- Have students skim the titles and images in the rest of the lesson. Ask volunteers to tell what two other topics they will learn about in the lesson. *(eclipses and tides)*

Investigate, p. 405

Write the word *planet* on the board. Display a picture of planets in the solar system. Point to a planet and say, "This is the planet _____." Stress the word *planet*. Then:

- Explain to students that the word *planetary* means "having to do with a planet."
- Tell students that the word *orbit* comes from the Latin word *orbis*, meaning "circle." Draw a dot on the board and draw a circle around the dot. Trace the path of the circle with your finger. Explain that you are *orbiting* the dot.
- Draw and label an *ellipse* with *two foci* on the board. Have students repeat the words. Discuss the relationship between the *foci* (plural of *focus*) and the shape of the ellipse.

Modify Instruction—Multilevel Strategies

Background/Experience Lead students in a discussion of how the movement of Earth and the moon affects their daily lives. You may want to start the discussion by having students relate the ways humans measure time in days, months, and years to specific movements of both Earth and the moon. Then ask students to hypothesize how their idea of time might be different if they lived on another planet such as Mars.

Beginning Have students draw a diagram showing Earth's relative position around the sun for each of the four seasons. Next to each season, students should draw a picture showing the type of weather experienced in their area during that time of year.

Intermediate Have students research time zones. Ask students to choose a place that they have been to (or would like to go to) that is in a different time zone than the one in which they live. Instruct students to draw pictures of what people in their chosen place might be doing at 12:00 P.M. in the student's time zone.

Advanced Have students who have seen tidal changes or an eclipse write a description of the event. If students have not experienced these events, have them research one event and write a description of what they think the event would be like.

For All Students Have students build a mobile that can be used to model how Earth moves around the sun and how the moon moves around Earth.

Extend

Have the students complete the **Show What You Know** activity on page 163 to demonstrate their understanding of the movements of Earth and the moon.

③ Apply and Assess

Modeling Eclipses

When to Use With Reading Review p. 413	Proficiency Levels
🕐 30 minutes	✔ Beginning ✔ Intermediate ✔ Advanced

Materials: balls of various sizes

Organize students into groups.

- Give each group a collection of balls of various sizes. Have students label balls to represent Earth, the moon, and the sun.
- Instruct the groups to use their balls to model how a solar eclipse and a lunar eclipse occur.
- Have students use their models to try to explain why a lunar eclipse does not happen every month.

Informal Assessment

Beginning	Intermediate	Advanced
Have students stand up. Tell them that their chair represents the sun and they represent Earth. Then have students enact Earth's revolution. *(Students should walk in circles around their chairs.)* Next ask students to enact Earth's rotation. *(Students should turn in circles in place.)*	Have students draw a picture of how Earth moves over the course of one day. *(Students should draw one rotation.)* Then have students draw a picture of how Earth moves over the course of one year. *(Students should draw one counterclockwise revolution of Earth around the sun.)* Have students label Earth's axis on both of their drawings.	Have students write a short paragraph explaining why many places on Earth experience seasons. *(Students' explanations should focus on the fact that Earth is tilted on its axis and this causes the intensity of the sun's rays to vary over the course of the year in certain areas.)*

© Harcourt

Name _____

Date _____

Movements of Earth and the Moon

Draw and label arrows indicating:

1. Earth's rotation
2. Earth's revolution
3. The moon's revolution

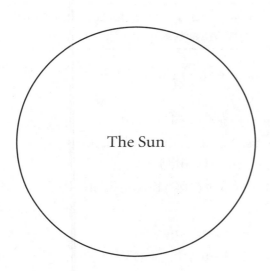

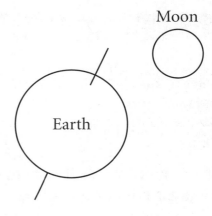

Moon

Earth

The Sun

School-Home Connection: Have children take this page home to share with family members. They can use this page to tell about the movements of Earth and the moon.

2 What Causes the Phases of the Moon?

① Build Background

Access Prior Knowledge

When to Use	Proficiency Levels
Before introducing the lesson 15 minutes	✔ Beginning ✔ Intermediate ✔ Advanced

Materials: photographs of lunar phases

Ask students if the moon in the night sky always looks the same. Students will most likely know that the moon changes in appearance. Ask students to describe or draw this change. After students have completed their descriptions, show students photographs of different lunar phases.

Preteach Lesson Vocabulary

> **new moon, first quarter, full moon, third quarter**

List the vocabulary words on the board.

Explain to students that all of the vocabulary terms refer to a phase of the moon. Then:

- Write the word *quarter* on the board. Ask students to describe what they think of when they hear the word *quarter*. Most students will say they think of a quarter coin. Explain to them that a 25 cent coin is called a quarter because 25 cents is a quarter, or one-fourth, of a dollar *(100 cents)*. Then write *quarter* = ¼ on the board.
- Ask students what a quarter of an hour would be. *(15 minutes)*
- Draw a box on the board and separate the box into four sections. Write one of the vocabulary terms in each of the boxes. Explain to students that lunar phases are separated into four main quarters. Each quarter represents ¼ of the lunar cycle.

Build Fluency

Have students work with a partner. Each team should draw the phases of the moon on four index cards. As one partner holds up a card, the other partner says the name of that phase. Have students reverse roles so that both students get a chance to say the terms.

② Scaffold the Content

Preview the Lesson

When to Use
With pp. 414–418

🕐 35 minutes

Proficiency Levels
✔ Beginning
✔ Intermediate
✔ Advanced

- Have students turn to p. 417 in their textbooks. Call out different phases of the moon and have students point to the named phase. Remind students that the moon is a sphere, so when they see half of the disk, they are really seeing a quarter of the moon. Point out the words *gibbous* and *crescent* in the captions. Ask students what they think these words mean. Elicit or explain the shape to which each word refers.

- Have a volunteer read the section title on page 418. Then tell students to look at the pictures. Point out similarities and differences between the phases of the moon and Venus.

Investigate, p. 415

- Give students time to read the materials list and the procedure, and to study the pictures in the Investigate.

- Display a calendar for the current month. Be sure students know what the word *calendar* means.

- If necessary, help students locate the moon phase information in the newspaper.

Modify Instruction—Multilevel Strategies

Language and Vocabulary Have students start their own moon log. They should use local newspapers to determine when the moon will rise in the evening.

- In their logs, they should record the time and date they observed the moon and make a drawing of what the moon looked like and where it was in the sky.

- If possible, have students continue their observations for at least a month so that they will be able to see a full lunar cycle.

- After students complete their observations, have them correctly label at least four of the phases they drew using the lesson vocabulary words.

Beginning Have students make an illustrated dictionary of moon phases. Next to the term for each lunar phase, students should draw a picture of what that phase looks like.

Intermediate Have students use a flashlight and a baseball to model the lunar cycle. As they model a new moon, first quarter moon, full moon, and third quarter moon, have them call out the name of the phase.

Advanced Have students write a description of each lunar phase, relating the phase to the positions of the moon, the sun, and Earth.

For All Students Have students make a flipbook showing the lunar cycle. Students should show their flipbook to the class. The class should attempt to call out the names of the phases as they see them.

Extend

Have the students complete the Show What You Know activity on page 167 to demonstrate their understanding of lunar phases.

③ Apply and Assess

Earth's Phases

When to Use	Proficiency Levels
With Reading Review p. 419	✔ Beginning
	✔ Intermediate
🕐 20 minutes	✔ Advanced

Materials: flashlight, two balls

Ask students if they think Earth would appear to have phases to somebody standing on the moon. Students should write down their hypotheses.

- Supply students with two balls and a flashlight in order to test their hypotheses. Make sure students understand that the flashlight should represent the sun and the two balls represent Earth and the moon.

- Have students model the movements of Earth and the moon and observe how the light from the flashlight falls on the model.

- After students complete their experiments have them determine whether their hypotheses were valid.

Informal Assessment

Beginning	Intermediate	Advanced
Have students draw the lunar cycle. *(Students drawings should resemble the photographs on page 417.)*	Show students pictures of the following phases and have students call out the correct name for each phase: new moon, crescent moon, first quarter moon, full moon, gibbous moon, and third quarter moon.	Have students make a graphic organizer that shows the cyclical nature of the lunar cycle. Students should include information about how long the cycle takes. *(29 days)*

© Harcourt

Lunar Phases

Draw a picture of the named lunar phase in each of the boxes below.

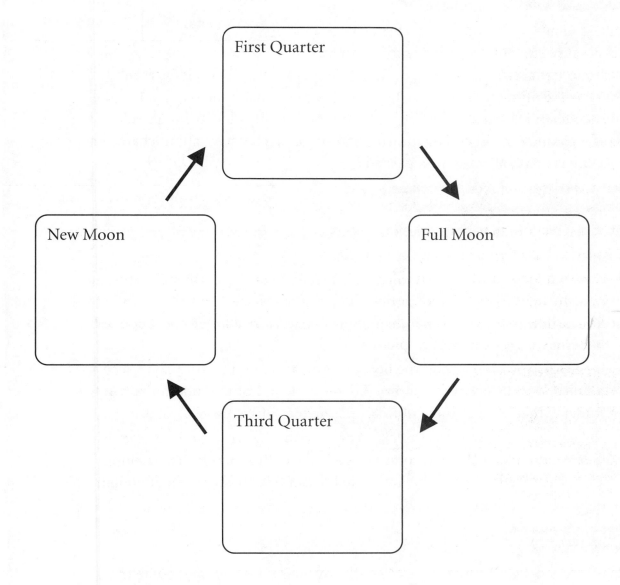

First Quarter

New Moon

Full Moon

Third Quarter

School-Home Connection: Have children take this page home to share
with family members. They can use this page to tell about how the moon goes
through phases.

What Is In the Solar System?

① Build Background

Access Prior Knowledge

When to Use	Proficiency Levels
Before introducing the lesson	✔ Beginning
⏱ 25 minutes	✔ Intermediate
	✔ Advanced

Ask students to draw a solar system. Check to make sure students' drawings show planets or other celestial bodies orbiting a sun (or multiple suns). If students aren't already aware of it, tell them that ours is only one of many solar systems in the universe. Then ask students to list the names of as many planets in our solar system as they know of. Elicit any information students may have about characteristics of the individual planets they listed.

Preteach Lesson Vocabulary

asteroid, satellite, meteor, comet

Materials: pictures of various celestial objects

List the vocabulary words on the board.

Show students pictures of asteroids, meteors, and comets. Help students match up the pictures with the correct terms. Once students have correctly identified the object in each image, go through the pictures once more and have students call out the term that goes with each picture. Then:

- Write the word *satellite* on the board. Show students a picture of a telecommunication satellite. Then show students a picture of the moon. Explain to students that both of these objects are satellites of Earth.

- Tell students that the word *satellite* comes from the Latin word *satelles*, which means "attendant." Have a volunteer read the definition of *satellite* aloud. Then have students discuss why a satellite can be considered an attendant of the body it orbits.

Build Fluency

Have students go through pages 422–425 of their textbooks and recite the names of the inner and outer planets by completing the following sentence: Planet _____ is a satellite of the sun.

© Harcourt

② Scaffold the Content

Preview the Lesson

- Have students skim the lesson. Invite volunteers to read the titles of each section.
- As you say each of the terms in the titles—*inner planet, outer planet, asteroid, meteor*, and *comet*—have students locate and point to a picture in the lesson that relates to that term.

Investigate, p. 421

Write the word *scale* on the board.

- Tell students that the word *scale* has many different meanings. Show students pictures of fishes and reptiles and point out the scales.
- A *scale* can also be an instrument used for measuring weight. Show students an example of this kind of scale.
- A third meaning of *scale* is the meaning used in the Investigate. In this meaning, scale is a proportion used in determining a relationship (in this case, distance). Show students various scales, such as those on maps, globes, or model planes.

Modify Instruction—Multilevel Strategies

Comprehensible Input Organize students into groups. Assign one or two planets to each student.

- Each student should compile a list of facts about his or her assigned planets.
- Instruct the groups to play a game: a student reads a fact about the planet he or she researched, he or she continues to read facts until the students have guessed which planet is being described, repeat the process until all of the students have taken turns reading clues.

Beginning Have students draw a diagram of the solar system. The diagram should include the following objects: the sun, all of the planets, asteroids, meteors, and comets. Make sure students place all of the objects in the correct positions.

Intermediate Have students choose a planet, asteroid, or comet and make a model of that celestial body. Students should label their models. Display the models for the rest of the class to view.

Advanced Have students make a booklet entitled, "Guide to the Solar System." The booklets should be illustrated and give information about all of the objects found in the solar system.

For All Students Have students choose a planet or comet. Students should make a poster about their chosen celestial bodies. Display the posters in class.

Have the students complete the **Show What You Know** activity on page 171 to demonstrate their understanding of the planets in the solar system.

③ Apply and Assess

Moving Model of the Solar System

When to Use With Reading Review p. 429	Proficiency Levels
⏱ 20 minutes	✔ Beginning ✔ Intermediate ✔ Advanced

Go to an open area such as a physical education field. Have students use their bodies to make a moving model of the solar system.

- One student can represent the sun.
- Each planet can be represented by a student.
- Group students together to represent the asteroid belt. Extra students can be comets and moons.
- After students are correctly arranged, have them begin to move in their orbits.
- Students may wear signs identifying the planets they are representing.

Informal Assessment

Beginning	Intermediate	Advanced
Show students a picture of a comet. Ask: Is this a meteor? *(no)* Is this a planet? *(no)* Is this a comet? *(yes)* Is this a satellite? *(yes)*	Have students draw and label a diagram of the solar system. Students should include all of the planets, the asteroid belt, and at least one comet.	Have students write a short paragraph describing how the inner planets are different from the outer planets. *(Answers will vary.)*

Name _____

Date _____

Listing the Planets

List the planets in order from closest to farthest from the sun.

Inner Planets

1. _____

2. _____

3. _____

4. _____

Outer Planets

5. _____

6. _____

7. _____

8. _____

9. _____

10. _____

Which of the planets listed above may *not* actually be a planet? _____

School-Home Connection: Have children take this page home to share with family members. They can use this page to tell about the planets in the solar system.

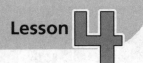
What Is Beyond the Solar System?

1 Build Background

Access Prior Knowledge

When to Use	Proficiency Levels
Before introducing the lesson 25 minutes	✔ Beginning ✔ Intermediate ✔ Advanced

Materials: a picture of a galaxy

Show students a picture of a galaxy. Invite volunteers to answer the following questions:

- What is the name of this structure? *(a galaxy)*
- What is a galaxy made of? *(many stars, or many solar systems)*
- Are there many galaxies in the universe? *(yes)*

Preteach Lesson Vocabulary

> **galaxy**

Write the vocabulary word on the board.

Pronounce the word aloud and have students repeat the word after you. Then:

- Have students turn to page 436 and look at the picture of the Milky Way Galaxy. Tell students that Earth and the solar system that Earth belongs to are found in the Milky Way Galaxy.
- Tell students that the term *galaxy* is a noun. The adjective form of *galaxy* is the word *galactic*, which means, "having to do with a galaxy." Have students use each word in a sentence.
- You may also wish to introduce other technical terms, such as *nebula*, *supernova*, and *Magellanic*. Point out that *nebula* is related to the Spanish word *nebulosa*. *Supernova* is a compound word, in which *super* means very large. Ask students who they think the Magellanic Clouds might be named after *(Magellan.)*

Build Fluency

Ask students the following questions and have students answer "stars" to each question: What is a galaxy composed of? What can be seen in the night sky? What begins as a nebula? What are suns? What is composed of glowing gases? The collapse of what causes black holes?

© Harcourt

② Scaffold the Content

Preview the Lesson

When to Use
With pp. 430–438

🕐 35 minutes

Proficiency Levels
✔ Beginning
✔ Intermediate
✔ Advanced

Have students examine the photograph on page 430 of their textbooks. Explain to students that they are looking at the birth of a star. Ask a volunteer to describe what is meant by the word *birth. (the beginning or start of)* Then:

- Tell students that they will learn more about how stars are born and how they die in this lesson.
- Instruct students to write down any questions they have about stars. Students should write down the answers to their questions as they go through the lesson.

Investigate, p. 431

Bring to class a lamp that can be dimmed. Turn the lamp on and ask students to describe how bright the lamp is.

- Increase or decrease the brightness of the lamp and ask students: Is the lamp now brighter or less bright than before?
- Repeat this activity several times. Then tell students that they were describing the *brightness* of the lamp.

Modify Instruction—Multilevel Strategies

Language and Vocabulary Remind students that comparative words often end in *-er*. For example, the comparative form of *big* is *bigger*. Superlatives often end in *-est*. The superlative form of *big* is *biggest*. Have students find other comparatives and superlatives in their textbooks from page 433 to 436. *(page 433: brightest, dimmer, hottest, coolest, greatest, dimmest, least, brighter, hotter; page 434: faster, biggest, shortest; page 435: longer, longest; page 436: closest)*

Beginning Have students order the following celestial bodies from smallest to biggest: galaxy, red giant, supernova, universe, and white dwarf.

Intermediate Ask students the following questions: What type of star is bigger than the sun? What is the smallest type of star? Will the universe be bigger tomorrow than it is today? Is the universe getting bigger or smaller?

Advanced Have students write a short paragraph that describes the Big Bang. Students should use at least three comparative or superlative words in their paragraphs.

© Harcourt

For All Students Have students turn to pages 432–433 and examine the H-R diagram. Ask students to name what type of star is the biggest star, what type of star is the smallest star, what type of star is the brightest star, what type of star is the hottest star, and what type of star is the coolest star.

Extend

Have the students complete the **Show What You Know** activity on page 175 to demonstrate their understanding of the life cycle of stars.

③ Apply and Assess

Making a Movie of the Life of a Star

When to Use	Proficiency Levels
With Reading Review p. 439 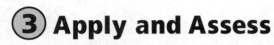 25 minutes	✔ Beginning ✔ Intermediate ✔ Advanced

Organize students into groups for this major project. Instruct the groups to use drawing paper, a computer program, or a video camera to create a "movie" that shows the Big Bang and the life cycle of a star that formed shortly after the Big Bang. Students should first draw a story board that shows the "scenes" in their movie. They should write a script that a narrator can read along with the movie. Have groups show their completed movies to the class.

Informal Assessment

Beginning	Intermediate	Advanced
Ask students to make a drawing of a galaxy. Have students point to the area of the galaxy that has the oldest stars. *(Students should point to the center of the galaxy.)* Ask students to point to the area of the galaxy that has the youngest stars. *(Students should point to the tips of the galaxy's arms.)*	Ask students the following questions: Is a neutron star bigger or smaller than a supergiant? *(smaller)* What is the name for a huge system of stars? *(a galaxy)* What theory describes the origins of the universe? *(the Big Bang Theory)*	Have students write a short story entitled, "The Story of the Universe." Students should include information about the origins of the universe, and what is taking place in the universe today. *(Stories will vary.)*

Name _____

Date _____

Life Cycle of a Star

Number each of the following events in the order they occur. Then draw a picture of the event described in the box.

_____ Birth of a Star

_____ A Neutron Star Forms

_____ A Supergiant Forms

_____ A Supernova Forms

School-Home Connection: Have children take this page home to share with family members. They can use this page to tell about the life cycle of stars.

12 Atoms and Elements

Develop Scientific Concepts and Vocabulary

In this chapter, students will define atoms, elements, and compounds. They will be introduced to the Periodic Table of Elements, which organizes elements by their atomic number. They will also learn about the states of matter and what causes a substance to change from one state of matter to another.

Preview Scientific Principles

Walk through the chapter with students, pausing to read aloud or to have volunteers read aloud the three questions that are lesson titles. Encourage students to briefly discuss each question and to tell what they already know that might help them answer the questions.

When to Use With Chapter Opener	Proficiency Levels
30 minutes	✔ Beginning ✔ Intermediate ✔ Advanced

Lesson 1: What Is Matter Composed Of?

- Ask students to imagine dividing something in half so many times that the pieces become so small they can't divide them anymore. Tell them to think of an *atom* as that remaining particle.

- Explain that atoms are extremely small. Ask students to think of one crystal of salt and guess if it contains about one atom, one thousand atoms, or one billion atoms. Students may be surprised to learn that there are billions of atoms in that one crystal.

Lesson 2: What Are Elements and Compounds?

- Display or distribute copies of the Periodic Table. Explain that all of the substances named in the table are *elements* and that elements are made of one kind of atom.

- Have students take turns reading element names and identifying familiar ones. Ask them to describe what they know about those elements.

- Explain that when two or more different elements combine, they make compounds.

© Harcourt

Lesson 3: What Are the States of Matter?

- Review the different states of matter—solid, liquid, and gas—and why substances change states. Explain that adding or removing heat can change the *state of matter*.
- Help students match the terms evaporation (liquid to a gas), condensation (gas to liquid), freezing (liquid to solid), and melting (solid to a liquid) to the state changes.

Practice

- Write the following pairs of words on the board: *nuclear: nucleus, electron: electric, atom: atomic, elementary: element, metallic: metal*. Discuss the relationship between the terms in each pair.
- Have students use the words in sentences to illustrate their different, but related, meanings.

Apply

- Display the lines below on the board or chart paper. Read them with students.
- Invite volunteers to underline the element in each line.
- Refer students to the Periodic Table. Have them find each element on it.
- Invite students to write their own examples of elements used in everyday life and share them with the group.

Elements in Everyday Life

You have an iron frying pan.
We played with the tin soldiers.
Our water flows through copper pipes.
I eat calcium to build strong bones.
The neon shines in bright lights at night.
My tooth has a silver filling.
My bracelet is made of gold.
Sulfur helps light matches.
I watched the mercury rise in the thermometer.
I breathe oxygen in the air.

What Is Matter Composed Of?

① Build Background

Access Prior Knowledge

When to Use	Proficiency Levels
Before introducing the lesson 20 minutes	✔ Beginning ✔ Intermediate ✔ Advanced

Ask students to tell what they know about *atoms*. Students may know that atoms are the smallest building blocks of matter that have the properties of that substance or that atoms break down into smaller particles called protons, neutrons, and electrons. Have students draw a model of what they think an atom looks like. Tell students that they will learn about the *atomic number* of a substance. Ask them to guess what the atomic number might be.

Preteach Lesson Vocabulary

> **atom, proton, nucleus, neutron, electron, atomic number**

List the vocabulary words on the board.

- Have students find *atom* on page 452 and review the definition of the term.
- Write the following prefix on the board: *sub-*. Review that it means "below" and ask volunteers to use this meaning to define *subatomic*. Summarize that subatomic particles are particles smaller than an atom. They are the particles that together form an atom.
- Have students search page 453 to identify the three subatomic particles—*proton*, *neutron*, and *electron*. Explain that protons and neutrons are found inside the *nucleus* of the atom. Ask where electrons are found. *(outside the nucleus)*
- Say that *atomic number* refers to the number of a certain subatomic particle in an atom. Ask partners to search page 453 to identify that particle. *(proton)* Ask students to define atomic number in their own words and share their definitions with the group.

Build Fluency

Have partners take turns interviewing each other with these questions and answers:

Q: What is an atom? *A: the smallest particle with the properties of a substance*

Q: What are the three subatomic particles? *A: proton, neutron, and electron*

Q: Which particles are in the nucleus? *A: proton and neutron*

Q: What is atomic number? *A: the number of protons in an atom*

② Scaffold the Content

Preview the Lesson

When to Use	Proficiency Levels
With pp. 450–456	✔ Beginning
⏱ 15 minutes	✔ Intermediate
	✔ Advanced

- Read the title on page 450 and review the meaning of *matter*. Ask students to describe the picture. Read the caption. Ask students what they can conclude about atoms from the picture and caption. Students should recognize that atoms are very, very small.

- Preview page 453 and review the three subatomic particles.

- Refer to pages 454–455. Read the section head and ask students to tell about the items on the timeline. Summarize that this section tells about different models of the atom.

- Have students read the topic heading on page 456. Explain that isotopes are varieties of atoms with the same number of protons but different numbers of neutrons.

Investigate, p. 451

- Before students begin the Investigate, write *mystery object* on the board. Ask students what a mystery is. Tell them that it is something unknown that you want to explain or understand. Ask them to share any books or movies they know that are mysteries.

- Explain that in this Investigate, students will observe a mystery object and use clues to guess what it is.

- Remind students that it is important to make drawings and keep good records of their observations.

Modify Instruction—Multilevel Strategies

Background/Experience Atoms are so small that they cannot be observed directly. This restriction makes it difficult to understand them. Learners will increase their understanding by identifying the parts of an atom and the history of its discovery.

Beginning Have students define *electron*, *neutron*, and *proton*. Ask them to write the words and definitions for each one on tag board sentence strips.

Intermediate Have students find five facts about atoms in the lesson and write them on tag board sentence strips.

Advanced Ask students to choose one of the following topics and write a paragraph about it: electrons; isotopes; the nucleus of an atom; John Dalton's atomic theory; Democritus; James Chadwick. They may need to consult an encyclopedia or other resources for information.

For All Students Have students continue to write facts about atoms on tag board sentence strips as they work through the lesson. Post the facts on a bulletin board.

Extend

Have the students complete the **Show What You Know** activity on page 181 to demonstrate their understanding of atoms.

③ Apply and Assess

Make a Dictionary

When to Use With Reading Review p. 457 🕐 20 minutes	Proficiency Levels ✔ Beginning ✔ Intermediate ✔ Advanced

Materials: small stapled books with lined pages

- Have students pick out the most important words from the lesson. Write the list on the board.

- Have small groups work together to write a definition for each term, then organize the words and definitions alphabetically in their dictionaries. Encourage them to illustrate the words, if possible.

- Ask them to design a cover and write a title for their dictionary.

- Give students time to add terms to their dictionaries as they complete the other lessons in this chapter.

Informal Assessment

Beginning	Intermediate	Advanced
Ask students to read aloud the words and definitions on the tag board strips. Have them exchange tag board strips with a partner and read them aloud. *(Answers will vary.)*	Ask students to tell you about the five facts they wrote. *(Answers will vary.)*	Ask students to write two comprehension questions about the paragraph they wrote. Then have them work in small groups, asking their questions to students and providing feedback to the other students' answers. *(Answers will vary.)*

Atomic Word Web

In each circle, write a key word or concept about atoms.

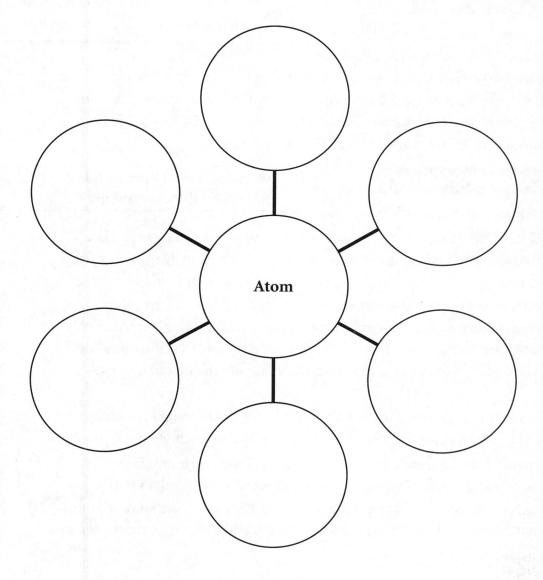

School-Home Connection: Have students take this page home to share with family members. They can use this page to tell about atoms.

What Are Elements and Compounds?

① Build Background

Access Prior Knowledge

When to Use	Proficiency Levels
Before introducing the lesson 20 minutes	✔ Beginning ✔ Intermediate Advanced

Explain that some substances are elements and others are compounds. Display a Periodic Table and ask students what they know about it. Ask how it is organized. Say that it organizes the elements. Say that some elements are metals and others are non-metals. Explain that water is a compound with the formula H_2O. Ask students what they know about the formula and what it tells about water.

Preteach Lesson Vocabulary

> **element, metal, nonmetal, periodic table, compound**

List the vocabulary words on the board.

- Have students find *element* on page 460. Explain that it means a substance made with only one kind of atom. Give examples, such as hydrogen, oxygen, gold, or sulfur.

- Ask students to find *metal* and *nonmetal* on page 461. Explain that some elements are classified as metals and some as nonmetals. Point out some of the properties of metals. Write the prefix *non-* and review that it means "not" or "no." Ask students to use this meaning to define *nonmetal* and describe the properties of a nonmetal.

- Preview the Periodic Table on pages 462 and 463. Say that the table organizes all elements by atomic number. Read the names of the first ten elements aloud.

- Write *compound* on the board. Help students list phrases with *compound*. (*compound word, compound fracture, compound microscope*) Explain that it means "things put together." Review that elements have only one kind of atom. Explain that compounds are substances that "put together" two or more atoms.

Build Fluency

Help students play the *Complete-the-Fact* game. Divide the students into two groups, one group reads the first part of the fact and the other responds with the correct ending.

Elements are...	*substances made of one kind of atom*
The Periodic Table...	*organizes the elements by atomic number*
Compounds are...	*substances that combine two or more kinds of atom*

② Scaffold the Content

Preview the Lesson

When to Use With pp. 458–466	Proficiency Levels
⏱ 15 minutes	✔ Beginning ✔ Intermediate ✔ Advanced

- Refer students to page 458. Read the title and have students discuss what they know about elements and compounds. Discuss the picture and read the caption. Ask students how they can tell that silk is a compound and not an element.

- Refer students to page 461 and preview the properties of metals. Point out that metals can conduct heat and electricity well, and form sheets and wires. Say that many, but not all, metals are shiny and have a silvery color. Ask students to describe nonmetals.

- Have students find the Periodic Table. Write *helium*, *sodium*, *gold*, and *aluminum* on the board. Help them find these elements and identify the atomic number of each.

Investigate, p. 459

- Before students begin the Investigate, explain that they will be observing and classifying different elements. Have students find the names of the elements that they will be studying—*graphite*, *sulfur*, *copper*, *iron*, and *aluminum*—on the Periodic Table. Explain that graphite is a form of carbon.

- Then have students find the categories they will use to classify the elements: *color*, *shininess*, *hardness*, *odor*, *texture*, *ability to bend*, and *attraction to a magnet*. Discuss the meanings of these categories.

Modify Instruction—Multilevel Strategies

Language and Vocabulary Knowing the names and symbols of the elements is an important step for studying elements and compounds, and later for studying chemistry. The names of the elements identify them; the symbols are used in chemical formulas. Some of the names may be familiar to students because of their everyday use. Others are unfamiliar, in part because they derive from Latin or other names. These activities will help students learn the names and symbols of common or commonly used elements.

Beginning Have students memorize the names and pronunciation of hydrogen, oxygen, carbon, aluminum, and silicon.

Intermediate Have students write the names of the first eight elements on index cards and the symbols for each on eight more cards. They can practice matching names and symbols in a Concentration game.

Advanced Have students make a three-column table listing the name, atomic number, and symbol for the first ten elements. Have them use the table to learn the names and symbols for those elements.

For All Students Have students compile a list of common elements and write the symbols for them on separate index cards. Use the cards to play a game. Ask volunteers to take turns writing a symbol on the board and have the rest of the students say what element it represents.

Extend

Have the students complete the Show What You Know activity on page 185.

③ Apply and Assess

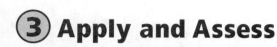

Parade of Elements

When to Use With Reading Review p. 467 ⏱ 25 minutes	Proficiency Levels ✔ Beginning ✔ Intermediate ✔ Advanced

Materials: markers, paints or colored pencils, butcher paper, string, tape

- Have each student select a different element from the Periodic Table. Have students write the name, symbol, and two or three phrases describing the element on a piece of butcher paper.

- Help students attach a string around the top of the paper so the poster can hang around their necks. Have a parade of elements so students can see the variety of elements.

- Then have students present their posters one at a time to the group and tell something about their element.

- Post the papers on a bulletin board entitled *Parade of Elements*.

Informal Assessment

Beginning	Intermediate	Advanced
Ask students to say the names of the elements they learned. *(hydrogen, oxygen, carbon, aluminum, and silicon)*	Show students a pair that includes an element name (first eight only) and a symbol. Ask if the pair matches. If it does not, ask the student to correct the name or symbol to match the pair. *(Answers will vary. Use the Periodic Table to choose pairs and check answers.)*	Say the name of an element (first ten only) and have students give the symbol or give a symbol and have students identify the name. *(Answers will vary. Use the Periodic Table to choose elements and check the symbols or vice versa.)*

Elements and Compounds Outline

Complete this outline by filling in the blanks.

I. Elements

    A. An element is made of _____.

        1. The element _____ has the symbol O.

        2. The element _____ has the atomic number 1.

        3. Elements can be classified as metals and _____.

            a. Metals

        1. conduct _____ and electricity

        2. form _____ and wires

        3. make up about _____ of all elements

            b. Nonmetals

        1. have _____ properties of metals

        2. are often _____ at room temperature

    B. Periodic Table

        1. organizes all of the _____ on Earth

        2. organizes elements by _____

II. Compounds

    A. A compound combines _____.

    B. Compounds _____ have the same properties
    as the elements that form them.

© Harcourt

School-Home Connection: Have students take this page home to share with
family members. They can use it to tell about elements and compounds.

What Are the States of Matter?

① Build Background

Access Prior Knowledge

When to Use	Proficiency Levels
Before introducing the lesson 20 minutes	✔ Beginning ✔ Intermediate Advanced

Ask students to recall the states of matter, reminding them that ice, water, and steam represent three common states of water if necessary. Discuss how states of matter change from one form to another. Explain that students will learn about a fourth state of matter called plasma and ask them to tell what they know about it. Ask students if they recall the term to describe changing a liquid to a gas (boiling) or a solid to a liquid (melting). Discuss what the boiling point or melting point temperatures of a substance might be.

Preteach Lesson Vocabulary

Materials: thermometers

> **melting point, boiling point, plasma**

List the vocabulary words on the board.

- Distribute thermometers and ask students to recall the temperature at which ice melts to liquid water. Point out that this temperature (32°F or 0°C) is the *melting point* of water. Explain that the melting point of any substance is the temperature at which the solid turns to a liquid. (This is the same temperature where the liquid turns to a solid.) Each substance has its own unique melting point.

- Repeat for the *boiling point* (liquid turns to a gas).

- Have students find these terms in their textbooks on page 472 and ask them to define each term in their own words.

- Ask students to find *plasma* on page 474. Explain that plasma is a fourth state of matter. Although it is rare on Earth, it is common in the universe. Plasma includes charged and uncharged atoms and electrons.

Build Fluency

Have students complete these sentence frames with the states of matter and say the sentences in a chanting rhythm.

_____ is one state of matter.   _____ is a second state of matter.

_____ is a third state of matter.   _____ is the fourth state of matter.

② Scaffold the Content

When to Use With pp. 468–474	Proficiency Levels
🕐 15 minutes	✔ Beginning ✔ Intermediate ✔ Advanced

Preview the Lesson

- Read the chapter title on page 468 and ask students to answer the question as well as they can. Discuss the picture and read the caption. Ask students to explain how glaciers represent three of the states of matter.

- Ask students to preview the section titles and then summarize the main topics of the lesson. Allow time for them to ask questions about unfamiliar terms.

- Have students scan the pictures and captions throughout the lesson. Ask them to describe what they see.

Investigate, p. 469

Materials: thermometer

- Before students begin the Investigate, explain that they will be observing the effect that salt has on the melting point of ice.

- Review the meaning of melting point.

- Tell students that they will be taking and recording temperature measurements every two minutes. Review how to use a thermometer.

Modify Instruction—Multilevel Strategies

Background/Experience Students will need a firm understanding of the basic meaning of *solid*, *liquid*, and *gas* in order to learn the more advanced concepts about these topics covered in this lesson. These activities will help students review the terms.

Beginning Have students copy and match these definitions with the correct terms.

1. Has definite shape and volume. *(solid)*

2. Has definite volume, but no fixed shape. *(liquid)*

3. Has no definite volume or shape. *(gas)*

Intermediate Have students make vocabulary flash cards with the terms on one side and a definition on the other. They can use the cards to quiz each other in small groups.

Advanced Have students use a pencil to write three sentences: one about solids, one about liquids, and one about gases. Have them erase the word *solid*, *liquid*, or *gas* from each sentence, then trade with a partner and fill in the missing term in each sentence.

For All Students Have students keep a journal where they record facts about solids, liquids, gases, and plasma on separate pages. They can add to the journals as they work through the lesson.

Extend

Have the students complete the **Show What You Know** activity on page 189 to demonstrate their understanding of the states of matter.

③ Apply and Assess

KWL Charts

When to Use With Reading Review p. 475 ⏱ 20 minutes	Proficiency Levels ✔ Beginning ✔ Intermediate ✔ Advanced

- Divide the students into small groups. Explain that they will be making their own KWL charts after they have a group discussion.

- Explain that *KWL* means *What I <u>Know</u>, What I <u>Want</u> to Know*, and *What I Have <u>Learned</u>*.

- Have groups review melting point, boiling point, and plasma. Then ask them to complete their own *KWL Chart* for each topic summarizing the content of their group discussions.

Informal Assessment

Beginning	Intermediate	Advanced
Read one of the definitions. Ask students to identify the state of matter. *(Solids have definite shape and volume. Liquids have definite volume but no fixed shape. Gases have no fixed shape or volume.)*	Ask students yes/no questions about the different states of matter to test their understanding. *(Answers will vary.)*	Have students define *solid, liquid,* and *gas. (Solids have definite shape and volume. Liquids have definite volume but no fixed shape. Gases have no fixed shape or volume.)*

States Change Table

Read across each row. Fill in the last column to identify the state of matter that results when you add or remove heat. Then write a definition for *boiling point* and *melting point*.

solid	add heat	
liquid	add heat	
gas	remove heat	
liquid	remove heat	

boiling point: _____

melting point: _____

School-Home Connection: Have students bring this page home to share with family members. They can use it to tell about states of matter.

13 Matter and How It Changes

Develop Scientific Concepts and Vocabulary

In this chapter, students will learn about how matter undergoes physical and chemical changes and what defines each type of change. They will learn to define a variety of mixtures, including solutions and suspensions. They will learn about acids and bases and how to rate the acidity or alkalinity of a substance on the pH scale.

Preview Scientific Principles

Walk through the chapter with students, pausing to read aloud or to have volunteers read aloud the four questions that are lesson titles. Encourage students to briefly discuss each question and to tell what they already know that might help them answer the questions.

When to Use With Chapter Opener	Proficiency Levels
25 minutes	✔ Beginning ✔ Intermediate ✔ Advanced

Lesson 1: What Are the Physical Properties of Matter?

- Display a classroom object and ask students to describe its color, texture, size, shape, hardness, and other physical properties.
- Have partners choose another object and take turns describing its physical properties to each other.

Lesson 2: What Are Mixtures?

Ask students what fruit salad, liquid cough medicine, cereal in milk, and a bucket full of different rocks have in common. Explain that the examples are all mixtures. Summarize that a <u>mix</u>ture <u>mix</u>es different substances together. Ask students for other examples.

Lesson 3: What Are Chemical Properties of Matter?

- Explain that a chemical reaction forms new substances.
- Show students how gas forms when an antacid tablet is added to water. Have students discuss how they know a chemical reaction is taking place.

Lesson 4: What Are Acids and Bases?

- Dip litmus or pH papers in an acidic solution, such as lemon juice, and a basic one such as liquid soap. Have students describe the results.
- Summarize that lemon juice is an acid and soap is a base.

Practice

Help students use the chapter vocabulary by exploring the multiple meanings of several key words. Write *base* on the board. See how many meanings of the word students can offer and write them on the board. Students may use a dictionary to expand their list. Possible meanings include: markers in a baseball game; bottom levels of a building or other structure; bottom coat of paint; geometry term; a center for activity; the root of a word; a substance that turns red litmus blue. Repeat the activity for *scale*. (a tool for measuring weight or mass; a system of measurement; a series of musical notes; overlapping skin or flake on fish or other animals; a ratio on a map or model)

Apply

Write the riddles from the chart below on the board.

Have students take turns reading individual lines.

When a reader gets to the line, "What am I?" have the rest of the group answer the question with a complete sentence: "I'm a _____." *(base; scale)*

Word Riddles

I'm the bottom of a sculpture.
I'm the bottom coat of paint.
Kids slide into me in baseball.
But in science, I'm the "opposite" of an acid. What am I?

I tell you how much you weigh.
I'm what you practice on a violin or flute.
I'm a tough plate on a fish or reptile.
But in science, I help tell the pH of things. What am I?

What Are the Physical Properties of Matter?

① Build Background

Access Prior Knowledge

When to Use	Proficiency Levels
Before introducing the lesson 20 minutes	✔ Beginning ✔ Intermediate ✔ Advanced

Ask a volunteer to define *matter*. Review that it means any substance that has mass and takes up space. Ask students to name examples of matter and nonmatter. Choose one of the examples of matter from the list of student examples. Ask students to describe its physical properties, including what they know about its mass, volume, and density. After listing some physical properties, ask students to guess what a physical change in matter might be.

Preteach Lesson Vocabulary

> **physical property, mass, volume, density, physical change**

List the vocabulary words on the board.

- Have students find *physical property* in the textbook and help them make a list of physical properties of matter, such as color, texture, shape, mass, and volume.

- Ask students to define the term. Guide them to the understanding that physical properties describe a substance as it is alone and not interacting with other substances. Ask students to describe the physical properties of an eraser, piece of paper, or crayon.

- Write *mass*, *volume*, and *density* on the board. Explain that these terms describe three physical properties of matter. Ask students to tell what they know about each one. Guide them to the understanding that mass is a measure of the amount of matter in an object, volume tells how much space it takes up, and density relates mass to volume.

- Explain that a *physical change* changes a substance, but does not make new substances. Crumple a piece of paper as an example of a physical change. Ask students to describe other ways they could make a physical change to the paper.

Build Fluency

Have two groups hold the following back-and-forth conversation, repeating the same question and creating new answers by substituting the words in italics.

Q: What is a physical property?

A: _____ is a physical property. (*Texture, Shape, Hardness, Density, State, Color, Mass, Volume*)

② Scaffold the Content

Preview the Lesson

When to Use
With pp. 484–492

🕐 15 minutes

Proficiency Levels
✔ Beginning
✔ Intermediate
✔ Advanced

- Preview pages 486–487 to show students that they will learn more about the physical properties of matter. Have them list terms that are physical properties.

- Have students preview the pictures on page 488 and tell what they show about mass and volume. Ask students to tell what they know about measuring each property.

- Have students study the data on page 489 and summarize the information. They should recognize that the density information for different substances is given.

- Preview pages 490–492 to show that they are about physical changes. Read the heading on page 492. Say that these terms describe types of physical change.

Investigate, p. 485

Materials: aluminum foil, wood block, book

- Before students begin the Investigate, explain that they will be observing physical properties of objects including measurements of mass and volume.

- Show a sample of aluminum foil and a wood block as you say the names and write the terms on the board.

- Students will need to measure the length, width, and height of the block to find its volume. Write *length*, *width*, and *height* on the board and demonstrate each aspect using the wood block or a large book.

Modify Instruction—Multilevel Strategies

Language and Vocabulary Have students use these activities to better understand the meaning of the vocabulary terms in the lesson.

Beginning Have students copy the following sentences then practice reading them aloud with a partner. *Matter is anything that has mass and takes up space. A physical property describes something by itself. Physical changes do not make new substances.*

Intermediate Have students write definitions for *physical property* and *physical change* on tag board strips.

Advanced Ask students to choose a classroom item and measure its mass and volume in front of the group, explaining their actions aloud.

For All Students Say key words from the lesson. Ask volunteers to give the meaning and draw a picture on the board, if applicable.

© Harcourt

Have the students complete the **Show What You Know** activity on page 195 to demonstrate their understanding of physical properties and physical changes.

③ Apply and Assess

Physical Properties Poster

When to Use	Proficiency Levels
With Reading Review p. 493	✔ Beginning
🕐 15 minutes	✔ Intermediate
	✔ Advanced

Materials: markers or colored pencils, tag board

- Have students draw a picture of a classroom object on tag board or poster board.
- Direct them to list categories of physical properties, such as color, shape, mass, hardness, and texture. Then have students list the properties of the object in each of those categories.
- Have students present their posters to the class, then post them on a bulletin board.

Informal Assessment

Beginning	Intermediate	Advanced
Erase one or two key words from each sentence, then ask students to tell what the missing words are. Ask them to read the complete sentences aloud. *(Answers will vary.)*	Have students read their definitions. *(Possible answer: A physical property describes a characteristic of matter of itself and not how it interacts with other things. A physical change does not make new substances.)*	Ask students to summarize what mass and volume are. *(Mass is the amount of matter in a substance. Volume tells the amount of space an object takes up.)*

Physical Properties Chart

A physical property of matter is listed in each row. Write a word, phrase, or sentence to describe the physical property.

Shape	
Texture	
Hardness	
State	
Mass	
Volume	
Density	

School-Home Connection: Have students take this page home to share with family members. They can use it to tell about physical properties.

Lesson **2** **What Are Mixtures?**

① Build Background

Access Prior Knowledge

When to Use	Proficiency Levels
Before introducing the lesson 15 minutes	✔ Beginning ✔ Intermediate Advanced

Write *mixture* on the board and ask students to identify any words they see within the term. Discuss what "mix" means and what a mixture might be. Ask students to think about combinations they could make with kitchen ingredients that would be mixtures.

Preteach Lesson Vocabulary

mixture, solution, suspension, colloid

List the vocabulary words on the board.

- Ask students to define *mixture* in their own words. Guide them to the understanding that a mixture combines two or more things that can be separated again.

- Have students find *proportion* on page 496 and read the term with them. Explain that the proportion in a mixture tells the relative amount of each ingredient.

- Have students find *solution* on page 498. Explain that in a solution, one substance dissolves evenly in another. Give the examples of sugar in hot tea or chocolate syrup in milk. Explain that an *alloy* is a special kind of solution made with two metals.

- Write *suspension.* Stir soil into water and explain that it is a suspension. Ask students to observe it and observe it five minutes later. Say that a suspension is a mixture with particles large enough to see that will separate from the liquid over time.

- Write *colloid.* Preview that a colloid, such as milk, is like a suspension but with particles too small to see.

Build Fluency

Write these lines on the board. Read the word. Have students read the definitions.

mixture: a combination of two or more substances that keep their own properties

solution: a mixture with substances that dissolve evenly

suspension: a mixture with large particles that don't stay mixed

colloid: a suspension with small particles

© Harcourt

② Scaffold the Content

When to Use With pp. 494–500	Proficiency Levels
⏱ 15 minutes	✔ Beginning ✔ Intermediate ✔ Advanced

Preview the Lesson

- Refer students to page 494. Discuss what they see in the picture and ask a volunteer to read the caption. Ask students how they know that paint is a mixture. Ask if they know what kind of mixture it is.

- Have students preview the section headings and pictures to identify the main topics of the lesson. Ask volunteers to read the section headings and tell what they know about each topic. Allow time for students to describe what they see in the pictures.

- Remind students that colloid is a type of mixture. Write *colloid*. Explain that it comes from the Greek *kolla*, meaning "glue." Ask what is "glue-like" about a colloid.

Investigate, p. 495

- Before students begin this Investigate, tell them that this Investigate asks them to *hypothesize*. Discuss what students know about a hypothesis and guide them to the understanding it is an idea that can be tested.

- Summarize that students will be testing ideas about how to separate mixtures back to their original ingredients.

- Make sure students understand the terms *filings* and *gravel* as "shavings or small pieces scraped off with a file" and "a mixture of pebbles and rocks."

Modify Instruction—Multilevel Strategies

Language and Vocabulary Use these exercises to help students better distinguish the subtle differences between different kinds of mixtures.

Beginning Have students copy this information to make a set of flash cards they can use to practice the vocabulary: <u>mixture:</u> *a combination of two or more substances that keep their original properties;* <u>solution:</u> *a mixture with all substances evenly distributed;* <u>suspension:</u> *a mixture that contains particles large enough to see that will eventually separate*

Intermediate Have students make a vocabulary card for each of these terms: *mixture, solution, suspension.*

Advanced Have students use each of the following words in a complete sentence: *mixture, solution, suspension.*

For All Students As students work through the lesson, have them extend the Multilevel Strategies to include the terms *colloid, alloy,* and *proportion.*

© Harcourt

Have the students complete the **Show What You Know** activity on page 199 to demonstrate their understanding of mixtures.

③ Apply and Assess

Vocabulary Lift-the-Flap Games

When to Use	Proficiency Levels
With Reading Review p. 501	✔ Beginning
🕐 25 minutes	✔ Intermediate
	✔ Advanced

Materials: two pieces of construction paper per student, ruler, pen, scissors, stapler

- Give each student two pieces of paper to create a lift-the-flap vocabulary game.
- On one piece of paper, have students mark six squares and then cut three sides of each square, leaving one side attached.
- Then have them staple or glue the second (uncut) piece of the paper under the first, along the edges of the paper.
- On the top of each flap, have students write one vocabulary word from the lesson. Folding the flap back to expose the paper underneath, have students write the definition of the word below.
- Have students make up games to use with their paper game boards.

Informal Assessment

Beginning	Intermediate	Advanced
Read aloud the definitions from the students' vocabulary cards and ask them to give you the word that is being identified. Then have students read aloud all of the definitions for you. *(Answers will vary.)*	Ask students to read their vocabulary cards. *(Answers will vary.)*	Ask students to define each term in their own words. *(mixture: a combination of two or more substances that keep their original properties; solution: a mixture with all substances evenly distributed; suspension: a mixture that contains particles large enough to see that will eventually separate)*

Name _____

Date _____

Mixtures Word Web

Complete the word web by writing a definition for each term in the ovals.

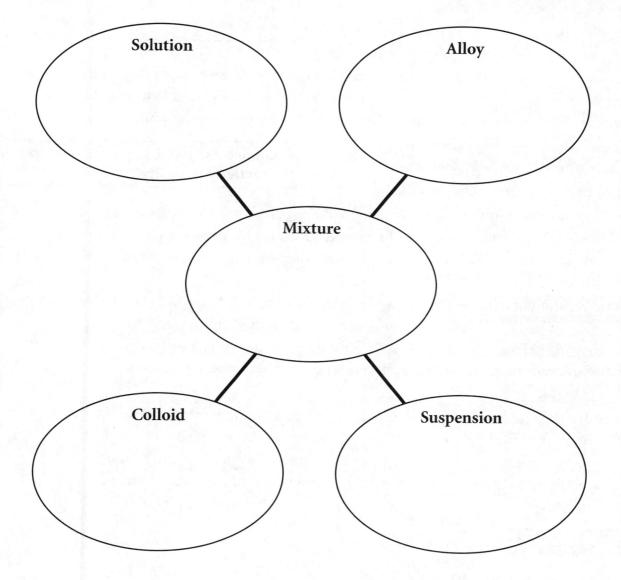

Solution

Alloy

Mixture

Colloid

Suspension

School-Home Connection: Have students take this page home to share with family members. They can use it to tell about mixtures.

© Harcourt

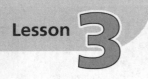

What Are Chemical Properties of Matter?

① Build Background

Access Prior Knowledge

When to Use	Proficiency Levels
Before introducing the lesson 20 minutes	✔ Beginning ✔ Intermediate Advanced

Review the meanings of *physical properties* and *physical changes* with students. Summarize that physical changes do not make new substances. Ask students what they think might happen during a *chemical change* and guide them to the idea that new substances will be made. Ask what they think chemical properties might be.

Preteach Lesson Vocabulary

> chemical change, chemical property, reactivity, stability

List the vocabulary words on the board.

- Remind students that physical changes do not create new substances. Explain that chemical changes occur when elements and compounds react to form new substances. Chemical properties describe how substances interact with other substances.

- Have students find *reactivity* and *stability* on page 505. Help students derive the meanings of these terms from "react" and "stable." Summarize that reactivity describes substances that easily undergo chemical reactions. Stability describes substances that do not. Ask students how these words relate. *(They are antonyms.)*

- Introduce the four kinds of chemical reactions: A *synthesis reaction* combines two or more substances into one new substance. A *decomposition reaction* is the opposite of a synthesis reaction. It separates one substance into two or more new substances. *Single replacement reactions* replace one substance with another. *Double replacement reactions* occur when two substances trade places.

Build Fluency

Divide students into two groups. Have Group 1 "call" the definition. Have Group 2 "respond" with the term. Students may contribute more examples to use.

Call: a change that makes new substances **Response:** chemical change (or reaction)

Call: a reaction that combines substances into one **Response:** synthesis

Call: opposite of stability **Response:** reactivity

© Harcourt

② Scaffold the Content

Preview the Lesson

When to Use	Proficiency Levels
With pp. 502–508	✔ Beginning
	✔ Intermediate
15 minutes	✔ Advanced

- Refer students to page 502. Read the lesson title and ask students to tell what they know that can help them answer the question. Discuss the picture and ask a volunteer to read the caption. Say that exploding fireworks are an example of a chemical change. Ask how students know a chemical change is taking place.

- Ask students to read the names of the four kinds of chemical reactions listed on pages 506–507. Ask them to summarize what they know about each kind.

- Read the topic heading on page 508. Ask students to think of some chemical reactions and then explain why they might want to stop them or slow them down.

Investigate, p. 503

- Before students begin the Investigate, remind them that they should wear safety goggles to protect their eyes and a lab apron to protect their clothes whenever they work with chemicals.

- Point out the title on the page: *Different Kinds of Changes*. Ask volunteers to name the four main kinds of chemical changes. Reinforce that a chemical reaction forms new substances.

- Explain that *infer* means "to use observations to make conclusions." Tell students that they will make inferences from observations they make in the Investigate.

Modify Instruction—Multilevel Strategies

Comprehensible Input Many of the terms in this lesson relate to more common or simpler root words. Students can use these relationships to help remember the meaning of the terms, especially when the words are long and unfamiliar.

Beginning Have students identify roots in *reaction*, *stability* and *replacement*. (*react*, *stable*, *replace*)

Intermediate Have students use root words to write definitions for *reaction*, *stability* and *replacement* on tag board strips or index cards.

Advanced Have students prepare a short oral presentation for other students identifying the roots of *reaction*, *stability* and *replacement* and using those roots to define each term.

For All Students Extend the activities to include terms like *reactivity*, *replacement*, *decomposition*, or other terms as students work through the lesson.

Have the students complete the **Show What You Know** activity on page 203 to demonstrate their understanding of chemical reactions.

③ Apply and Assess

Make a Chemical Reaction Chart

When to Use	Proficiency Levels
With Reading Review p. 509	✔ Beginning
⏱ 30 minutes	✔ Intermediate
	✔ Advanced

Materials: markers or colored pencils, butcher paper or poster board

- Tell students that they will make a chart showing the four main kinds of chemical reactions.
- Divide students into small groups.
- Have them write the names of the four main reaction types: synthesis, decomposition, single replacement, and double replacement. Have them write a summary of each type using words or symbols (synthesis: A + B → C) or give an example.
- Have groups present their work and then display the posters in the classroom.

Informal Assessment

Beginning	Intermediate	Advanced
Have students name the root in one of the terms and relate it to the meaning of the term. *(reaction: react; stability: stable; replacement: replace)*	Read the definitions and ask students to identify the matching term. *(Answers will vary)*	Ask students to summarize how the roots help them understand and remember the meaning of the terms. *(Answers will vary)*

Definition Boxes

Write a definition in each box. Below each pair of boxes explain how the terms are different from each other.

Physical Change	Chemical Change

_____

_____

_____

Reactivity	Stability

_____

_____

_____

School-Home Connection: Have students take this page home to share with family members. They can use it to tell about chemical changes.

What Are Acids and Bases?

① Build Background

Access Prior Knowledge

When to Use	Proficiency Levels
Before introducing the lesson ⏱ 20 minutes	✔ Beginning ✔ Intermediate Advanced

Write the words *acid* and *base* on the board. Ask students to tell what they know about each term. Ask them to describe what a lemon tastes like. Say that lemon juice is an example of an acid and that acids often taste sour. Ask them to describe what soap feels like. Say that soap is an example of a base and that bases often feel slippery. Explain that scientists can classify many substances as acids or bases. Ask students to name other examples.

Preteach Lesson Vocabulary

> **acid, base, pH scale, indicator**

List the vocabulary words on the board.

- Have students find *acid* and *base* on page 512 and scan the page to find examples in each category. Ask them to find a definition for each term and point out that the terms are opposites. Say that litmus paper is a special paper that shows if a substance is an acid or base. Acids turn blue litmus paper red and bases turn red litmus paper blue.

- Tell students that when acids and bases react with each other, they neutralize or cancel each other out. Tell students that *neutral* means "neither an acid nor a base."

- Have students find *indicator* on page 514. Explain that an indicator "indicates" or tells if a substance is an acid or base. Litmus paper is one kind of indicator.

- Preview the pH scale on pages 514–515. Remind students that the Mohs' scale rates the hardness of minerals. Explain that the pH scale is a different scale that rates how acidic or basic a substance is. Ask students to identify the range of numbers on the scale, and the numbers for most acidic, most basic, and neutral on the scale.

Build Fluency

To reinforce the concept of pH, model this chant of common solutions. You may also do this activity as a call-and-response. Students may give their own examples.

pH 0: battery acid   pH 2: lemon juice   pH 3: vinegar

pH 7: distilled water   pH 10: cleaning liquids   pH 11: ammonia.

② Scaffold the Content

When to Use
With pp. 510–516

⏱ 15 minutes

Proficiency Levels
✔ Beginning
✔ Intermediate
✔ Advanced

Preview the Lesson

- Read the lesson title on page 510 and ask students to tell what they know about acids and bases. Discuss what the picture shows about acids.
- Review that acids turn blue litmus paper red, and bases turn red litmus paper blue. Ask students what they think acids do to red litmus paper or what bases do to blue litmus paper. *(They don't change them.)*
- Refer students to page 515. Tell them that *indicators* can test solutions for acidity or alkalinity (how basic they are).

Investigate, p. 511

- Before students begin the Investigate, have volunteers read aloud the list of eight household solutions that they will be testing for acidity and alkalinity.
- Remind students that they should wear safety goggles and a lab apron. They should not touch any of the solutions.
- Explain that they will not dip the litmus paper in the solutions, but will use a dropper to put each solution onto the paper.
- Explain that students will switch to wide-range indicator paper to determine the pH of each solution after they have tested the solutions with litmus paper.

Modify Instruction—Multilevel Strategies

Background/Experience The main goal of this lesson is to define acids and bases and to identify the pH of a variety of substances. The following exercises provide opportunities for students to build vocabulary they can use to discuss acids and bases and to practice classifying acids and bases.

Beginning Have students fold a piece of paper in half and label one side *acid* and the other side *base*. Then ask students to write the following solutions in the correct column, according to whether they are an acid or a base: *soap, vinegar, lemon juice, detergent, car battery acid, ammonia, baking soda, disinfectant.*

Intermediate Have students write sentences on tag board sentence strips, using the following words from the lesson: *acid, base, pH, indicator, litmus paper.*

Advanced Have students research the history and development of the pH scale. Allow them to use an Internet search engine or other resources for information. Have them write a paragraph or draw a timeline to represent the information they found.

For All Students Have students begin an "Acids and Bases" bulletin board. Have them divide the bulletin board into two sections and attach pictures or names on index cards of substances that belong in each category.

Extend

Have the students complete the **Show What You Know** activity on page 207 to demonstrate their understanding of acids and bases.

③ Apply and Assess

Make a Wide-Range Indicator Paper Model

When to Use With Reading Review p. 517  30 minutes	Proficiency Levels ✔ Beginning ✔ Intermediate ✔ Advanced

Materials: a long strip of white butcher paper, ruler, markers

- Have groups divide the paper into 15 equal-size sections and label them from 0 to 14. Then ask students to write or draw a substance in each section that has the pH shown in that section.
- Ask students to present their work to the class. They should explain what the pH scale represents and what the different numbers mean.

Informal Assessment

Beginning	Intermediate	Advanced
Read the words aloud to the students and have them respond by telling you whether each one is an acid or a base. *(Answers will vary.)*	Say each of the words aloud for students and ask them to give you the definition in their own words. *(Answers will vary.)*	Ask students to summarize their research. *(Answers will vary.)*

Table of Acids and Bases

Read the substance in the first column of each row. Write *acid* or *base* in the second column to classify it. In the third column, describe how the substance changes litmus paper. The first row is completed to show you how.

Substance	Acid or Base	Change to Litmus Paper
Vinegar	acid	changes blue litmus paper red
Baking soda		
Orange juice		
Battery acid		
Liquid soap		
Ammonia		
Detergent		
Antacid tablets		
Lemon juice		
Disinfectant		

School-Home Connection: Have students take this page home to share with family members. They can use it to tell about acids and bases.

14 Energy

Develop Scientific Concepts and Vocabulary

In this chapter, students will learn about different forms of energy and how some forms travel in waves. They will learn about the parts of a wave. They will read about the way that light behaves, learning how the characteristics of different objects affect the way we see (or don't see) light.

Preview Scientific Principles

Walk through the chapter with students, pausing to read aloud or to have volunteers read aloud the three questions that are lesson titles. Encourage students to briefly discuss each question and to tell what they already know that might help them answer the questions.

When to Use With Chapter Opener	Proficiency Levels
20 minutes	✔ Beginning ✔ Intermediate ✔ Advanced

Lesson 1: What Are Some Forms of Energy?

- Have the class brainstorm a list of items that use electricity to work.
- Hold a ball in the air. Ask students if they think the ball has energy. Then ask students if they think the ball has energy now as you drop the ball.
- Talk about the different types of fuels that cars and trucks use (diesel, gasoline, electricity).

Lesson 2: What Are Waves?

- Draw a wave on the board. Ask students to point to the part of the wave they think is the top, or crest, and the part they think is the bottom, or trough.
- Have about nine students stand in front of the classroom and demonstrate the stadium wave. Then have students show parts of a wave: the first student kneels, the second student stands half-way, the third student stands, the fourth student stands half-way, the fifth student kneels, and the sixth student sits.
- Ask the rest of the class to identify the students that represent the top and bottom of the wave. *(the third and sixth students)*

© Harcourt

Lesson 3: How Does Light Behave?

- Use a prism to show students the way that light can be split into its separate colors. Allow students to ask questions or describe what they see.
- Have students look at the rainbow from the prism or a picture of a rainbow. Make sure they can name all of the colors in English.

Practice

Define *kinetic energy* and *potential energy*. Then have students use the terms to describe their energy as they move or hold an elevated position.

- Have students take turns performing your commands to run around a desk, jump up and down, do jumping jacks, sit on a chair, or stand on a step.
- When a student is sitting on a chair or standing on a step, the class will say, "That's potential energy."
- When a student is running or jumping, the class will say, "That's kinetic energy."

Apply

Have students sing the following song to the tune of *London Bridge*. Have them act out sitting and waiting or always moving as they sing the song. You may wish to have them add lines to the song after they learn more about different forms of energy.

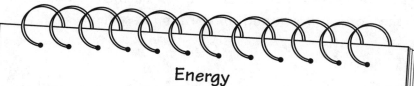

Energy

Potential energy sits and waits, sits and waits,
sits and waits.
Potential energy sits and waits,
Potential energy.

Kinetic energy always moves, always moves,
always moves.
Kinetic energy always moves.
Kinetic energy.

What Are Some Forms of Energy?

① Build Background

Access Prior Knowledge

When to Use	Proficiency Levels
Before introducing the lesson 10 minutes	Beginning ✔ Intermediate ✔ Advanced

Ask students to think of different forms of energy they are familiar with. If they need help, you may prompt them to think about how we power our cars, make our computers and appliances work, and heat our homes.

Preteach Lesson Vocabulary

energy, potential energy, kinetic energy, law of conservation of energy

List the vocabulary words on the board.

- Explain that potential energy is energy that is due to the position or condition of an object. To describe something's potential energy, you often need to describe its position, or where it is located.

- Students are likely to see the word *conservation* in other contexts, especially ones dealing with the environment and recycling. Help students identify the word *conserve* in *conservation*. Explain that *conserve* means "to save or protect." Conservation is the saving or protecting of something. It is what people do when they save something from being harmed or wasted. Have students use the words *conserve* and *conservation* in sentences.

Build Fluency

Since potential energy is dependent upon position, give students practice asking about and describing someone's position. Have student pairs move around the room and talk about their partner's position. One partner asks, "What is my position?" The other partner describes the partner's location. Partners should take turns asking and answering questions.

② Scaffold the Content

Preview the Lesson

When to Use
With pp. 526–532

⏱ 15 minutes

Proficiency Levels
✔ Beginning
✔ Intermediate
✔ Advanced

Have students read the lesson title and study the pictures in the lesson. Have them use their preview of the lesson to try to answer the title question. Tell students to look for answers to the question as they read.

Investigate, p. 527

Before students begin the Investigate:

- Students may be unfamiliar with the phrase *clear space* in step 1. Use tape to mark the floor area around a doorway. Say that, in order to open, the door needs this "clear space," or area with nothing in it. Explain that students should do the Investigate in a large empty space.

- Simplify the language of questions 1 and 2 by asking:

  "How far did the cart go the first time? How far did it go when you raised the height?"

  "What things changed each time you did the experiment?"

Modify Instruction—Multilevel Strategies

Comprehensible Input In a dictionary, show students the many different definitions for *run*. Discuss the following meanings of run.

- *To move quickly on foot.* Demonstrate this meaning by jogging in place.

- *To compete in a political race for office.* Talk about the people who run for president, vice president, and so on. Show a sample ballot from a recent election.

- *To flow, as water from a faucet.* Turn the sink faucet on and then off.

- *To operate or enable to work.* Turn on an unplugged appliance. Then plug it in and try turning it on again.

Beginning Use the word *run* in a sentence, such as, "When the snow melts, water runs down the side of the mountain." Ask the student to act out, draw, or pantomime the meaning you are using. *(Answers will vary.)*

Intermediate Act out one of the meanings for *run*. Have the student describe what you are doing by using *run* in a sentence of his or her own. *(Answers will vary.)*

Advanced Ask students to think of other ways they have heard *run* used. Have them look up the definition in the dictionary. Help them interpret the meaning by simplifying the vocabulary and definition.

For All Students Discuss the meaning of *run* as used on page 529—people and machines *run* on different forms of energy.

Extend

Have students complete the Show What You Know activity on page 213 to demonstrate their understanding of one common use of *run*.

③ Apply and Assess

Group Things That Run

When to Use	Proficiency Levels
With Reading Review p. 533 15 minutes	✔ Beginning ✔ Intermediate ✔ Advanced

Materials: magazines, paste, paper, scissors

- Have students work in small groups. They should look through magazines to find and cut out pictures of things that run.
- Have students group their pictures by the different meanings for *run*.

Informal Assessment

Beginning	Intermediate	Advanced
Take one of the pictures from the activity above and ask the student to put it with other pictures that represent the same meaning for *run*. *(Answers will vary.)*	Tell one meaning for *run*. Ask the student to choose a picture from the activity above that shows this meaning. *(Answers will vary.)*	Ask the student to explain why, in the activity above, they chose to put certain pictures together in the same group. *(Answers will vary.)*

What Can Run?

Look around your home or school. Find one thing that can run. Draw a picture of it below. Try to write a sentence to tell what you see. Use the word *run* in your sentence.

What can run?

_____

_____

 School-Home Connection: Have students take this page home to share with family members. They can use it to tell about energy and things that run on it.

What Are Waves?

① Build Background

Access Prior Knowledge

When to Use	Proficiency Levels
Before introducing the lesson 15 minutes	✔ Beginning ✔ Intermediate ✔ Advanced

Materials: long jump rope

Have two volunteers demonstrate a wave using a jump rope. Each student holds one end of the jump rope. One student carefully holds his or her end still. The other student pulls the rope up and then down. Have the class observe how the rope moves. Explain that this is one example of a wave. Elicit from students other kinds of waves, such as an ocean wave and the wave of a hand.

Preteach Lesson Vocabulary

> **wave, wavelength, amplitude, frequency, electromagnetic spectrum**

List the vocabulary words on the board.

- On the board, draw a single wave. Explain that this is what one wave looks like.
- Show a photo of or draw an animal feeding trough and identify it. Point out the large depression. Then point to the low point in your drawing of a wave and explain that this drop in a wave is called a *trough*. Encourage students to visualize a feeding trough to help them remember the trough of a wave.
- Show a photo of or draw a mountaintop. Point to the very top of the mountain and explain that this is called a crest. Then point to the high point in your drawing of a wave and explain that this high part of a wave is called a crest. Encourage students to visualize a mountain crest to help them remember the crest of a wave.

Build Fluency

Help students become more comfortable with the words *wave, crest*, and *trough*. Have partners draw waves and point to the wave parts as they take turns describing them to each other using these model sentences:

This is a wave. This is the crest of the wave. This is the trough of the wave.

© Harcourt

② Scaffold the Content

Preview the Lesson

When to Use
With pp. 534–542

20 minutes

Proficiency Levels
✔ Beginning
✔ Intermediate
✔ Advanced

Have students read the lesson title. Give students a chance to name and describe any waves they know about. Then have students look through the lesson and predict what kinds of wave they will learn about.

Investigate, p. 535

Before students begin the Investigate:

- Have a volunteer stand in front of the class with you and act as your partner. As you read aloud the directions step-by-step, demonstrate for students what to do.
- Simplify the phrase "measure and record the time it takes" by saying, "find out how long it takes and write this down."
- For question 2, tell students to compare the time it took for each wave to reach their partner. Remind students that *hypothesize* means "to make a guess based on what you've already seen."

Modify Instruction—Multilevel Strategies

Language and Vocabulary Ask students what *pitch* means in baseball. Discuss the meaning of *pitch* as a verb (to throw the ball to the batter) and as a noun (the throw to the batter).

Explain that in science, the word *pitch* is a noun that means "how high or low a sound is." Use a guitar to demonstrate this meaning of *pitch*. Pluck a single guitar string. Ask students if they would describe the sound as high or low. Then press on the string to shorten it. Pluck the string again, then ask students if they would describe this sound as higher or lower than the first one. Explain that the second sound has a higher pitch and sounds higher because the frequency is higher. A sound with a higher frequency vibrates faster.

Beginning Pluck two different guitar strings. Ask, "Which string had a higher pitch? Which had a higher frequency?" (*Students should point to the same string each time, the string that made the higher sound.*)

Intermediate Pluck two guitar strings and ask students to tell if the pitch of the second sound was higher or lower than the pitch of the first. (*Answers will vary.*)

Advanced Ask students to tell how pitch and frequency are related. (*Answers may include: The higher the frequency of a sound, the higher the pitch.*)

For All Students Encourage students to remember the demonstration of the term *pitch* as they read about sound energy.

Extend

Have students complete the **Show What You Know** activity on page 217 to demonstrate their understanding of the phrase "measure and record the time it takes."

③ Apply and Assess

Make Sound

When to Use With Reading Review p. 543 🕙 20 minutes	Proficiency Levels ✔ Beginning ✔ Intermediate ✔ Advanced

Materials: empty bottles with different neck lengths

- Give pairs of students a few bottles with different neck (or air column) lengths. Have students arrange the bottles by neck length from longest to shortest. Instruct students to draw this arrangement and label it "Length of Air Column."

- Ask students take turns blowing across the mouths of their bottles while their partner listens to the sound.

- Have students arrange the bottles by pitch from highest to lowest. Instruct students to draw this arrangement and label it "Pitch." Have them compare their drawings and tell how pitch is related to the length of the column of air.

Informal Assessment

Beginning	Intermediate	Advanced
Point to two bottles from the activity above and ask, "Which one will make the sound with the higher pitch?" (Students should point to the bottle with the shortest neck.)	Have a volunteer choose any two bottles from the activity above and blow across them. Ask students to tell which sound had a higher pitch. (Answers may include: The first sound had a higher pitch.)	"How can you tell by looking at the bottles which one will make a sound with a higher pitch?" (The bottle with the shorter neck will make a sound with a higher pitch.)

How Much Time Does It Take?

1. Choose three activities from the list below. Write them in the chart.

2. How long does it take you to do them? Measure and record in the chart the time it takes for each activity.

Daily Activities

brushing teeth

tying shoelaces

eating breakfast

getting dressed

combing hair

	Activity	Time
1.		
2.		
3.		

 School-Home Connection: Have students take this page home to share with family members. They can use this page to tell how to "measure and record the time it takes."

How Does Light Behave?

① Build Background

Access Prior Knowledge

When to Use	Proficiency Levels
Before introducing the lesson	✔ Beginning
⏱ 10 minutes	✔ Intermediate
	✔ Advanced

Materials: flashlights

Allow groups of students to practice making shadows with their hands using the flashlights. Then have volunteers tell what they think makes a shadow. Tell students that a shadow is caused by certain characteristics of an object and the way that light behaves. This lesson will explain how light waves behave.

Preteach Lesson Vocabulary

reflection, refraction, diffraction, transparent, translucent, opaque

Materials: bowl, pitcher of water, large sponge, small paper towel

List the vocabulary words on the board.

- Working over a bowl, pour water on the sponge. Explain that the sponge absorbs the water. *Absorb* means "to soak up or take in." Tell students that light can be absorbed too. When light waves hit an object the waves are soaked up by the object. Objects that absorb all the light that hits them are called opaque.

- Pour water on the paper towel. Explain that again the water was absorbed. Point out that the sponge and paper towel absorb different amounts of water. In the same way, different objects absorb different amounts of light. Objects that only absorb some of the light that hits them are called translucent.

- Bounce a ball off the floor, and tell students light bounces off some things, too. Explain that the bouncing of light off something is called reflection.

Build Fluency

Have students practice describing the way that something bounces. Use a small ball that won't bounce too far or do this activity in a gymnasium or outside. Explain that in English we can say that something, like the ball or light, "bounces off of" something or that it "bounces into" something. Have groups of students practice bouncing a ball into a wall and describing the ball's movements using the word *bounce*.

© Harcourt

② Scaffold the Content

Preview the Lesson

When to Use	Proficiency Levels
With pp. 544–550	✔ Beginning
20 minutes	✔ Intermediate
	✔ Advanced

Have students read the lesson title and the **Fast Fact** on page 544. Simplify the language in the Fast Fact for your students. Say, "Ctenophores are a group of ocean animals. They use tiny hairs to move. Those hairs are called cilia. When the hairs move, they scatter the light. This makes a rainbow appear in the water. This rainbow happens because light diffracts. Light also reflects. You will learn about this in the Investigate."

Investigate, p. 545

Before students begin the Investigate:

- Read the directions through, step-by-step. Clarify any language that may be cumbersome for ESL students.
- For question 1, ask students, "How far was the mirror from the first pin? How far was the mirror from the place where the two lines met?"
- For question 2, say, "Think about where an object is located. Think about where its reflection seems to be located. How do these compare?"

Modify Instruction—Multilevel Strategies

Comprehensible Input Use this activity to help students understand how light moves in reflection, refraction, and diffraction.

- Draw a simple diagram showing how light behaves, or moves, when it strikes an object. (Draw a simple shape indicating the object light strikes. Then use a line with an arrow to show how light travels when it is reflected, refracted, or diffracted.)
- Have one student at a time mimic the movement of light. For reflection, they should move up to an object and then back away from it.
- For refraction, they should move to the object and then behind it in a slightly different direction.
- For diffraction, they can move to the edge of the object and then around its edge and continue going away from it.

Beginning Have one student choose a light movement to demonstrate. Then have another student tell the word for that type of light movement.

Intermediate Name one of the ways light moves. Have the student mimic the movement.

Advanced Have the student describe what happens when light is reflected, refracted, or diffracted.

For All Students Tell students to think about how light moves when they read about reflection, refraction, and diffraction.

Extend

Have students complete the **Show What You Know** activity on page 221 to demonstrate their understanding of how light behaves.

③ Apply and Assess

Find Real-Life Examples

When to Use With Reading Review p. 551 20 minutes	Proficiency Levels ✔ Beginning ✔ Intermediate ✔ Advanced

Take the class for a walk around the school yard or nearby park.

- Divide the class into six groups, making sure each group has students of differing English language abilities. Assign each group one of these words: *opaque, translucent, transparent, reflected, refracted, diffracted.*

- Tell students to find examples of their word and draw pictures of what they find.

- Encourage groups to use words to label their drawings. For example, the opaque group may draw and label leaves and trees. The reflected group may draw and label a metal window frame or a piece of mirror on the ground.

- Bring the class together and have the groups report on what they found.

Informal Assessment

Beginning	Intermediate	Advanced
Ask each student to show you an opaque object or a picture of one. *(Answers will vary.)*	Point to a reflective object in the classroom and ask, "Is the light being reflected or refracted by this object?" *(reflected)*	Ask the students to explain what happens to light when it hits an opaque object. *(The light is absorbed.)*

© Harcourt

Name _____

Date _____

How Does Light Move?

Look around your home or classroom.

1. Find one example of light that is reflected. Draw a picture or use words to describe what you see.

2. Find one example of light that is refracted. Draw a picture or use words to describe what you see.

3. Find one example of light that is diffracted. Draw a picture or use words to describe what you see.

1. Reflection	**2.** Refraction	**3.** Diffraction

© Harcourt

School-Home Connection: Have students take this page home to share with family members. They can use this page to tell how light behaves, or moves.

15 Heat and Electricity

Develop Scientific Concepts and Vocabulary

In this chapter, students will study heat, or the transfer of thermal energy, and three ways that thermal energy can transfer from one object to another. They will also learn about static and current electricity, how electricity is produced, and how to build a circuit.

Preview Scientific Principles

Walk through the chapter with students, pausing to read aloud or to have volunteers read aloud the three questions that are lesson titles. Encourage students to briefly discuss each question and to tell what they already know that might help them answer the questions.

When to Use With Chapter Opener	Proficiency Levels
⏱ 30 minutes	✔ Beginning ✔ Intermediate ✔ Advanced

Lesson 1: How Is Thermal Energy Transferred?

- Ask if students ever drank a hot drink from a Styrofoam cup or paper cup. Which cup kept the drink warm longer? Which cup protected their hand from the heat better?

- Ask students what happens when food is heated in a metal pan. Discuss which parts of the pan you can and cannot touch. Discuss how a potholder makes it safe to touch the hot pan and why.

Lesson 2: What is Electricity, and How Is It Produced?

- Have students describe lightning and explain how it forms. Ask why hair can stand up after brushing it or why people can get a "shock" after walking on carpet. Explain that lightning, hair "static," and rug shocks are forms of *static electricity*.

- Ask students what kind of energy runs lamps, ovens, and other appliances. Point out that current electricity, or electrons moving through wires, powers these tools.

© Harcourt

Lesson 3: What Is a Circuit?

- Tell students that electricity flows through circuits. Explain that *circuit* comes from the Latin word meaning "to go around."
- Tell students that when they flick a switch to turn on a light, they are actually <u>completing a circuit</u> that allows electricity to flow through wires to the light.

Practice

To help students become more aware of things that run on electricity, have them read aloud the letters in *electricity*. Beneath each one, have them write the name of an item that operates on electricity and begins with that letter.

You can brainstorm with students a list of words to use in this exercise. (Examples: e: electric blanket, l: lamp, e: elevator, etc.)

Apply

Write the following rhyming lines on the board. Read the lines aloud, and then do a choral reading with the group. Point out that each line includes words that rhyme. Discuss any new terms, and ask volunteers to explain the rhymes. Invite volunteers to write the rhyming words on the board. Then ask if students can think of other words that rhyme.

Rhyme Time!

To flip a switch, there is no glitch.
In certain weather, static is automatic (and dramatic).
Do you need the electromagnet? You bet!
The sun's radiation needs no power station.
Opposites attract, and although abstract, it is a fact.
If you want to keep your house hot, you'll have to pay a lot per watt.
Do you need to dry your hair? A circuit will work it.

How Is Thermal Energy Transferred?

① Build Background

Access Prior Knowledge

When to Use	Proficiency Levels
Before introducing the lesson 25 minutes	✔ Beginning ✔ Intermediate ✔ Advanced

Ask students what a thermometer is used for. Ask them to describe any experiences using a thermal blanket. Have students who use a thermos raise their hands and explain how it works. Then ask if any students have heard about hypothermia and what this condition involves. Write the terms thermometer, thermal, thermos, and hypothermia in a column on the board. Ask students what root these words have in common. Explain that the common root *therm* comes from the Greek meaning "heat."

Preteach Lesson Vocabulary

> **thermal energy, heat, conduction, convection, radiation, insulation**

List the vocabulary words on the board.

- Review the meaning of *kinetic*, as in kinetic energy. Be sure students understand that *kinetic* means "about motion" or "causing motion." Have students read the definition of *thermal energy* on page 562. Introduce thermal energy as the kinetic energy of the particles in matter.

- Explain that heat is the transfer or movement of thermal energy from one object to another. Relate this meaning to bus, money, or job transfers.

- Have students find *conduction*, *convection*, and *radiation* on pages 564 and 565. Summarize that these terms describe the three ways thermal energy can transfer from one object to another. Ask students to tell what they know about each method.

- Ask students for examples of *insulation*, such as in a home attic, winter coat, or Styrofoam cup. Ask students to use the examples to try to define what insulation might be. Summarize that insulation prevents the transfer of thermal energy.

Build Fluency

Practice the following lines as a *call-and-response* to reinforce key concepts.

What is heat?	...the transfer of thermal energy
What is conduction?	...the transfer of thermal energy when two solid objects touch
What is radiation?	...the transfer of thermal energy as waves
What is insulation?	...a substance that does not conduct thermal energy well

② Scaffold the Content

Preview the Lesson

- Read the lesson title on page 560 with students and ask them to name the three ways thermal energy is transferred. Ask them what the picture shows about thermal energy.
- Ask students to find *thermal energy* on page 562 and try to define it.
- Write *conduction*, *convection*, and *radiation* on the board. Use the pictures on pages 564–565 to preview that conduction transfers thermal energy between solid objects, convection transfers it through a fluid, and radiation transfers it as waves.
- Discuss with students how a winter coat insulates people from the cold. Have them find the term *insulation* in the textbook and ask what it means.

Investigate, p. 561

- Before students begin the Investigate, review with them how to set up a line graph.
- Tell them that they will be graphing changes in the temperature of a liquid in two kinds of cups.
- Write the following terms on the board: *beaker*, *fishing sinker*, *graduated cylinder*, *thermometer*, and *stopwatch*. Tell students that these materials are used in the Investigate. Have students come to the board and draw each item. Then ask them to describe it and tell how it is used.

Modify Instruction—Multilevel Strategies

Background/Experience Give students experience working with the topic of heat by having them complete the following exercises. Encourage students to refer back to the lesson for any information they need to complete the exercises.

   Beginning Have students work in pairs asking and answering the following lines:

   How does conduction work? *by transferring heat between solid objects*

   How does convection work? *by transferring heat through a fluid*

   How does radiation work? *by transferring heat as waves*

   Intermediate Ask students to give an example of each of the kinds of thermal energy transfer: conduction, convection, and radiation. Have them illustrate each example.

Advanced Have students make a list of words or phrases containing the root *therm*. They may use the textbook and/or a dictionary for this activity. Then ask students to use three of the words in complete sentences and illustrate as many of the words as possible.

For All Students Refer students to page 563. Put some examples on the board of the same temperature measured in both Celsius and Fahrenheit. Ask for volunteers to identify similarities and differences between the two scales and explain how they relate.

Extend

Have the students complete the Show What You Know activity on page 227 to demonstrate their understanding of the transfer of thermal energy.

③ Apply and Assess

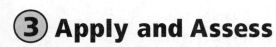

Design a Bulletin Board Display

When to Use	Proficiency Levels
With Reading Review p. 567	✔ Beginning
🕐 30 minutes	✔ Intermediate
	✔ Advanced

Materials: paints or markers, butcher paper, glue

- Assign the following main topics to different groups:

  What is thermal energy?

  What is convection?

  What is conduction?

  What is radiation?

  What is insulation?

- Have each group design one section of the display. Direct them to include definitions, illustrations, labels, applications, and/or examples. Each section should include a title.

- Ask groups to present their section to the rest of the students.

Informal Assessment

Beginning	Intermediate	Advanced
Ask students to memorize one of the question/answer pairs to recite aloud. Ask them *yes/no* questions about the information in the sentences. *(Answers will vary.)*	Read each definition and ask students to name the type of thermal transfer. *(Answers will vary.)*	Have students play a guessing game with their *therm* words. Put the students into teams. Have one team show an illustration of a term, while the other writes or guesses the word. Teams alternate roles to continue the game. *(Answers will vary.)*

Thermal Energy Transfer Word Web

In each oval, write the ways to transfer thermal energy. In the rectangles around each oval, write a definition, an example, or an application, and draw a picture to illustrate the process.

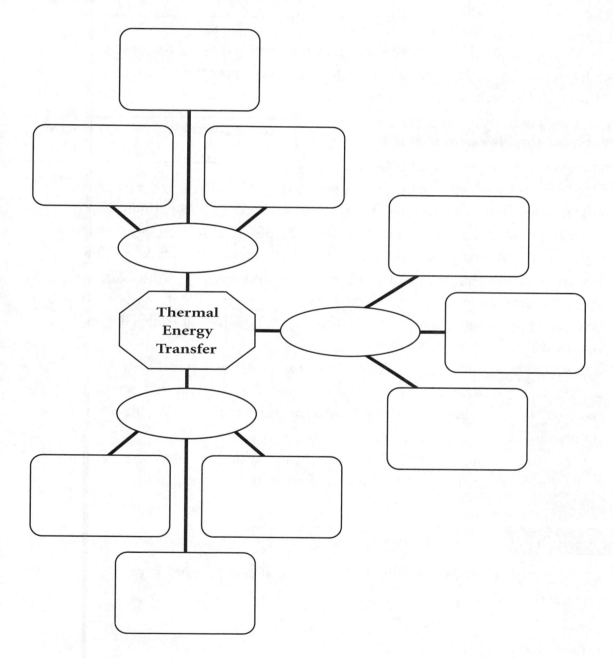

School-Home Connection: Have students take this page home to share with family members. They can use it to tell about the transfer of thermal energy.

Lesson 2 What Is Electricity, and How Is It Produced?

1 Build Background

Access Prior Knowledge

When to Use	Proficiency Levels
Before introducing the lesson 20 minutes	✔ Beginning ✔ Intermediate ✔ Advanced

Ask students to describe any experiences with a power outage. Did they notice how many appliances and other tools need electricity to run? Ask them to imagine living before the invention of the electric light. Ask them how they think that invention has changed and shaped how people live.

Preteach Lesson Vocabulary

> **static electricity, current electricity**

List the vocabulary words on the board.

- Have students find *static electricity* on page 570. Ask students to define static as something still or unmoving. Ask them what word electricity might come from and guide them to the understanding that it relates to "electron." Help volunteers summarize that static electricity involves electrons that do not flow.

- Remind students that antonyms, such as *attract* and *repel*, are words with opposite meaning. Ask students if they have used bug repellent. Invite a volunteer to give the meaning of the word *repel*. Explain that static charges can attract or repel.

- Allow time for students to tell different meanings of *current* and help them understand that one meaning is "flow" or movement. Explain that *current electricity* involves the movement of electrons. Have students find the term on page 572.

- Write *conductor* and *insulator*. Explain that conductors pass electric current easily. *Insulators* are the opposite of conductors; they do not pass electric current easily.

Build Fluency

Lead the group in reciting the following lines about current electricity:

- It is the flow of electrons through a wire.
- Metals conduct electricity well.
- Rubber and plastic are good insulators.
- Current electricity runs appliances at home.

② Scaffold the Content

Preview the Lesson

When to Use With pp. 568–576	Proficiency Levels
🕐 30 minutes	✔ Beginning
	✔ Intermediate
	✔ Advanced

- Read the title on page 568 and ask students what they know about electricity and how it is produced. Have students tell what the picture of lightning shows about electricity.

- Have students use the pictures and captions on page 570 to determine when charges attract and when they repel.

- Have students preview the graphic on page 572. Ask volunteers to read aloud the sequence of events that allows an electric light to be turned on.

- Have students scan pages 574–576 to identify different ways electricity is produced. *(hydroelectric, fossil fuels, nuclear power plants, wind, solar, tides, geothermal)*

Investigate, p. 569

Materials: balloon attached to long string, wool

- Before students begin the Investigate, explain that they will study static electricity.

- Review the definitions of *static electricity*, *attract*, and *repel*.

- The directions tell students to let balloons hang "freely" and rub them "vigorously" with wool. Ask volunteers to act out with props or pantomime these actions.

- To help students preview the content, write these questions on the board and discuss them with the group. *What causes charge on the balloons? What kinds of charge attract each other? What charges repel?*

Modify Instruction—Multilevel Strategies

Background/Experience This lesson focuses on electricity. The following sentences summarize some of the key facts from the lesson. Copy them onto the board and use them for the following activities, which will help prepare students to master the content in the lesson.

- Static electricity involves charged particles.
- Like charges repel. Unlike charges attract.
- Current electricity involves the flow of electrons through wires.
- Current electricity runs appliances in homes and businesses.

Beginning Have students copy two of the sentences and practice reading them aloud with a partner.

© Harcourt

Intermediate Have students copy the four sentences. Working with a partner, have them take turns reading a sentence aloud but omitting a key word. Have the other partner provide the missing word.

Advanced Ask students to copy the sentences. Then for each one, have them write a related sentence on the same topic.

For All Students Have students copy the sentences onto tag board strips. Display the strips on a bulletin board. Have students write new sentences and add them to the bulletin board as they work through the lesson.

Extend

Have the students complete the Show What You Know activity on page 231 to demonstrate their understanding of electricity.

③ Apply and Assess

When to Use	Proficiency Levels
With Reading Review p. 577 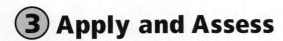 30 minutes	✔ Beginning ✔ Intermediate ✔ Advanced

Energy Sources Posters

Materials: paints, markers or colored pencils, five pieces of poster board

- Divide students into five groups. Assign each group one of the following topics: solar energy, hydroelectric power, wind power, fossil fuels, and nuclear energy.
- Have students in each group make a poster for their topic, including a title, definition, details from an encyclopedia or online source, and a representative picture.
- Invite volunteers to share the information on the group's poster, and then display them on a bulletin board entitled *Different Sources of Energy*.

Informal Assessment

Beginning	Intermediate	Advanced
Have students summarize the information in the two sentences. *(Answers will vary.)*	Read the sentences aloud to students, leaving out one or more words. Ask students to provide the missing words without referring to their papers. *(Answers will vary.)*	Ask students to read aloud their new sentences. To test comprehension, ask them questions about the content in their sentences. *(Answers will vary.)*

© Harcourt

Key Concepts of Electricity

Fill in the word map by writing key words or phrases in each bubble that tell about electricity and how it is produced.

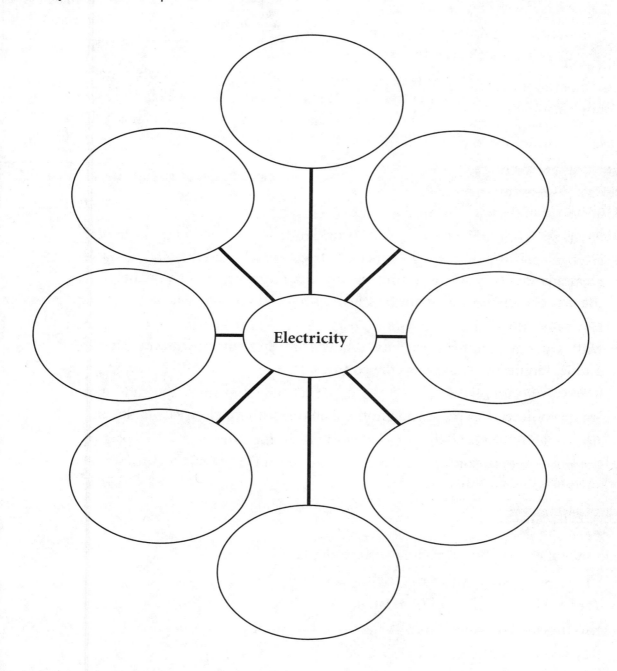

School-Home Connection: Have students take this page home to share with family members. They can use it to tell about electricity.

What Is a Circuit?

① Build Background

Access Prior Knowledge

When to Use Before introducing the lesson 20 minutes	Proficiency Levels ✔ Beginning ✔ Intermediate ✔ Advanced

Tell students that this lesson is about electrical circuits. Ask them if they know how electricity is able to travel from one point to another and to tell what they know about circuits. Explain that they will learn about two kinds of circuits, *series* and *parallel*. Ask them to name some things that appear in a series. Then ask them to describe or draw two parallel lines.

Preteach Lesson Vocabulary

circuit, series circuit, parallel circuit, electromagnet

List the vocabulary words on the board.

- Begin by defining the term *circuit* for the students. Tell them that a circuit is a continuous path through which electrical current can flow. Discuss the meaning of *continuous* as unbroken or without openings. Let students preview the shape of a circuit by studying the pictures on page 580.

- Have students find *series circuit* on page 582. Ask them to define it as a circuit with only one path for electricity to flow. Have students preview the shape of a series circuit by referring to the pictures.

- Repeat for a parallel circuit on pages 582-583. Guide students to the understanding that a *parallel circuit* provides more than one path for electricity to flow.

- Ask students to guess what an *electromagnet* is, focusing on the two parts of the word—*electro* and *magnet*. Summarize that an electromagnet uses electric current to make a magnet.

Build Fluency

Do the following choral reading with students:
- **Circuits** are paths where electricity flows.
- **Terminals** are at the end of a battery.
- **Circuits** are controlled by switches.
- **Resistors** resist the flow of electrons.

© Harcourt

② Scaffold the Content

When to Use
With pp. 578–584

⏱ 30 minutes

Proficiency Levels
✔ Beginning
✔ Intermediate
✔ Advanced

Preview the Lesson

- Explain that the lesson focuses on the two types of circuits—series and parallel. Refer students to page 578 and ask them what circuits have to do with the picture.
- Have students look at the graphics on page 581. Tell them this page shows electrical meters and explains how electricity is measured.
- Have students turn to page 584. Explain that electromagnets are created by electrical current flowing through a coiled wire. Draw a coil on the board and have students describe it. Explain that electromagnets are used in doorbells, televisions, motors, high-speed trains, and many other applications.

Investigate, p. 579

Materials: insulated wire, wire cutters

- Before students begin the Investigate, explain that they will build a circuit.
- Discuss the materials students will use. Describe the way batteries are classified according to their size. Ask a volunteer to define *insulated*, as in *insulated wire*. Show how insulation can be removed from a wire to expose the metal underneath.
- Write *reattach* and *unhook* on the board and tell students that these terms appear in the Investigate. Point out the prefixes *re-* and *un-* and discuss their meanings. *(re: again; un: not, the opposite of)*

Modify Instruction—Multilevel Strategies

Language and Vocabulary The main components of a circuit are the battery, wires, and switch. A circuit that lights a bulb, for example, would also include a bulb; a circuit that sounds a ringer would also include a bell. Review the purpose of each part of a circuit then draw on the board a simple schematic of a series circuit with a battery, bulb, wires, and switch. Students can use the diagram in the following activities to reinforce the names of circuit components.

Beginning Have students copy the circuit and label the battery, wires, and switch.

Intermediate Have students copy the circuit and label the battery, wires, and switch. Then ask them to write one or two sentences about what a circuit does or how it works.

Advanced Have students copy the circuit. Ask them to label the battery, wires, and switch, and then write a summary of the purpose of each component.

For All Students Have students extend their Multilevel activity to a parallel circuit.

Have the students complete the **Show What You Know** activity on page 235 to demonstrate their understanding of circuits.

③ Apply and Assess

Circuit Models

When to Use	Proficiency Levels
With Reading Review p. 585	✔ Beginning
⏱ 25 minutes	✔ Intermediate
	✔ Advanced

- Explain that students are going to dramatize the two different kinds of circuits.

- Divide students into two groups. Assign one group the series circuit and the other group the parallel circuit.

- Have students discuss how to represent the circuits by putting themselves into either a loop or parallel formation. Refer them to the textbook for diagrams of each layout.

- Have the groups demonstrate their circuits in front of the class, then show what happens to the circuit when the electricity is interrupted.

Informal Assessment

Beginning	Intermediate	Advanced
Ask students to share their pictures with the class. *(Answers will vary.)*	Ask students to display their pictures and give an oral presentation about what a circuit is. *(A circuit is a continuous path for electricity to flow.)*	Ask students to display their pictures and give an oral presentation about how each part of a circuit works and what it does. Then have them answer any questions other students have about their work. *(The battery supplies the electricity, the wires provide the path, and the switch opens and closes to complete or break the circuit.)*

Fill in the Blanks

Read each definition. Write the word that matches it by putting one letter on each line.

electricity flows around it

— — — — — — —

temporary magnet made by running current through a wire coil

— — — — — — — — — — — — — —

opens and closes a circuit

— — — — — —

circuit with only one path

— — — — — —

circuit with more than one path

— — — — — — — —

School-Home Connection: Have students take this page home to share with family members. They can use it to tell about circuits.

16 Forces and Motion

Develop Scientific Concepts and Vocabulary

In this chapter, students will study the motion of objects. They will learn about different kinds of forces, including the force of gravity. Students will also learn how objects react to various kinds of forces as well as how forces interact with each other.

Preview Scientific Principles

Walk through the chapter with students, pausing to read aloud or to have volunteers read aloud the three questions that are lesson titles. Encourage students to discuss briefly each question and to tell what they already know that might help them answer the questions.

When to Use With Chapter Opener	Proficiency Levels
🕐 25 minutes	✔ Beginning ✔ Intermediate ✔ Advanced

Lesson 1: How Do Forces Affect Us?

- Write *force* on the board. Explain to students that *force* is derived from the Latin word *fortis*, which means "strong."

- If possible, take students to the gym and have them throw a basketball against the wall with only a small amount of force. Have students slowly increase the amount of force they use to throw the ball and observe how this increased force affects how the ball moves.

- Ask students to describe how they can make a bike go faster or slower.

Lesson 2: How Do Forces Interact?

- Write *interact* on the board. Have a volunteer look up *interact* in a dictionary and read the definition to the class. Then instruct students to write a definition of *interact* in their own words. Have students share their definitions.

- Have pairs of students pantomime different ways people interact with each other.

- Discuss how students think forces might interact with each other.

Lesson 3: What Is Gravitational Force?

- Slowly pronounce *gravitational* for the class. Have students repeat the word after you. Tell students that *gravity* is the root of the word *gravitational*.
- Write *gravity* on the board. Tell students that *gravity* is derived from the Latin word *gravitas*, which means "heavy." Explain to students that things that are heavy exert more gravitational force than things that are light.
- Drop a book. Ask students what force pulling on the book made it fall.

Practice

Explain to students that without Earth's strong gravitational force pulling them toward the center of the planet, they and all the objects on Earth's surface would float above the ground. Make a class list of things students would not be able to do if they did not have this strong force acting on them. For example, tell students they would not be able to swing back-and-forth on a swing or play a game of horseshoes without Earth's gravitational force pulling the swing and horseshoe back down toward the ground.

Apply

Copy the chart below on the board. Tell students gravitational force increases with mass. Have students list the objects in order from those that exert the greatest gravitational force to those that exert the least gravitational force. Then have them use objects on the list to complete the following sentence: _____ exerts more gravitational force than _____.

Mass vs. Gravity

Object	Mass
apple	16 g
baseball	142 g
beach ball	47 g
book	479 g
boot	254 g
bowling ball	4,671 g
brick	2,323 g
sandwich	22 g

How Do Forces Affect Us?

① Build Background

Access Prior Knowledge

When to Use	Proficiency Levels
Before introducing the lesson	✔ Beginning
⏱ 30 minutes	✔ Intermediate
	✔ Advanced

Lead students in a discussion about the word *force*.

- Have students describe what they think *force* means. Encourage students to use *force* in a sentence or to pantomime the meaning of the word.
- Tell students that the scientific meaning of *force* is different than its common meaning. Have a volunteer read the textbook glossary definition of *force*.

Preteach Lesson Vocabulary

> **velocity, force, acceleration, inertia**

List the vocabulary words on the board.

Have students write down the vocabulary words for the lesson. As homework, instruct students to use a lexicon to find the equivalent terms in their native language. Then:

- Write *velocity* on the board. Tell students that this word is derived from the Latin word *velox*, which means "swift, or very fast." Have students draw a picture of something that can move very fast.
- Write *acceleration* on the board. Tell students that this word is derived from the Latin verb *celerare*, which means "to hasten, or move faster."
- Instruct students to walk around the room (or take students to a track). Have students start by walking slowly. Then ask them to accelerate or increase their speed. Repeat this command several times until students are at a running speed. Then tell students that in science, *accelerate* can also mean "slow down" or "change direction."

Build Fluency

Tell students that when you describe an object's velocity, you are describing both its speed and the direction it is moving in. Show students a map of your state and go over cardinal directions (north, south, east, west, northwest, southeast, and so on). Have them indicate the town they live in. Then select other towns across the state and ask students to call out the direction they would have to travel in order to reach the town.

© Harcourt

② Scaffold the Content

When to Use	Proficiency Levels
With pp. 596–602	✔ Beginning
35 minutes	✔ Intermediate
	✔ Advanced

Preview the Lesson

Materials: small balls

Give students small balls. Have students toss a ball up in the air or bounce it on the ground. Instruct students to observe how the ball is moving and then to describe that movement. Help students describe the ball's movement by asking: "Is the ball moving fast or slow?" "Is the ball changing speeds?" "Which direction is the ball moving in?" "What causes the ball's direction or speed to change?" Read aloud the lesson title and tell students that, in this lesson, they will find out how forces can cause an object's direction or speed to change.

Investigate, p. 597

Before students begin the Investigate:

- Write *speed* on the board. Tell students that this word can be used as both a noun and a verb.
- Explain that the past tense of the verb *speed* is irregular. Write the following information on the board:

  Present tense—The car speeds.

  Future tense—The car will speed.

  Past tense—The car sped.

Modify Instruction—Multilevel Strategies

Background/Experience Take students outside and have a race.

- From the starting line, have students run as fast as they can for 15 seconds.
- At the end of 15 seconds, have students drop an object to mark their stopping points; use a meter stick to measure how far they ran from the starting line. Show students how to use a compass to find the direction they ran.
- Help students use this information to calculate their velocity.

Beginning Have students repeat the activity above, this time running in the opposite direction from the starting line. Then have them calculate and state their velocity.

Intermediate Have students repeat the activity above, this time running in the opposite direction from the starting line. Have them calculate their velocity. Have students draw a diagram using arrows to represent the velocities they calculated.

Advanced Have students repeat the activity above, this time running in the opposite direction from the starting line. Have them calculate their velocity. Have students write a paragraph comparing their motion during both races.

For All Students As you continue with the lesson, relate students' experiences with the race (their motion and the forces that acted on them) to what is being described in the lesson text.

Extend

Have the students complete the Show What You Know activity on page 241 to demonstrate their understanding of velocity and acceleration.

③ Apply and Assess

Describing Movement

When to Use	Proficiency Levels
With Reading Review p. 603	✔ Beginning
🕐 20 minutes	✔ Intermediate
	✔ Advanced

Materials: balls

- Give each student a ball. Tell students to apply force to the ball. Have them describe the result. *(The ball moved.)* Ask students what overcame the ball's inertia. *(The force applied by their muscles.)*

- Instruct students to roll the ball slowly on the floor. While the ball is rolling, have students accelerate the ball in several different ways. Then have students describe how the ball's motion changed. *(Answers may include: The ball's speed increased. The ball's speed decreased. The direction in which the ball was moving changed.)*

Informal Assessment

Beginning	Intermediate	Advanced
Have students draw an example of acceleration that they witnessed today. *(Answers will vary.)*	Have students act out or describe an example of acceleration that they witnessed today. *(Answers will vary.)*	Have students write a definition for the following terms using their own words and experiences: *velocity, force, acceleration, inertia.* *(Answers will vary.)*

© Harcourt

Name _____

Date _____

Calculating Velocity and Acceleration

Calculate the velocity of Object A and the acceleration of Object B. Show your work in the space provided.

Object A	Object B
Direction: east	**Direction:** down
Distance traveled: 16 km	**Starting speed:** 0 km/hr
Time traveled: 4 min	**Current speed:** 8 km/hr
Velocity: _____	**Time to reach current speed:** 12 sec
	Acceleration: _____
Show your work here:	Show your work here:

School-Home Connection: Have students take this page home to share with family members. They can use this page to tell about velocity and acceleration.

Lesson 2 — How Do Forces Interact?

1 Build Background

Access Prior Knowledge

<table>
<tr><td>When to Use
Before introducing the lesson
 25 minutes</td><td>Proficiency Levels
✔ Beginning
✔ Intermediate
✔ Advanced</td></tr>
</table>

Tell students to pantomime a person who is very cold. Look for a student who is rubbing his or her hands together or rubbing his or her hands over their arms. Point out the student's actions to the rest of the class. Ask students why people who are cold rub their hands together. Then ask if any students know why rubbing their hands together heats up their hands. Some students may know that rubbing their hands together creates friction.

Preteach Lesson Vocabulary

Materials: balance with two scales

> balanced forces, unbalanced forces, friction

List the vocabulary words on the board.

- Write *balanced* and *unbalanced* on the board. Ask students to compare the words. Students should note that the words are the same, except one of them has the prefix *un*. Remind students that the prefix *un* means "not."

- Show students a balance. Place two objects of equal mass on the balance. Say, "These two objects are balanced." Next place two objects of different masses on the balance. Say, "These two objects are unbalanced." Have students use this demonstration to infer the meanings of the terms *balanced forces* and *unbalanced forces*.

- Write *friction* on the board. Tell students that *friction* is derived from the Latin word *fricare*, which means "to rub." Explain to students that when two objects rub against each other, friction results. Have students rub two objects together and repeat the word *friction*.

Build Fluency

Place different common objects on a balance. If the objects are balanced, have students say, "The _____ and the _____ are balanced." If the objects do not balance, have students say, "The _____ and the _____ are unbalanced." Repeat this exercise at least 10 times.

© Harcourt

② Scaffold the Content

Preview the Lesson

When to Use
With pp. 604–610

🕐 35 minutes

Proficiency Levels
✔ Beginning
✔ Intermediate
✔ Advanced

Materials: rope

Have students preview the heading and art on page 606. Use a rope to hold a tug-of-war tournament. If one team wins a match, hold up a sign that says, "Unbalanced Forces." If a match is a tie, hold up a sign that says, "Balanced Forces."

Investigate, p. 605

Before students begin the Investigate:

- Write the word *estimate* on the board. Tell students that they will need to estimate, and explain that estimating is guessing an approximate amount. Model how to estimate the length of the classroom. Then write the following estimate on the board:

   I estimate the classroom is _____ meters wide.

- Have students complete the sentence to estimate the width of the classroom. Then have them measure to see if their estimate was correct.

Modify Instruction—Multilevel Strategies

Comprehensible Input Give each student a plastic cup and 10 centimeters of colorful sewing thread. Have students fill the cups with water and then carefully place the thread on the water's surface. Have students describe what they observe. Lead students in a discussion relating what they observe with the balanced forces of gravity and surface tension acting on the water strider on page 608.

Beginning Have students use arrows to draw the forces acting on the thread and label them as balanced forces or unbalanced forces.

Intermediate Have small groups of students prepare skits about a water strider trying to go for a swim. The skit should focus on the forces that prevent the strider from getting below the water's surface. Encourage students to make the skit as humorous as possible. Then have students perform their skits for the class.

Advanced Have students write a paragraph comparing the forces acting on the thread and the water strider on page 608.

For All Students Give students a variety of small objects. Have students carefully place them one at a time on the water's surface. Have them state whether the forces of gravity and surface tension acting on each object are balanced or unbalanced.

Have the students complete the **Show What You Know** activity on page 245 to demonstrate their understanding of balanced and unbalanced forces.

③ Apply and Assess

Demonstrating Force

When to Use	Proficiency Levels
With Reading Review p. 611	✔ Beginning
🕐 25 minutes	✔ Intermediate
	✔ Advanced

Materials: large plastic cup, water, magnets, feather, small wooden blocks

Organize students into groups. Give each group a variety of materials, and have each group find a way to demonstrate the following forces:

- buoyant force
- friction
- gravitational force
- magnetic force
- surface tension

Informal Assessment

Beginning	Intermediate	Advanced
Hand students a ball. Ask them to demonstrate unbalanced forces acting on the ball. *(Students should make the ball move in some way.)* Then ask students to demonstrate balanced forces acting on the ball. *(Students should make the ball stay still.)*	Ask students to list three different types of forces. *(Answers may include: nuclear force, buoyant force, friction, gravitational force, magnetic force, electric force, surface tension, a push, a pull.)*	Have students write a sentence explaining how friction can be reduced between two objects. *(Answers may include: Grease or oil can be put on the objects to lubricate them and reduce friction.)*

© Harcourt

Determining Net Force

The arrows below represent two forces acting on an object and the direction they are acting. Calculate the net force and write whether the force is balanced or unbalanced.

12N + 12N = _____

23N + 23N = _____

7N + 13N = _____

School-Home Connection: Have students take this page home to share with family members. They can use this page to tell about balanced and unbalanced forces.

What Is Gravitational Force?

① Build Background

Access Prior Knowledge

When to Use	Proficiency Levels
Before introducing the lesson	✔ Beginning
🕐 25 minutes	✔ Intermediate
	✔ Advanced

Materials: ball

Hold out a ball in your hand and ask students what will happen if you let go of the ball. Then let the ball drop to the ground and ask if anybody knows why this happens. Elicit that Earth's gravitational force pulls the ball towards Earth's surface. Then ask what other objects exert a gravitational force. Tell them anything with mass can exert a gravitational force.

Preteach Lesson Vocabulary

gravitational force, weight

Materials: video or picture of astronauts floating in spacecraft

List the vocabulary words on the board.

- Have students write down the vocabulary terms. Allow students a moment to study the terms, then have them close their notebooks. Give students a quick spelling quiz using the two terms.

- Show students a video or a picture of astronauts floating in a spacecraft. Explain to students that people often say objects are *weightless* in space because they are able to float around. Tell students that the suffix *less* means "not having." Ask students to hypothesize why astronauts are weightless in space.

- Write *weight* and *wait* on the board. Pronounce the words and have volunteers use a dictionary to describe the difference in their meanings.

- Underline the *gh* in *weight* and explain that in many words such as *weight*, *light*, *height*, *right*, *fight*, and so on, the *gh* is silent.

Build Fluency

Provide students with scales and have them find the weight of various objects. After they weigh each object, they should state the following sentence aloud: "The weight is _____ newtons."

② Scaffold the Content

When to Use	Proficiency Levels
With pp. 612–618	✔ Beginning
	✔ Intermediate
🕐 35 minutes	✔ Advanced

Preview the Lesson

Read aloud the lesson title. Encourage students to use what they learned in the previous lesson to answer the question in a class discussion. Then have students set a goal of reading the lesson by encouraging them to write down what else they would like to know about gravitational force.

Investigate, p. 613

Before students begin the Investigate:

- Write *spring* on the board. Tell students the word has many meanings. Show students some different examples of coiled metal springs. Tell students that spring scales often include springs such as the ones that you showed them.
- Explain that *spring* is also used to describe the season that comes between winter and summer. Challenge students to name the season that comes after summer. *(fall, or autumn)*
- Another meaning of *spring* is a natural fountain or flow of water from the ground. If possible, show students a picture of this type of spring.

Modify Instruction—Multilevel Strategies

Language and Vocabulary Write *gravity*, *mass*, and *weight* on the board. Explain to students that understanding the meanings of these three terms is key to understanding what gravitational force is. Have students make a three-columned chart. In the first column, they should write down the three terms. In the second column, they should write down the definition of the terms. And in the third column, they should record the unit of measurement used to measure each quantity.

Beginning Have students draw three diagrams illustrating the meanings of *gravity*, *mass*, and *weight*.

Intermediate Have students describe the meanings of *gravity*, *mass*, and *weight* to a partner.

Advanced Have students write a short paragraph explaining how *gravity*, *weight*, and *mass* are related to each other.

For All Students Give each student an object. Students should determine the weight and mass of their object and then tell why the weight and mass of the object are different.

Have the students complete the **Show What You Know** activity on page 249 to demonstrate their understanding of gravitational force.

③ Apply and Assess

Gravity Riddles

When to Use	Proficiency Levels
With Reading Review p. 619 ⏱ 25 minutes	✔ Beginning ✔ Intermediate ✔ Advanced

- Write the following terms on the board: *gravitational force, inertia, weight, mass.* Model for students how to make up a riddle for one of these terms. For example, say, "I get weaker when two attracting objects get farther apart. What am I?" Then have a volunteer answer the riddle. *(gravitational force)*

- Have pairs of students write a riddle that ends with "What am I?" for each of the terms on the board. Then have pairs take turns reading their riddles to the class.

Informal Assessment

Beginning	Intermediate	Advanced
Give students a variety of small objects, a spring scale, and a balance. Have students determine the weights and masses of the objects. Then have students identify the object that can exert the greatest gravitational force. *(Answers will vary.)*	Have students make a poster showing the difference between weight and mass. *(Posters will vary.)*	Have students write a short story about how their weight and mass would or would not change if they traveled to the moon. Instruct students to use the term *gravitational force* at least once in their paragraph. *(Answers will vary.)*

Name _____

Date _____

Strength of Gravitational Forces

Determine which of the objects in the table below would experience the strongest gravitational forces. Rank the strongest gravitational forces "1," the next strongest "2," and the weakest "3."

Rank	Gravitational Force Between Objects

School-Home Connection: Have students take this page home to share with family members. They can use this page to tell about gravitational force.

© Harcourt

ESL Support 249

17 Work and Simple Machines

Develop Scientific Concepts and Vocabulary

In this chapter, students will learn about work and simple machines. They will explore how levers and other simple machines help us do work. They will also learn what inclined planes are and what some of the most common examples are.

Preview Scientific Principles

Walk through the chapter with students, pausing to read aloud or to have volunteers read aloud the two questions that are lesson titles. Encourage students to briefly discuss each question and to tell what they already know that might help them answer the questions.

When to Use With Chapter Opener	Proficiency Levels
🕒 20 minutes	✔ Beginning ✔ Intermediate ✔ Advanced

Lesson 1: How Do Levers Help You Do Work?

- Conduct a class discussion on work and simple machines. Explain that levers are simple machines that help us make things move.

- Have students discuss balances and scales. Have them use the words in sentences and explain how they are alike and different.

- Help students name simple machines that may be in the room or in their homes, such as carts, pencil sharpeners, doorknobs, bicycles, and tricycles.

- Discuss playground equipment with students and ask them what simple machines such equipment includes. Elicit that a playground has many simple machines, such as seesaws.

Lesson 2: What Are Inclined Planes?

- Have students tell what they think the similarities and differences between levers and inclined planes might be.

- Have students discuss what happens to the speed of a car on a road that gently starts going uphill. Then discuss what happens when the car starts going downhill.

- Have students discuss what kind of inclined plane they think a doorstop is. Elicit that it is a type of wedge.

- Have students tell what they think the similarities and differences between a nail and a screw are.

To help students use vocabulary from the chapter's topic, involve them in contributing to a giant word web around the central words *WORK AND SIMPLE MACHINES* on the board. Encourage students to dictate or write related words around the focus words. Words might be *pulley, wedge, force, seesaw, lever, inclined plane,* and so on. Then have students choose words from the web to use in sentences about work and simple machines. Encourage them to read their sentences aloud.

Apply

Write the sentences from the following chart on the board and have students take turns echoing or reading a line aloud. You may wish to model how to pantomime some of the actions described in the sentences. Then ask students to search old magazines for pictures of different simple machines and have them cut out and paste the pictures on a sheet of paper to create a collage. Finally, have each student select one picture of a simple machine to write or tell about.

Work and Simple Machine Sentences

When we exit the highway, we go up a ramp, which is an inclined plane.

A pole-vaulter uses a pole, which is a kind of lever.

We use a doorstop to keep the door open.

When I push a chair and it moves, I do work.

When I push a chair and I can't move it, I don't do any work.

Riding a simple machine, such as a bicycle, is good exercise.

A pair of scissors is an example of a simple machine.

The television, the computer, and many other things in this room were put together with screws.

How Do Levers Help You Do Work?

① Build Background

Access Prior Knowledge

When to Use	Proficiency Levels
Before introducing the lesson 15 minutes	✔ Beginning ✔ Intermediate Advanced

Give students an opportunity to use sentences as they talk about their personal experiences related to levers and work. Have them discuss what they understand the words *levers* and *work* to mean. Explain to students that they already know that many words have multiple meanings. Discuss that many words have ordinary meanings and scientific meanings. The word *work* is one of them.

Preteach Lesson Vocabulary

> **work, lever, fulcrum, pulley, wheel-and-axle**

List the vocabulary words on the board.

Have students look at pages 630 through 635 to find the vocabulary words.

- Ask students which word on the board is a hyphenated compound word. Ask students if they know what the words *wheel* and *axle* mean by themselves. Explain that the compound word refers to a simple machine that uses a small and a large wheel.

- Point to the word *fulcrum* and have students say the word with you. Explain that a *fulcrum* is the fixed point of simple machines, such as scales, and of playground equipment, such as seesaws.

- Point to the word *lever* on the board and have students say the word with you. Ask students if they know the meaning of the word. Discuss that a *lever* is a like a bar or rod that turns around a fixed point, or fulcrum.

- Have a volunteer point to the word *pulley*. Have them repeat the word with you. Discuss that a *pulley* is a simple machine consisting of a wheel with a rope or a chain.

Build Fluency

Have students work in pairs. Model dialogues by completing questions and answers such as the following:

What is a _____? It's the fixed point of a scale or a lever. *(fulcrum)*

What are _____? They are simple machines that use a wheel, a rope, or a chain. *(pulleys)*

② Scaffold the Content

When to Use	Proficiency Levels
With pp. 628–636	✔ Beginning
⏱ 20 minutes	✔ Intermediate
	✔ Advanced

Preview the Lesson

- Ask students to point to the title on page 628 as you read it aloud. Explain to them that they will find the answer to this question in the lesson. Discuss the picture.

- Have students look pages 629–636 and tell what is happening in each picture.

- Ask students to share their experiences with balances. Have them explain what balances are used for and the kinds they are familiar with.

- Discuss simple machines with students. Have them describe their experiences with simple machines such as pulleys, levers, and wheels-and-axles. Elicit that the wheels of bicycles are examples of wheels-and-axles.

- Ask students to discuss the similarities and differences in meaning between *work* as it refers to jobs, chores, or tasks, and *work* as it is used in science.

Investigate, p. 629

Before students begin the Investigate:

- Write the word *scale* on the board and have students say the word with you. Ask for volunteers to explain the meaning of the word. Elicit that a *scale*, such as the spring scale on page 629, is a measuring instrument.

- Explain that the word *scale* is a word with multiple meanings. Ask students if they know any other meaning for the word. Elicit that *scale* can refer to, among other things, an order or rank for grading, such as a "scale from one to ten."

- Explain that the plates or pans of a balance are also called *scales*. Have students point to the scales that the statue depicted on page 628 is holding.

Modify Instruction—Multilevel Strategies

Language and Vocabulary Write the phrase *steering wheel* on the board and have students say the phrase with you. Have them find it in the text. Ask them on what page the phrase appears for the first time. Elicit that *steering wheel* appears on page 635.

Ask students what they think *steering wheel* means. Discuss that it is the hand wheel used to steer or direct a car in a particular direction.

Beginning Have students point to words or phrases such as *steering wheel* and *automobile* in the text. You may also point to the words and have students identify each word by name or say the word with you.

© Harcourt

Intermediate Ask students simple questions that require one-word answers or very simple sentences. For instance, you may ask: *What is a lever?* Help them answer with a complete sentence such as: *A lever is a simple machine.*

Advanced Have fluent readers read the section **Wheels-and-Axles** on page 635. Have them sum up what they read by describing the main idea and details of the paragraphs.

For All Students Continue the lesson by reminding students to think about the scientific meaning of *work*, and how useful it is that simple machines such as levers help us perform that work.

Extend

Have students complete the Show What You Know activity on page 255 to demonstrate their understanding of simple machines and work.

③ Apply and Assess

Make a Presentation

When to Use With Reading Review p. 637 20 minutes	Proficiency Levels ✔ Beginning ✔ Intermediate ✔ Advanced

Materials: encyclopedias, magazines, scissors, construction paper, paste, markers

- Have students in groups of three to five work together to research and find pictures of different types of simple machines in encyclopedias, in magazines, or on the Internet.

- Have them organize the pictures they can cut out or print out by type of machine, such as levers, pulleys, and wheels-and-axles.

- Ask the groups to paste the pictures organized by type of machine on construction paper and to label them with any appropriate information.

- Have the groups present their findings to the class and then display their work on a section of the bulletin board entitled *Simple Machines at Work.*

Informal Assessment

Beginning	Intermediate	Advanced
Ask individual students to identify levers, pulleys, and wheels-and-axles by pointing to pictures of them. Or, you may point to some of the pictures depicting these items and ask students to identify each one.	Have each student complete or write a sentence to describe levers or pulleys. *(Answers will vary but may include: A pulley is a simple machine.)*	Have each student describe aloud wheels-and-axles, pulleys, or levers using complete sentences. *(Answers will vary but may include: A wheel-and-axle is a large wheel and a small wheel that turn together.)*

Compare Levers and Pulleys

Complete the Venn diagram to show how levers and pulleys are alike and different.

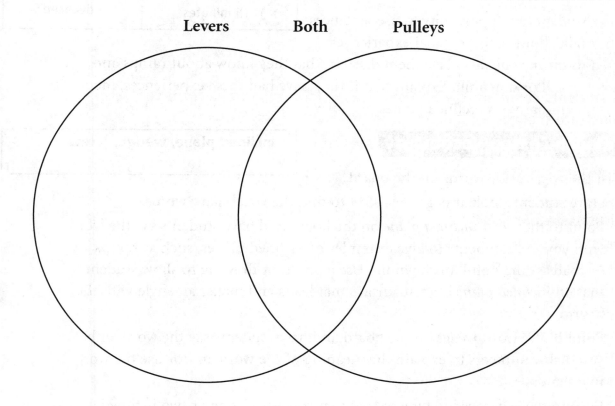

Levers Both Pulleys

School-Home Connection: Have students take this page home to share with family members. They can use this page to tell about simple machines that perform work.

What Are Inclined Planes?

① Build Background

Access Prior Knowledge

When to Use	Proficiency Levels
Before introducing the lesson 15 minutes	✔ Beginning ✔ Intermediate Advanced

Give students an opportunity to use sentences as they talk about their personal experiences related to *inclined planes*. Have them discuss what they know about ramps and driving uphill or downhill. Explain that if they have had these experiences, then they are familiar with inclined planes.

Preteach Lesson Vocabulary

> inclined plane, wedge, screw

List the vocabulary words on the board.

- Have students look at pages 640–644 to find the vocabulary words.
- Point to the word *inclined plane* on the board and have students say the word with you. Ask students to give examples of inclined planes, such as ramps or roads going uphill or downhill. Use a photo or drawing to show students that an *inclined plane* is a flat surface that leans and makes an angle with the horizon.
- Point to the word *wedge* on the board and have students say the word with you. Ask volunteers to explain the meaning of the word and/or use the word in a sentence.
- Explain that a *wedge* is a type of tool that consists of one or two inclined planes and has many uses. Give some examples of wedges such as axes and kitchen knives.
- Ask volunteers to read the last vocabulary word: *screw*. Have students repeat the word aloud with you. Have students discuss the meaning of the word and come up with sentences of their own using the word. Explain that screws are used in many devices, such as toys and CD players.

Build Fluency

Have students work in pairs. Model dialogues by completing questions and answers such as the following:

What type of plane is a ramp? It's an _____. *(inclined plane)*

Do you know what a _____ is? It's a kind of inclined plane that has one or two sloping sides. *(wedge)*

© Harcourt

② Scaffold the Content

When to Use With pp. 638–644	Proficiency Levels
🕐 20 minutes	✔ Beginning ✔ Intermediate ✔ Advanced

Preview the Lesson

- Ask students to point to the title on page 638 as you read it aloud. Explain that they will find the answer to this question in the lesson. Have students discuss the picture.

- Ask students to look at the pictures on pages 639–644 and tell what is happening in the images.

- Ask students to share their experiences with screws and screwdrivers. Have them relate what they did with them or what they saw being done with them.

- Ask students to share their experiences with ramps. Ask them if they have ever seen a moving truck being loaded. Discuss that the flat leaning surface used to load items into the truck is a ramp and, therefore, an inclined plane.

- Ask students to point to the needle, the sledgehammer, and the butcher's knife on pages 642 and 643. Ask students what kind of machine these are. Discuss with students what makes these items wedges.

Investigate, p. 639

Before students begin the Investigate:

- Write the word *friction* on the board and have students say the word with you. Ask for volunteers to explain its meaning or use it in a sentence. Elicit that *friction* means the force one body exerts on another when they rub against each other.

- Explain that when friction occurs, sometimes it can slow down or stop a body that is moving, such as the cart going up the ramp in the Investigate.

- Explain that the amount of friction depends on the contact surfaces (whether they are smooth or rough) and the amount of force pushing the bodies together.

Modify Instruction—Multilevel Strategies

Comprehensible Input Write the word *force* on the board and have students say the word with you. Have volunteers point to several instances in which the word is used in the text and mention the page numbers. Discuss the different meanings of the word *force*, and have students use the word in sentences. Explain that the word *force* in science usually refers to a push or pull applied to cause movement.

© Harcourt

Beginning Have students point to words such as *force* and *friction* in the text. You may also point to the words and have students identify each word by name or say the word with you.

Intermediate Ask students simple questions that require one-word answers or very simple sentences. For instance, you may ask: "What is force?" Allow them to answer with one word, such as *push*, but help them answer with a complete sentence, such as: "It's a push or pull."

Advanced Have fluent readers read the section **Screws** on page 644. Have them sum up what they read by describing the main idea and details of the paragraphs.

For All Students Continue the lesson by reminding students to think about inclined planes and how useful they are to us in everyday life.

Extend

Have students complete the **Show What You Know** activity on page 259 to demonstrate their understanding of inclined planes.

③ Apply and Assess

Make a Presentation

When to Use With Reading Review p. 645 ⏱ 20 minutes	Proficiency Levels
	✔ Beginning
	✔ Intermediate
	✔ Advanced

Materials: encyclopedias, magazines, scissors, construction paper, paste, markers

- Have students in groups of three to five work together to research and find pictures of different types of inclined planes in encyclopedias, magazines, or on the Internet.
- Have them organize the pictures by type of inclined plane, such as ramps, wedges, and screws.
- Ask the groups to paste the pictures organized by type of inclined plane on construction paper and to label them with any appropriate information.
- Have the groups present their findings to the class and then display their work on a section of the bulletin board entitled *Types of Inclined Planes*.

Informal Assessment

Beginning	Intermediate	Advanced
Ask individual students to identify ramps, wedges, and screws by pointing to pictures of them. Or, you may point to some of the pictures depicting these items and ask students if they can identify each one.	Have each student complete or write a sentence to describe wedges or screws. (*Answers will vary but may include: A wedge is a kind of inclined plane.*)	Have each student describe screws, wedges, or inclined planes using complete sentences. (*Answers will vary but may include: As a screw turns around its cylinder, it moves up and down.*)

Draw an Inclined Plane

In each row, read the words. Then draw a picture that shows the inclined plane.

Inclined Planes

Ramp
Wedge
Screw

 School-Home Connection: Have students take this page home to share with family members. They can use the pictures to tell about what they learned about inclined planes.